Exploring
Contradictions

Exploring Contradictions

Political Economy in the Corporate State

Edited by

Philip Brenner
Robert Borosage
Bethany Weidner

David McKay Company, Inc.,
New York

For Marc and David, Kristy, and Erika, Jaime and Noah—with love.

Exploring Contradictions: Political Economy in the Corporate State

COPYRIGHT © 1974 BY David McKay Company, Inc.

ISBN: 0-679-30256-5 (paper)
       0-679-30255-7 (cloth)
Library of Congress Catalog Card Number: 74-78902
MANUFACTURED IN THE UNITED STATES OF AMERICA

Design by Bob Antler

Acknowledgments

The editors would like to thank the authors, periodicals, and
publishers for their kind permission to reprint the following
copyrighted material:

"Inflation, Fiscal Crisis and the American Working Class," by James
O'Connor. Reprinted from *Socialist Revolution*, no. 8 (March-
April 1972). By permission of the author.

"Global Corporations: Their Quest for Legitimacy," Copyright ©
1974 by Richard Barnet and Ronald Müller. By permission of
the authors.

"Money Crises and the Operation of Multinational Firms," by the
U.S. Tariff Commission. Printed by the U.S. Government
Printing Office.

"Basic Facts: Distribution of Personal Income and Wealth in the
U.S." by Nancy Lyons and Letitia Upton. Copyright © 1972

by the Cambridge Policy Studies Institute. Reprinted by permission.

"Character and Work in America" by Michael Maccoby and Katherine A. Terzi. Copyright © 1974 by Michael Maccoby and Katherine A. Terzi. By permission of the authors.

"Federal Chartering and Corporate Accountability" by Ralph Nader and Mark Green. Copyright © 1974 by Ralph Nader and Mark Green. By permission of the authors.

"Notes Toward a Pluralist Commonwealth" by Gar Alperovitz. Copyright © 1974 by Gar Alperovitz. Reprinted by permission of the author.

"Reclaiming America: Land Reform as a Means of Reconstruction" by Geoffrey Faux. Reprinted from *Working Papers*, 1, no. 2 (Summer 1973) by permission of the author.

Preface

This book is about political economy. Both students and teachers of politics and economics have come to recognize with increasing frequency that the two subjects are linked; that to explain the link requires more than a mere mention of the one subject while teaching the other. Yet there is a dearth of material available to assist us in detailing the complexity of the political economy of the United States. The essays here contribute to the slowly enlarging literature on this topic.

Some will find these essays useful to introduce the subject of political economy in basic courses in both economics and politics. The discussion in part 1 provides a good overview of the relationship between economics and politics. In part 2 the authors analyze three fundamental problems that affect both the politics and economy of the United States: the relations between the government and the two sectors in the private economy; the nature of the modern corporation (which in effect means the multinational corporation); and the nature of our work and our character as workers. Part 3 discusses alternatives, to the present political economy. These proposals are examples of the type of pragmatic and programmatic thinking in which we must engage if we want to realize a different and better way of living and working.

Others may use this volume in advanced courses on public policy or economic policy—or on political economy. Each essay is a work of scholarship, and some are based on empirical research. Together they provide a dynamic analysis of the political economy of the United States that points to the critical questions which are emerging in the mid-1970s. The tensions identified by the authors make clear that the United States is entering a period of dramatic transformation.

For the troubled citizen, these essays can serve to describe the process of transformation and to provide possibilities for action. The section on alternatives offers healthy caveats with regard to some "radical" approaches to our various dilemmas, and positive reforms that might be pursued in working our way out of "crisis."

We planned this book in conjunction with a series of seminars which we directed for congressional staff assistants, under the auspices of the Institute for Policy Studies. We wish to thank those individuals who spoke at congressional seminars and whose presentations are not included in this collection. Without their participation, the seminars would have covered the political economy much less completely, and would have lacked a dimension of activist criticism and reporting which, ultimately, distinguished them from other discussions. To two friends, Margot White and Susan Berner, who helped generously—and expertly—to prepare the manuscript, we repeat our warm thanks. To Tina Smith and Alyce Wiley, from whom we borrowed time, tools, and tolerance, we are also grateful. We are indebted, as well, to Marcus Raskin, who served as initiator, participant in, contributor to, and unflagging supporter of the congressional seminar project from the time the first invitations went out, through the months of the seminars, to the completion of this book. We relied on the brightness of his vision, and his spirit.

About
the
Editors

Philip Brenner teaches political science at Trinity College, Washington, D.C. A member of the editorial board of *Politics and Society*, he was educated formally at Columbia University and Johns Hopkins University. He was co-director of the Washington Mini-School, an experimental project in political education, and is the author of articles on education and Congress.

Robert Borosage is a lawyer in Washington, D.C. where he is involved in poverty law. A graduate of Michigan State University and Yale University Law School, he has been a visiting fellow at the Institute for Policy Studies, where he worked on research regarding national security questions. He is the co-editor of *Executive Power* (1974) and the author of articles on war crimes and the national security state.

Bethany Weidner is a research associate at the Institute for Policy Studies, where she has worked with fellows on the history of participation in early American politics and on issues in postwar economic policy. She is a graduate of Reed College and a regular contributor to her community newspaper.

About the Contributors

Gordon Adams is on the staff of the Social Science Research Council and is a member of the editorial board of *Politics and Society*. He is completing a book on the role of the state in advanced capitalist countries.

Gar Alperovitz is a fellow of the Institute for Policy Studies and co-director of the Exploratory Project for Economic Alternatives. He is the co-author, with Staughton Lynd, of *Strategy and Program*.

Richard J. Barnet is co-director of the Institute for Policy Studies, and the author of several works on political economy.

Ronald E. Müller teaches economics at American University. He is the author of several articles on the economics of dependency in the Third World.

Joseph Collins is an associate at the Institute for Policy Studies and lectures widely on Latin America. Their article derives from three years of joint research in preparation for a book on multinational corporations.

Geoffrey Faux is co-director of the Exploratory Project for Economic Alternatives. He was formerly director of Economic Development for the U.S. Office of Economic Opportunity. The original version of his essay appeared in *Working Papers*

(Summer 1973) and has been revised by the author for this volume.

Nancy Lyons is a fellow of the Cambridge Policy Studies Institute and managing editor of *Working Papers for a New Society*.

Letitia Upton is an associate fellow of the Cambridge Policy Studies Institute.

Michael Maccoby heads the Harvard Project on Work, Technology and Character and is a fellow of the Institute for Policy Studies. He is completing a book on corporate managers.

Katherine A. Terzi is a member of the Harvard Project and is involved in an experimental study on humanizing work.

Ralph Nader is a public-interest lawyer in Washington, D.C. He is the author of *Unsafe at Any Speed*.

Mark Green is director of the Corporate Accountability Research Group and is the co-editor (with Mr. Nader) of *Corporate Power in America*.

James O'Connor teaches economics at California State University, San Jose. He is U.S. coordinating editor of *Kapitalistate* and the author of *Fiscal Crisis of the State*.

Marcus Raskin is co-director of the Institute for Policy Studies. He is currently at work on a book to be called *Democracy: The New Social Contract*, and is the coordinator of the *Encyclopedia for Social Reconstruction*.

Introduction

Philip Brenner
Robert Borosage
Bethany Weidner

Barrington Moore once asked why no society has ever been as decent to its members as it could have been, given existing technology and resources. In response, he speculated that it was because too many members of the society were good citizens; they accepted existing economic and political arrangements and dutifully obeyed rules established in accordance with these.

Moore may be correct in his analysis, but we believe that people have been obedient subjects rather than good citizens. A good citizen is not one who accepts an ongoing institutional arrangement that creates an indecent society. A good citizen in America today is one who seeks ways to create a decent (not necessarily a perfect) society—and so challenges the structure of our political economy.

This book derives from what might be called an effort at good citizenship. In the spring of 1973, the Institute for Policy Studies sponsored a series of seminars for congressional assistants on the political economy. The seminars were designed not to stimulate legislation, but to investigate and raise questions about the assumptions that underlie most · legislation. To this end, we invited individuals and groups working to reconstruct society to discuss their ideas and activities with members of congressional staffs. We hoped that knowledge of the energy and intentions of these non-established groups would, cumulatively, lay the groundwork for the staff to consider policies which would contribute to the achievement of that more humane, more nearly just, society.

Several essays in this book were first presented orally at the seminars. Others were distributed as background material. But, as with any book based on the activities of people, this work took on a life of its own with a distinct purpose. Our intention here is to provide a set of essays that will be useful to you because of the connections it might help you make in your own life.

The approach of this book is one linking politics and economics. This breaks from the tendency in both the established political science and economics disciplines to segregate their respective subject matters. The traditional disciplines fail to help us understand how a supposedly affluent society could be plagued by hunger, unemployment, endemic war, energy shortages, widespread corruption, deep-seated worker dissatisfaction, and a general sense of loss and failure—of something gone wrong.

Political scientists and economists have labored for approximately ninety years—from the time they founded their professional associations—to carve out their own intellectual turf. Political scientists accomplished their task by confining their studies to questions about governing. Most of them further circumscribed the discipline by identifying as "political" only those phenomena which could be used to explain how government operates. Thus, these scholars focus on the institutions of government, the behavior of those in government, or on the way in which nongovernmental bodies and citizens affect the government. Research about corporate power, alienation, or the nature of work and social relations tends to be judged as meaningful political science only if it can be used to explain how government works. Even recent attempts to broaden the field by making the study of corporations "legitimate" limit themselves to the question of governing—that is, to the question of how a few people can most successfully govern the many.

Similarly, economists created a professional identity by divorcing economic questions from questions of power, a move most symbolized by changing the name of their academic department from political economy to economics. Economics became the study of laws of production, distribution, exchange and consumption. Questions such as the relation of economic arrangements to the nature of man, or to the organization of the polity, or indeed, to a decent society, became "nonprofessional" concerns for economists after the nineteenth century.

In contrast, we are loath to isolate the question of governance from that of economic relations. Institutions of government are rooted in the same premises that determine the nature of other social institutions. The interrelationships between alienated work and the facility with which the government uses violence; between the distribution of wealth and the legitimacy of hierarchic patterns of authority; or between the sanctity of private property and the loss of political community suggest that economics and politics cannot be neatly distinguished.

A further problem has been that economists and political scientists aspired to be policy advisers. Powerful people in government and corporations tend to have very specific questions, however; questions that assume a structure of social inequality and a system of power. There was seldom occasion to offer advice that challenged any of those assumptions. Even well-intentioned scholars often became celebrators and rationalizers of the distribution of wealth and power in the society.

Only by understanding that what is economic is political can we get to the bottom of questions about wealth and power or poverty and oppression. Even in the context of exclusively governmental decisions, the connection between the two dimensions is clear. The government acts within an economic framework that limits its alternatives and often defines its activities. First, the federal government has accepted the responsibility for economic prosperity. But second, it is guided by the dictum that prosperity can only be achieved by fostering the growth of concentrated corporate power and personal wealth. Thus it is wrong to characterize the President and Congress as caretakers for the rich or pawns of campaign financiers. As the "society" has an interest in avoiding the distress of depressions or recessions, the President and Congress see themselves as acting in the interests of society when they act on behalf of the wealthy.

The value of the political economy analysis is equally clear with regard to questions not wholly concerned with governing. For example, corporate organization and political bureaucracies are viewed as neutral institutional arrangements because hierarchic structure is seen as a natural and inevitable feature of any advanced economy. But if bureaucrats and workers demanded the right to work cooperatively without hierarchy, the question would immediately become political. Activists and organizers in the 1960s learned well that the structure of the economy is not a given, but is the consequence of the several mechanisms that serve to reproduce it from one generation to the next, and of the exertion of power to ensure its maintenance.

As with any functioning system, the American economy and the American state operate within a fairly consistent logic. Yet we also find growing inconsistencies in the system, which we have called *contradictions*. In using this term, we do not intend the same meaning as Marx intended, though we use it in the same spirit.

To Marx, a contradiction was a dynamic tendency that was an inherent and defining characteristic of a system; it was an element arising from the system and undermining its stability. For example, Marx explains that high productivity—a virtue of capitalism—is achieved as a result of workers laboring together in alienating circumstances. But by being pressed together, workers are better able to recognize their oppression and to overcome it, than if they were kept apart. Similarly, the essays in this book highlight contradictory forces in the political economy. Yet we make no claim for these as dynamic patterns which necessarily exist in corporate capitalism, and which will eventually lead to its destruction. We do no more than contend that they are clearly important inconsistencies, and that they are manifestly prevalent.

We are not sanguine about the possibility of humanistic change. People's efforts toward humanistic change are often subverted by the exigencies of working through existing institutions; or their efforts are suppressed; or their energies are sapped by a constant battle to survive. Still, we share the optimism of our authors that the visibility of the contradictions they point out has prompted people to begin working to bring about a decent society, and that good citizenship as we define it is on the rise. We hope that the discussion of alternatives juxtaposed with an examination of the present strains on the political economy will stimulate both the visionary thinking and the practical activities necessary to bring about humanistic change.

Contents

Overview

In *Being and Doing* (New York: Beacon
Press, 1973), Marcus Raskin outlined a novel
conception of the structure of our society.
He argued that we live our lives within the
confines of four colonies: violence colony,
plantation colony, channeling colony, and
dream colony. Each colony is hierarchically
structured, and together the four encompass
all aspects of our lives—school, work, home
life, leisure—from infancy to death. Upon
introduction into this system, an individual
learns how to relate to hierarchy; she or he
develops a hierarchic-other, a type of
alter-ego that drives one to respond to
demands that are external to oneself, that are
"besides oneself." Raskin thus focused on the
fundamental problematic in Marx's
work—alienation—and examined its
ramifications in a modern context. The
hierarchic-other is a construct that attempts
to explain alienation in terms of a nonclass
structure of society.

1

The colonies overlap, of course; they are not distinct, unrelated entities. For Raskin, the richest area for investigation seemed therefore to be the factors which reinforce this interrelationship. A major factor is knowledge—the knowledges which are developed to teach individuals how to act and what to expect. The type of knowledges appropriate to a colonized reality, and certainly the type of knowledges necessary for a reconstructed society, thus became a critical subject for consideration. This was the impetus for the work Raskin is doing now, and which is reflected in his essay here.

Raskin describes the assumptions and values which form the foundation for traditional views on the economy and the state. He suggests that they have served to create and reinforce a colonized reality. The feelings of frustration and unease which we experience reflect the contradiction between our felt experiences and our accepted knowledges, between human impulses and hierarchical structures. Raskin suggests that this dissonance provides the basis for developing new knowledges and institutions which might reflect human values rather than colonized control.

1

Linking Liberation and Politics

Marcus Raskin

In recent years, say, the last decade, Americans have wondered what the moral basis is for our institutions and our "knowledges." We are like surfers riding the tidal waves of profound value shifts and institutional instabilities. Because of this unease, there is an attempt to understand anew and to develop paths and models predicated on somewhat different assumptions of human nature and action than those by which American institutions operate.

Our assumptions and values are embedded in the knowledges of economics and political science, just as these same knowledges are a mirror of our faulty institutions. There is a mutually reinforcing and only partially dialectical relationship between the types of knowledges developed and the kinds of institutions fostered by a society, and especially by its ruling groups. From time to time—when there is the felt sense and the objective appearance of a systemic break, or when a new class (conscious of itself as a class) reaches for power, or when there is a realization that the old definitions of class do not apply because most people both subjectively and objectively realize they are in the same situation—new modes of knowledge come into being and new institutional arrangements are attempted and discussed.

This volume of essays is in part a recognition and representation of this changed situation in American practical and intellectual life. In this essay, I attempt to outline the knowledge-value assumptions of the present system. I suggest that they are objectively faulty and rather frightening in their consequences; that they foster elements of behavior that, when mediated through institutions and roles and finally mechanical categories, are similar to the behavior of the Ik tribe. The Ik, made famous in the United States by Colin Turnbull, survived, but only as individuals *against* other individuals; the residue of decency dissolved. I then make some observations about the nature of the state and about assumptions concerning the nature of man which are revealed in the state. In particular, I discuss the prevailing assumptions about man which caused the development of the kind of state the people of the United States now have—with the understanding that this state has annulled its own social contract. Thus, we require quite a different social order, and current events—from war to Watergate to consumer crises such as fuel, to unemployment—point up this need with a brutal force.

How Did All "This" Start?

As Erich Kahler has pointed out, the modern concept of the economy as a particular sphere of human activities and conditions is relatively recent, dating from the eighteenth century and growing out of the work and thought of Adam Smith.[1] There was, however, a crude system of economics, mercantilism, which operated before the development of the so-called free economics of Adam Smith.

1. Erich Kahler, *Man the Measure* (New York: George Braziller, 1956).

Unrecognized mercantilist beliefs persist today. The individual leader and his clique must identify the state's interests with their own so that they can be free of challenge from other individuals and groups within their own borders. Thus, the English mercantile kings—for example, Edward IV and Henry VII—built up their own fortunes "using their position for obtaining personal privileges" to grow rich and independent of Parliament. Laws and policies were fashioned accordingly. Modern American politicians have attempted to use their positions for similar purposes. This is especially true for those leaders whose political power far exceeded their economic power; those who represented groups (or themselves) that had not solidified their economic power, but had thrust themselves into the councils of political power. Nixon, for example, attempted to solidify his own and his group's financial and long-term political position by developing new fortunes for himself and encouraging his cronies to do the same.

It is an old story for people in power to accrue to themselves as many different kinds of power as possible. This is reflective of a long-standing political (and ethical) belief in the supremacy of power values in the real world. As Thrasymachus noted to the idealistic Socrates, what counted was power, and those who had power decided on the meaning of justice.

The ideologues of capitalist economics over the last several hundred years have not been quite so crude in dealing with power as it worked its will in the world. According to Adam Smith, acquisitiveness—one other name for the power position—was an invariant human condition which stemmed fron nature and reason. Consequently, it was acceptable and legitimate. Walter Weisskopf points out that the translation of Adam Smith's position in practice meant that this inherent acquisitive attitude, mediated through a very specific economic system, necessitated a continuous striving.

> The striving was for more and more money, wealth,
> possessions, and riches [which] developed against fierce
> resistance because it ran counter to the entire Occidental

tradition. Moneymaking for its own sake, the taking of interest,
buying cheap and selling dear, exploiting the fluctuations of
supply and demand for one's own advantage—all these and
other activities which form the daily routine of economic life in
the modern economy were considered morally reprehensible
throughout Western civilization until the advent of capitalism.[2]

The theorists of free enterprise had hoped that such behavior
was not depraved in its consequences. Men like Ricardo and Smith
wanted to reward the hard worker, the striver, and the independent
minded. In effect, they encouraged—as the European discovery of
other parts of the world had encouraged—a new definition of self and
a clear definition of interest which could readily be understood,
weighed, and quantified in the marketplace. In other words, such
ideas were the perfect rationale for a new class which wanted to
undercut and limit the power of the aristocracy. The economic
knowledge, which both described and promoted this way of life,
assumed, as Weisskopf points out, that nature and reason "instilled"
people with the drive or instinct of economic self-interest; monetary
gain was accomplished through hard work, producing more products,
and selling them to others. Perhaps more important, each of the little
self-interests were additive because they resulted in national economic growth, the production of all things that can be bought, sold,
or used by the society.

From the eighteenth century onward, another principle was
developed from the assumption of an inherent attitude of acquisitiveness in man. Partly grandiose and partly scientific, this attitude
claimed that it was crucial for man to move beyond merely
understanding nature; that, hereafter, man must master and conquer
nature. It was to be exploited for use. Nature became a resource not
only for man but for his economic profit. The schools and
universities, through the knowledges they developed and the beliefs
they advocated, bolstered this attitude for the benefit of capitalism.
The horrendous result was a new form of imperialism which said that

2. Walter Weisskopf, "Image of Man in Economics," *Social Research* (August
1973): 552.

those who were satisfied to live with nature and would not join in conquering it would themselves have to be conquered. Such people were seen as primitive in their tools, attitudes, and consciousness.

By the nineteenth century, Darwinism reflected this principle of survival and reward for the "fittest." After all, if all human endeavor could be framed in terms of nature, reason, and inexorable economic laws of history, then businessmen did not need to justify themselves on moral or religious grounds. By mid-twentieth century, a bloody world war was fought by nations and leaders on both sides who emulated the Darwin-Spencer school of survival of the fittest. Was it really possible that those principles so fundamental to the Manchester liberals were also crucial to the twentieth-century Fascist totalitarians? Mussolini praised the herioc and power-oriented inclinations which seemed to be present in the ideas of the Benthamite and the Manchester School. Even Bentham's reform of the prison was little more than a totalitarian scheme for remaking the individual into a mirror of the correcting institution.

The Manchester liberals placed their faith in two trends which theoretically seemed sound but in practice turned out to be disastrous. One theme, the labor theory of value, asserted that reward should "increase in proportion to effort." Another was that exchange was a good unto itself if the values exchanged were equal. The problem in both cases was that people had different operational definitions of what should be rewarded, what was really "effort," and what was value. So long as people themselves were seen as usable commodities who rented out their lives, then supply and demand became more important than the issue of how hard a man, woman, or child worked; or what the products were that were made. It meant that those who had capital and power had to live within an "as if" or representational system of value and exchange (usually through the money price) which colonized themselves as well as those who became the commodities.

The colonizers, however, became used to a situation in which there was always an army of "unemployed" waiting to rent or sell themselves out so they could eat. In most cases, the bourgeois accepted the "as if" reality, finding it easier to justify than to change for one more natural and humane. The state itself could be counted on to step into the picture and to justify the rich, powerful, and wellborn by assigning them splendid missions to be carried out through entities known as corporations to which the state would grant charters. The creation of the corporations was the very means to avoid personal liability and risk. It was also the way to produce and encourage accumulation which was unearned. The corporations would be treated as individuals. Like the children's books that grant human qualities to Donald Duck and Bugs Bunny, the corporation itself, over the years, became anthropomorphic. With the corporation, money and the market became the mask to hide the intrinsic worth of things and people. In its daily operations with the bourgeois class, the state was both a willing agent and the principal for protecting the rights of particular cliques to sell dear and buy cheap. This was all accomplished by the state through the issuance of charters and licenses for monopoly or corporate activity.

Yet, it was never contemplated in English law that corporate charters would be open-ended or perpetual. Indeed, it was assumed that the state had the power to regulate the corporations although it advocated the corporate form as the better way for individuals to be productive and for them to create personal wealth. Many of those who received such charters actually purchased them. No doubt members of the same family occupied places in the state apparatus as well as in their own corporations, each helpful to the other. More resourceful bourgeois were in both places at the same time. Nevertheless, charters were more than pro forma, in perpetuo privileges. They could be revoked, although there was, it seemed, great peril in doing so. In 1684, Charles II compelled the London Livery Corporation to "surrender their charters and accept in place of them new charters in which it was provided by a special clause that the wardens' and clerks' names were first to be presented to the King for his approval, and if rejected, that the courts of assistants were to elect others, and so on, from time to time, until his Majesty should be satisfied, any election contrary to such provisions to be void." The king also reserved the power of removing any wardens, assistants, or clerks.[3] It was widely believed that the attempt of King James II to enforce this principle of chartering led to tyranny and, indeed, to the Revolution of 1688.

In the United States, it is only relatively recently that, for all intents and purposes, charters have been granted in perpetuo. At one time, the New York State constitution "required a two-thirds vote of both houses before a charter could be granted, while other States went so far as to demand ratification by popular vote where banking powers were concerned." [4] One wonders what the political result would be if the states decided to call back the charters or if the United States decided to "federalize" each corporation, placing limits on what was made, the nature of participation among workers and "investors." Would the upper managers and the very rich see such a move as "tyrannical"? Would they throw in with the armed forces to "right" such an injustice? Would workers and consumers see such chartering as liberating and revolutionary? But let us not get ahead of our story. These are endings that the reader will have to supply. Instead—back to the interplay of knowledge and the state and the economic system.

Modern political economy—or economics—is predicated on the assumption of division of labor and the development of markets of exchange. Such divisions assume that in fact people will not only do each task well but will find a noncoercive means of working together. Indeed, those very social cooperative modes that were necessary for production among the producers were of necessity predicated on cooperation and the kind of property that was better shared. Yet the thought of Ricardo or Adam Smith assumed a kind of interest and motivation which, as Marx said in the *Economic and Philosophic Manuscripts of 1844*, was not humanity but egoism.[5] The system of

3. John P. Davis, *Corporations* (New York: Capricorn Books, 1961), p. 22.
4. Henry A. Wallace, *Whose Constitution?* (New York: Reynal & Hitchcock, 1936), p. 156.
5. Karl Marx, *Economic and Philosophic Manuscripts of 1844* (Moscow: Foreign Languages Publishing, 1959), pp. 151–53.

interests and egoism, as it developed the modern market—or, indeed, the modern oligopolistic system—was powerful enough to perpetuate the system of private property through the modern corporation. The modern corporation maintained enough of a "public" character as to appear to be a collective or cooperative venture. Of course, in its practice, nothing could have been further from the actual mechanics of the modern corporation. Rather than its having a corporate soul, which was cooperative and public, it developed sophisticated mechanisms for exploitation over its own employees and the buyers of their products. The corporation was pyramidal and functional.

In Europe, the nineteenth-century workers could no longer be satisfied with or accept the theories and ideology of the bourgeois class. Between 1837 and 1848, the English Chartists organized themselves into a conscious group with a clear program. They aimed at the limitation of the working day and the right of the worker to enjoy the fruits of his labor. The Chartists identified the ruling class as the owners and viewed the government itself not as a disinterested observer, but as a force for the ownership class. The Chartists did not see their work as replacing the parliamentary system. They developed a social program within the framework of parliamentarism and capitalism, calling for universal suffrage, secret voting, and equal electoral districts.

Socialist thought and action was the necessary outgrowth of the dialectical tension between workers, reformers, profits, needs, and force. The socialists argued that the political freedoms which were "won" in the English, the American, and the French revolutions were incomplete because new forms of dependencies had already occurred. Thus, the transformation of the political system to guarantee rights in one sense mocked the way that people actually had to live. Ideas of private property which were to be guaranteed and protected by the state—because they were imputed as being the sine qua non for other liberties—meant that those who were aggressive, inventive, corrupt, or had large inheritances could insulate themselves against the poor and the wretched. They had to exchange nothing and do less in terms of the market. Even the "honest" merchants were, by the nature of the system, corrupt. It was not the modern schoolmen, the socialists, who made this discovery. It was the Thomists who said that the honest businessman, a pure merchant who dealt absolutely fairly with everyone and who became rich as a result of his ability, was not exchanging anything with the society. "All the wealth went one way. Through a succession of actions, each of which was entirely lawful, wealth leaked out of society." [6]

The socialists hoped to end this systemic corruption through the collectivization of wealth so that the worker, the producer, could in fact receive his just due. Yet there was the belief that capitalism was a necessary stage to socialism. Saint-Simon had argued that politics was a secondary function, that socialism would become a world movement just as irreversible as the industrial revolution and would spread throughout the world. He believed that property and economic wealth determined politics and value, using as one proof that the political constitution of France had changed ten times in twenty-five years without any visible positive result to the human conditions of the French. (Yet one must be somewhat diffident in automatically accepting the view that economics precedes politics in the modern state. If the United States were to adopt a new constitution, it is doubtful that the present economic forces would survive intact. The political struggle that would emerge around rewriting the Constitution would make clear that independent economic power would have to bend to the will of the community.)

The debate about value, intrinsic and extrinsic, continues today and is reflected in these essays. In the United States, a question has been asked over the past several decades about what, in fact, is work or "meaningful" work. Once we say that work is something more than what another is willing to pay for, we can begin to evaluate work according to a set of criteria that is substantially different from that which comes to us from the seventeenth and eighteenth centuries. For example, does a person work as a "producer" in the Marxist sense if he is a salesman or an accountant? There are

6. Yves Simon, *Philosophy of Democratic Government* (Chicago: University of Chicago Press, 1951).

indications in Marx's writings that such people would be seen more as parasites who were living lived lives. In a modern society such as the United States, one which is overdeveloped and now begins to recolonize itself, it may well be the case that most "jobs" are parasitical jobs without purpose or, in fact, having negative productive purposes. It may be that literally millions of people are working at things which should not be done in the first place. Does that mean that employment by the state or the corporation should be "disvalued"? Or is all work to be seen as value no matter what its content, so long as another pays for it?

The picture that Marx and the Marxists emphasized was the potentiality of man and the determinism of history which would bring into being that potentiality, away from foolish or meaningless work. While Marx also believed in reward for work, he saw such questions as secondary to the fundamental ones. He saw the capitalist system as making people into things; people became hobbled and finally commodities for rent and sale. There was nothing noble or ennobling about them within the context of a capitalist system. "The real, active orientation of man to himself as a species being, or his manifestation as a species being (i.e., as a human being), is only possible by his really bringing out of himself all the powers that are his as the species man—something which in turn is only possible through the totality of man's actions. . . ." [7] It is through labor, according to Marx, that man should be able to prove himself. It can be the labor of creativity on an individual basis, or a group project. But in the capitalist form, Marx maintains, labor is alienating. Thus, the work that people do in the capitalist system is the attempt to come to themselves through alienated labor. As long as they do not own or control the means of production, their labor must be alienated—that is, they must sell their labor. People can never come to themselves or to others except in an alienated way because of capitalism. Marx has said that "The great beauty of capitalist production is that it not only reproduces wage labourers as wage

7. Marx, *Economic and Philosophic Manuscripts,* p. 156. et seq.

labourers, but that it produces in relation to the accumulation of capital continuously a relative overpopulation of wage labourers." [8]

It is clear, then, that in Marx's definition, class is a set of human definitions which constantly change, take on different forms, and are therefore hard to follow as the technological and political base of the society also changes and the outward manifestations of class relationships mask the identities that one person has with another in a pyramidal structure. The last chapters of *Capital I*, tell the story of an E. G. Wakefield, who wanted to develop systematic colonization in the United States. By this he meant a way of producing and reproducing workers. He brought some three thousand people to the United States who then escaped his clutches to become workmen or farmers. As Marx said, "Capital is not a thing, but a social relationship between people mediated by things." Colonization clarifies the social role which capital plays whether it is seen horizontally—as the Mother Country "protecting" and "exploiting" another country—or vertically—as an internal system of exploitation and illegitimacy. In this sense, wealth and capital are merely one constituent part of a complex system of hierarchic relationships between the user and the used, the living and the lived.

It is assumed that in no way can any but the few, the most talented, be admitted from the masses into the society of the colonizer. There is, of course, no way for the colonized to escape, since they are trapped territorially and economically in fulfilling the tasks of the colonizer. Such traditional ideas of the social hierarchy were accepted among the American founding fathers. Alexander Hamilton often noted that the society was divided into the few and the many. If a person had economic position, property, education, he was identified as a permanent member of the political community— one of the few. On the other hand, the many are thought of as children, unsteady, immature, impulsive, ignorant, easily swayed by flattery and unable to plan their lives. Consequently, it was altogether reasonable that the contours of the state would be set by

8. Marx, *Capital* (Moscow: Progress Publishers) 1:796.

the few. Only in the voting mechanism might there exist a relationship, an interaction, between the few and the many. As Jefferson wrote in a letter to Abbe Arnoud, July 19, 1789,

> We think in America that it is necessary to introduce the people into every department of government as far as they are capable of exercising it. . . . 1. They are not qualified to exercise themselves the Executive Department, but they are qualified to name the person who shall exercise it. With us therefore they choose this office every four years. 2. They are not qualified to legislate. With us therefore they only cause the legislators.[9]

Thus, it was thought that the colonized had by nature different appetites and consciousness. They were more transitory, superficial, and unserious, whereas the colonizer, the guardian if you like, had plans and made connections. Indeed, it was said that the colonizer had *gravitas,* which was later manifested through his demeanor and bank account. In practice, a different reality developed. Such comments and assumptions about human nature turned out to be prescriptive ones which effectively protected the powerful against the powerless by encouraging the development of national institutions, and a national psychology and consciousness, which programmed people to accept such attitudes and behavior in their everyday lives. In this way, as I have said elsewhere, the colonized developed a *beside-himself,* a way of being in the world which would make it easy to exist within the prescriptive contours outlined by the philosophy of the oligarchs, the colonizers. Yet this view was mixed with the strain of another spirit.

The original theory of the American state was not merely to supply the rationalizing system for capitalism or to accept the colonizing principle of user-used. The state was the ideological and psychological essence which people were to believe in because it identified rights within a group and gave liberty to seek other spaces. As Lenny Bruce once said, "My forefathers came to this country so

9. *Works of Jefferson* (Ford ed.), 5:105.

they could be obscene." [10] Literally, this meant off-the-scene, the development of their own representatives and institutions. As one constitutional scholar, W. W. Crosskey, has said, the state, which encapsulated the United States, was in fact the people. The notion that the nation had to be set against the state as in the French revolution—where the nation was set against the king—was inapplicable in the American system. On the other hand, the United States, as a state, operated according to certain capitalistic principles which allowed capitalist economics to take precedence over politics. (Finally, the political principles of oligarchy gave rise to the economic principles of oligopoly.)

Chief Justice John Marshall interpreted the commerce clause of the Constitution to mean that the United States was to have a "national" commerce, one huge common market without internal state tariffs or burdens which could cut down the free flow of goods. Goods (bads) were the new king or sovereign. They were to move into any market guarded by the state, symbolically and literally. Workers were to be able to have the "liberty of movement" so that they could in fact become commodities, interchangeable, individuated, and quite alone, chasing capital—that is, wherever capital decided there would be a job for the worker. The history of geographic mobility of Americans is caused by more than the weather. Americans move for job "opportunity."

Since the Second World War, the United States, operating as a state, had another function to play for the economy. The state was expected to use the new economic knowledges which held that depressions could be deferred through deficit spending. The knowledges developed during this period in economics also had to assume the stability of the modern corporation. Modern economics equated growth with progress and assumed that the instrument for growth (of whatever kind) was the corporation. It was also believed that the state's economic policies could develop growth patterns for the economy that would take up any corporate slack.

10. Lenny Bruce in conversation with his lawyer arguing his defense against charge of obscenity in a New York nightclub performance.

While the elephantine military and national security establishment is in part a result of the psychology of fear and the imperial view—that to play a great role as the number-one imperial power it is necessary to have a huge military—it is also true that military spending has served as an outlet for Executive or state spending. It was unlikely that a Congress made up of local bourgeois would develop a program much beyond that of social control over the poor classes; it was even more unlikely that an Executive or a President who must play to the largest interests in the country—as they are—could develop a social program which causes turbulence to those interests. Thus, it became easier to spend on military hardware and manpower than on either social programs or public enterprise which competed with the economic corporate interests.

The government's economists had hoped that deficit spending would create new purchasing power among the people; in other words, people would buy goods (bads) they did not need even as their real needs and services—health, education, the community— atrophied. The problem of deficit spending, beyond the fact that the people have been spending for things which should be theirs by right, and spending on products which have turned each person into a little unit of consumption, is the overall and fundamental fact that state power cannot easily control capitalist excesses. It seems that deficit spending is usually accompanied by inflation. This means, of course, a flexible dollar worth less (exchange manipulation). As a tool of state intervention into the internal economy, a flexible mechanism is "necessary." However, there is a contradiction between such a use of the dollar—which endeavors to change the intrinsic and extrinsic worth of things on a continuous basis—and the one which was assigned to it at the end of the Second World War at Bretton Woods. The economic diplomats at that conference anointed the dollar as being as stable as gold, and therefore the standard for the world's monetary system. In other words, the world's social system, the relationship of one social class to another, was to remain relatively constant. As Ernest Mandel has said, "The contradiction between the dollar as an anticyclical device in the United States and the dollar as money of account on the world market has already become insurmountable." [11]

American liberal economists who historically have seen the state as their major client are caught on the philosophic and political dilemma of value, exchange, interest, and market. These words no longer fit the reality they are intended to describe. There are, of course, more "practical" concerns. Economists and politicians are confronted by the development of the multinational corporation which owes its patriotic commitments to no single country, but to the capitalist system. It is relatively free of the residue of patriotic belief that seemed to motivate earlier capitalists. If the corporation no longer "needed" the nation-state, and the people felt alienated from those governing processes which the state projected, where did this leave the state itself? Could the state be more than a repository and initiator of violence, or an employer of last resort, picking up the debris left behind by itself and other corporate institutions? Could it project itself as something more than an instrument of terror holding the people hostage in games of nuclear chicken or pursuing imperial wars which had neither interest nor purpose attached to them?

Each act of the American state seemed to reflect a fundamental weakness. While its bureaucracy at the lower levels attempted to develop a maintenance system for the society, the managers and operators in the upper reaches of government have devised a new spoils system which corrupts the offices they hold either through contracting out the government to corporations under the guise of their "know-how" or merely through stealing. Meanwhile, the process of voting is successively extended. It is not proved, however, that the extension of the vote causes any reallocation of power or participation in the daily economic and political operations of American life. There is a historical reason for this.

In the development of the American political system, voting was originally meant to reflect individual status as a taxpayer. Property

11. Ernest Mandel, *Marxist Economic Theory* (New York: Monthly Review Press, 1968), 2:532.

qualifications were, in many places within the United States, required for participation in an election. In the western United States, where everyone was a landowner and recent immigrant, equal suffrage was introduced in the early nineteenth century. By 1850, all white men were able to vote and, after the Civil War, according to myth, blacks were able to vote. Following the First World War, women, having embarrassed Wilson through street struggles and organizing, also received the vote. And by the 1970s, people eighteen years of age and over were given the right to vote.

This suggested that power and sovereignty rested with the people, and seemed to assure a uniform or single class of electors. Nothing was further from the truth as economic power protected itself from the voters by inventing ways of keeping their power and accumulation intact and beyond the reach of the political process. Simultaneously, the President, through the elective process, became the only citizen with the legal power to destroy himself and the world. Yet there is a blind faith in the American system, perhaps that residue which is so important for people "thrown" into a world which allows them few moorings and little comprehension of their place. The social contract of obeisance for protection ended with Kennedy when, as President, he risked the lives of the people at the Cuban missile crisis, arrogating sovereign power to himself and removing it from the people.

The most obvious alternative to this is socialism, although in practice there seem to be severe drawbacks. The practice in most socialist countries may not be relevant to the American experience or necessarily liberating. Indeed, as pointed out in certain of the essays (Adams), socialism in the form of nationalization may not in fact transform anything within the society in terms of control and decisional power. In other cases, when socialism is mediated through state power, as in the East European countries, it becomes a cover for unrequited forms of state oppression. Political concepts of ruler over ruled remain intact. Thus, in considering socialism, its context and relationship to traditional—and frightening—forms of state power must be understood so that power can in fact be deflected and transformed. One cannot forget that hierarchy, violence, threat are endemic to all forms of the state which have developed during the twentieth century. People must find those social forms and develop social institutions which link freedom, liberty, and self-sufficiency to the practice of sharing, empathy, and cooperation.

This requires a path of epistemology and action which will develop a system of linking principles and linking knowledges. By this I do not mean that concepts are tied dialectically like love and hate, which then in some wondrous way yield a synthesis. I mean linking in a structural sense (is it biological or "natural"?) where one strand without another leaves us incomplete or crippled. For example, freedom and sharing, liberty and empathy, self-sufficiency and cooperation are concepts which in a healthy society need to be linked or coupled. They have a practical (in the sense of good end) and prescriptive result that does not set the self against others. It assumes shared and voluntary authority among people. Surely it is time to jump over the Cartesian hurdles of "I think therefore I am" which, for no necessary reason, has set political philosophy and analysis of social events in the contextual frame of individualism.[12]

Most important, if we do not develop or find such principles, we will not be able to curtail pharaohistic power whether it comes in the form of the state or the corporation. The result will be that the fundamental contribution of the twentieth century to the lives of people and to political thought will be totalitarianism: rule by direct or indirect terror in ever larger, hierarchic, pharaohistic units which are pathological. It is our unfortunate reality that modern organization fosters institutions predicated on the obliteration of personal space without the coincident development of social or public space. (Thus, drugs.) The result is a cruel removal of limits that define our humanity and what we as people can and will do. An economic and political system operating with terror as its ever-present instrument whether aimed at the internally colonized or the externally colonized threatens people with the loss of their humanity. It causes people to

12. Contrary to what some of the Right may believe, individualism, egoism, and existentialism, a person's understanding of being in the world, are not the same.

lose touch with human limits, which are crucial to decent actions. Films such as *Modern Times* and *Dr. Strangelove* have caught the contradictions inherent in the modern economic and political system. They show how organization makes people mad in ideological "roles" they only wear as attempts are made to obliterate their spaces.

In the United States, what people feel about their situation creates a consciousness for a transformed social order. The necessary stage of muckraking is coming to a close. Indeed, mere muckraking could become a barrier to translating consciousness into reconstructive knowledge and action since after a certain level, muckraking has the effect of sapping people of energy to act or to see things in new ways. They begin to believe that "corruption" is an invariant condition of man. As the Marquis d'Argenson said (quoted by Rousseau in *The Social Contract*), "Learned researches in public law are often nothing but the history of ancient abuses; and to devote much labor to studying them is misplaced pertinacity." Scholarship and journalism as well need to move to another stage. This requires the development of reconstructive knowledge related to the economy and the state. We might begin by returning to ancient definitions of economy, which would help us to define value: What exchanges are necessary and why are they necessary? What is power, creativity, and participation? What is the purpose of a so-called political economy? And what is "need" beyond consumerization and consumption? In other words, economics and political science would become a clearly stated system of normative principles.

It is important to note that when knowledges are stated clearly as part of an external interest or consequence, we are much more able to identify their dangers. It is then that we are able to judge both their explicit purpose and their internal coherence. As Habermas has said, the Nazi attempt to develop a German physics or the Soviet attempt to develop a Marxist genetics became clearly laughable and challengeable. The reason, of course, was that it became possible to judge its form, content and consequence. We are, however, chary about judging the "neutral" sciences because we assume that they are outside class, system and purpose. Yet we know that nothing exists in such pure form, let alone phenomena which scientists arrange conceptually for purposes of practical action. The result is that we are not easily able to judge the effects of such neutral science before its pernicious effects are known. Because it is operational and many times descriptive of the way nature is and the way people act, we are deluded into judging its meaning and think that there is no other way of comprehending phenomena, arranging its meaning conceptually, and applying it in new ways. This is wrong. The task of reconstructive knowledge is to show that it can be done otherwise.[13]

While these words were meant to apply to the natural sciences, they are especially applicable to the social sciences. Those who will do the new political science and economics must be aware of the influence upon them of their own changing consciousness and the practical ground upon which each question of economics and political science of necessity stands. They will need to rethink about value, interest, exchange, power, and their modes of representation in the everyday world of each of us. Thus, the new scholars will not fear to analyze hierarchic authority, prejudices which in fact lead to horrifying results and those empty technologies and workings that have no purpose except their own reproduction and expansion. We seek to develop reconstructive knowledges and linking principles. As well, we must find ways of criticizing each other's work as a permanent basis of our scholarship and practice. One mode of that criticism must include existential questions: Can we go beyond our present faulty institutions and colonizing knowledges to the development of livable new structures which create a decent society? Can we develop an economy and a social contract from I-in-We and empathetic relationships? We shall see.

13. Marcus Raskin, "Answer to Critics," *Philosophy Forum* 12 (1972): 165–93. Symposia on *Being and Doing* by Marcus Raskin.

II

Contradictions in the Political Economy

As the various phases of the administration's economic policy follow one upon the other; as prices rise while wages are controlled; as balance-of-payments crises seem to occur with taxing regularity, we can sense that the political economy is entering a period of confusion and transition. The selections in this section provide some indications of the maladies of the political economy, exploring four disparate but essential aspects: the relationship between the state and the "private sector," distribution of income and wealth, the implications of burgeoning multinational corporations, and the nature of work.

Government intervention has been crucial to the operation of corporate capitalism throughout the twentieth century. Regulation, the provision of capital, and caring for the unemployed and unemployable exemplify governmental

23

activity. But, as James O'Connor contends, such services are
increasingly difficult to finance through taxation. Federal, state, and
local governmental levies already try the patience of the taxpayer.
Meanwhile, corporate decisions with regard to technology and plant
location create increased unemployment at home. The resulting fiscal
crisis threatens the postwar relationship between the state and the
powerful corporation, and the corporation and organized
labor.

A second source of transformation and tension is described by
Richard Barnet, Ronald Müller, and Joseph Collins: the global
corporation. The corporate form—originally an offspring of the
state—now has pretensions that transcend the boundaries of nations.
Barnet, Müller, and Collins discuss the implications of a world
economy in which five hundred global corporations can dictate
national economic policies (and so affect the state) without control by
state leaders. For example, global corporations increasingly transfer
production facilities out of the United States to countries with cheap
labor. America imports an increasing percentage of its finished
industrial goods and exports agricultural products. The combination
describes the situation of an "underdeveloped" country.

The deleterious effects of global operations are also described in
the United States Tariff Commission's study of multinational
corporations. Though the authors struggled valiantly to show how
MNCs benefit the economy, they also demonstrate the havoc that
global corporations can wreak on national financial arrangements.
Since 1967, we have witnessed a continuous succession of
international monetary crises. Nixon, in his famous speech to the
nation on August 15, 1971, blamed the monetary crisis on
international "speculators" who irresponsibly sought to profit from
America's distress. The image of gnomes plotting in the counting
houses of Zurich does not stand up, however. The Tariff
Commission study shows that global corporations have both the
capacity and the motive to engage in short-run financial speculation
on currencies.

In their effort to increase profits or to protect against losses, multinationals create runs on the money market that lead to further selling of an already weak currency. Even small transactions by multinationals can overwhelm the international monetary system. The resulting instability undermines the trading position of the United States and contributes to growing inflation in this country and elsewhere.

The postwar evolution of the political economy has helped create continuous economic growth, and what politicians like to call "prosperity" for the United States. The literal cornucopia of goods and services produced is an accomplishment which should not be dismissed lightly. However, the benefits of this outpouring have never been shared with any semblance of equity. The data presented by Letitia Upton and Nancy Lyons demonstrate that the distribution of income and wealth has not changed significantly over the last twenty-five years. The simple fact remains that while one-fifth of the American population enjoys unparalleled wealth, one-fifth lives in poverty and hunger and another fifth lives at or below what the Labor Department defines as a minimal budget for family existence.

Even Americans who have steady employment and consider themselves middle- and upper-middle-class workers find their lives hollowed out, their minds colonized by the operation of a hierarchical corporate structure. Instead of participating in a creative, enlightening, and productive process, increasingly both blue- and white-collar employees find themselves limited to assigned tasks and routine operations. Work fulfills no needs, but is merely a means to acquire resources to fulfill needs. The best portion of a person's life is thus bartered away in meaningless activity.

Michael Maccoby and Katherine A. Terzi present evidence, gathered during a three-year study, of incompatibility between the character of the American worker and the nature of his work. This is the third contradiction we identify in the political economy. Workers whose "independent" character found expression in such occupations as farmer, craftsman, or small businessman are forced into routinized office and service jobs which allow little autonomy. At the same time, the study discovered workers in every occupational sector whose character is more independent and more demanding. These two developments become more significant in the context of a world where even professional and white-collar work affords less and less room for worker discretion.

Maccoby and Terzi conclude with a discussion of what principles must guide changes in the nature of work if we are to reconstruct our political economy and create a more humanistic one.

The five essays in this section do not encompass a full discussion of the dynamics of the American political economy. We do not touch on militarism, for example, nor on the roles played by racism or sexism. But the articles do examine three fundamental strains in the political economy. These contradictions form the basis for the growing tax revolt; for the increasing chaos in international monetary arrangements; for loss of employment in the United States; and finally, for growing worker alienation that is evidenced by increasing labor strikes, sabotage, and absenteeism. The authors thus make clear that economic matters can no longer be considered problems simply of technical adjustment.

Inflation, Fiscal Crisis, and the American Working Class

James O'Connor

Economic Structure of Modern Capitalism

Economic activities in modern capitalist societies may be classified into two broad groups: industries that are organized by private capital and those that are organized by the state. Production and distribution organized by private businessmen fall into two subgroups: competitive industries and monopolistic industries. In reality, there is considerable overlap between the three groups of industries (or sectors of the economy). Moreover, each sector depends on the other sectors in various ways. Nevertheless, each has its own distinguishing features.

In the competitive sector, the capital-to-labor ratio and output per worker (or productivity) are low, and the growth of production depends less on capital investment and technical progress than on the growth of employment. Production is typically small-scale and markets are normally local or regional in scope. Familiar examples of competitive industries producing for local or regional markets and organized by small businessmen are restaurants, drug and grocery stores, service stations, and many other branches of distribution; garages, appliance repair shops, and other business services; and many light manufacturing industries such as clothing and accessories and commercial displays. Familiar exceptions are textbooks and ethical drugs, which are sold in national markets. Roughly one-third of the American labor force is employed in competitive industries, the largest proportion in services and distribution (or trade).

The significance of low ratios of capital to labor and of low productivity is twofold: first, wages in competitive industries are relatively low; second, there is a tendency toward overcrowding because of the relative ease of setting up business. More, competitive industries are largely confined to producing for markets (or, in the case of trade, selling in markets) that are seasonal, subject to sudden changes in fashion or style, or otherwise irregular or unstable. The irregular nature of product markets means that small businessmen have little opportunity to stabilize production and employment. And since very little capital is invested per worker, there is little incentive for them to do so (even when the opportunity presents itself). The reason is that business losses from excess physical capacity and time lost in setup and shutdown operations are relatively small.

Unstable and irregular product markets and unstable and irregular labor markets go together in competitive industries. Employment in the competitive sector tends to be not only relatively low paid, but also casual, temporary, or seasonal in nature. Workers who are unable to find full-time, year-round, well-paid work in the monopolistic or state sectors flood the competitive sector seeking employment on almost any terms. In the United States, the chief examples are black and other minority workers cut off from "mainstream" opportunities by racism and discrimination; women excluded by sexism from good jobs and good pay; and older workers retired involuntarily from high-wage industries (most compulsory retirement rules are laid down by high-wage firms and industries). The supply of labor in competitive industries is further inflated by workers who do not want regular, year-round employment and who are willing to accept lower wages in order to obtain irregular work. Married women, students, and retired workers all voluntarily seek part-time, temporary, or seasonal work. It has been estimated that about 45 percent of the American work force is "peripheral" or marginal (either out of choice or necessity) and consists largely of blacks and other minorities, women, and youth.[1] In smaller communities, social discrimination and oppression create "relatively large reserves of labor" available to small firms.[2]

The social characteristics of the work force, the highly elastic supply of labor, the multitude of firms in a particular industry, and the small-scale, localized nature of production all combine to obstruct the organization of strong labor unions. More, highly competitive product markets, rapid business turnover, and small profit margins all make it costly for employers to recognize unions that are trying to get established. As a result, the labor movement in the competitive sector is relatively underdeveloped; many labor agreements are "sweetheart" contracts; and established unions are unable to exercise a strong influence on wage rates.

Excepting some competitive industries, the outstanding feature of the competitive sector is that workers are condemned to relative material impoverishment. In 1968, there were more than 10 million workers (about one-seventh of all employed workers) earning less than $1.60 per hour, including 3.5 million paid less than $1.00 hourly. Two-thirds of these workers were employed in retail trade and service industries and more than one-tenth were employed in agriculture, forestry, or fishing. Trade, services, and agriculture are all highly competitive, and are all low-wage industries.[3]

1. Dean Morse, *The Peripheral Worker* (New York: Columbia University Press, 1969).

2. Richard C. Wilcock and Irvin Sobel, *Small City Job Markets* (Urbana, Ill.: University of Illinois Press, 1958).

3. The remaining workers (comprising about one-quarter of the total) were employed in manufacturing, mining, and other industries. Our guess is that most of them worked in the competitive sector, although there is no way to establish this (U.S. Department of Labor, *Manpower Report of the President, 1968* [Washington, D.C.: Government Printing Office, 1968], pp. 83–84). To underline the fact that the

Not only are wages low in competitive industries, but working conditions tend to be poor, and unemployment and underemployment tend to be high. Normally, incomes are insufficient to allow workers to accumulate savings to cover contingencies such as unemployment, indebtedness, sickness, and death. Weak or corrupt labor organizations are not able to win company-paid health, retirement, and other fringe benefits. The result is that the work force in the competitive sector is compelled to look to the state to provide the means of subsistence that it cannot provide for itself, and which private business cannot provide. Workers in competitive industries are condemned to be partial or full dependents of the state, the recipients of income supplements in the form of public hospital services and health care, subsidized housing, welfare and relief, old age assistance, food stamps, and transportation subsidies.

MONOPOLISTIC SECTOR

In the monopolistic sector, the capital-to-labor ratio and productivity are relatively high, and the growth of production depends less on the growth of employment than on increases in capital per worker and on technical progress.[4] Production is typically large-scale and markets are normally national or international in scope. Common examples of monopolistic industries producing for national or international markets and organized by big businessmen are capital goods industries such as steel, copper, aluminum, and electrical

---

competitive sector is the location of a great deal of poverty (which is *created* by the functioning of capitalism as a whole), we quote from the report cited above: "The employed poor—with earnings below the poverty-line even for full-time work—now represent a larger problem, at least in terms of numbers, than the unemployed" (ibid., p. 35).

4. The conclusion of one study is that industries with high concentration ratios (i.e., monopolistic industries) have more technological change than unconcentrated industries (i.e., competitive industries) (Almarin Phillips, "Concentration, Scale and Technological Change in Selected Manufacturing Industries, 1899–1939," *Journal of Industrial Economics* 4 [June 1956]). In another study, it was established that high productivity is associated with larger firms, although there were many exceptions (Karl Borch, "Productivity and Size of Firm," *Production Measurement Review* 12 [February 1958]).

equipment; consumer goods industries such as automobiles, appliances, soap products, and various food products; transportation industries such as railroads, airlines, and branches of shipping. About one-third of the American work force is employed in monopolistic industries, the largest proportion in manufacturing and mining.[5]

The significance of high ratios of capital to labor and high productivity is twofold: first, wages in the monopolistic sector are relatively high, even in the smaller "fringe" firms that coexist with the giants in some monopolistic industries. Second, there exist various barriers to the entry of new capital and hence a relatively stable industrial structure (high capital requirements and overhead costs, advertising and brand loyalty, product differentiation, and costly distribution systems are among the factors that make it difficult to set up business in the monopolistic sector). The large amounts of capital invested per worker give management strong incentives to regularize production and employment in order to avoid losses attributable to unused productive capacity. The complexity of modern technology and work processes also compels management to minimize arbitrary or unexpected elements in production and distribution. Planning is extended downward to ensure the availability of raw materials and other supplies at stable prices and upward into wholesale and retail activities in order to control demands. For these reasons, the demand for labor is relatively stable and work is available on a full-time, year-round basis. White adult males, the dominant social group in society as a whole, have a firm hold on the jobs in the monopolistic sector, especially the better-paid, lighter, and more secure "good" jobs.

The social makeup of the work force, the relatively inelastic demand for labor, and the physical and geographic concentration of production units all facilitate the growth of powerful labor unions in

5. The five hundred largest manufacturing and mining corporations employ about two-thirds of all workers in manufacturing and mining industries. This is a crude measure of the number of workers in the monopolistic sector because many of these corporations sell some of their outputs in competitive markets. On the other hand, many smaller corporations sell in monopolistic markets.

monopolistic industries. More, monopolistic product markets, stable industrial structures, and large profit margins all make it relatively inexpensive for corporations to recognize unions that are trying to get established. As a result, since the 1930s and early 1940s, when workers in most monopolistic industries forced employers to recognize and bargain with their unions, the labor movement in the monopolistic sector has been relatively well developed.

The outstanding feature of the monopolistic sector is that neither prices nor wages are determined solely by the forces of the market. It has long been known that prices are administered in monopolistic (or oligopolistic) industries. It is less well known that wages are also administered.

Wages in monopolistic industries are not tied to productivity in the economy as a whole (as they would be in a system of competitive markets), but rather to productivity in the monopolistic sector. According to the author of the most sophisticated empirical investigation of the subject to date, "productivity gains are more likely to go to the workers the more unionized and concentrated [i.e., monopolized] the industry." [6] Summarizing several studies, another economist writes "the high and low-wage industries . . . correspond in large measure to well and poorly organized and to higher and lower degrees of concentration." [7] Wage increases in one industry in the monopolistic sector spill over to other industries within this sector. [8] But uniformity in wage increases and pattern trends are confined to the monopolistic sector and do not "trickle down" into the competitive sector. In the competitive sector, money wages (and

6. Sara Behman, "Wage Changes, Institutions, and Relative Factor Prices in Manufacturing," *Review of Economics and Statistics* 51 (August 1969): 236.

7. E. Robert Livernash, "Wages and Benefits," in Woodrow Ginsburg et al., *A Review of Industrial Relations Research* (Madison, Wisc.: Industrial Relations Research Association, 1970). The key study is Albert Rees and Mary T. Hamilton, "Postwar Movement of Wage Levels and Unit Labor Costs," *Journal of Law and Economics* 6 (October 1963).

8. "Similarity in wage change has been particularly noted among a group of highly concentrated highly organized industries as found by Harold M. Levinson. E. Maher demonstrated a high degree of uniformity in wage change in 23 large key-bargain situations. . . . Lloyd Ulman found a strong correlation of wage change with wage level from 1948–1962" (Livernash, "Wages," p. 110).

prices) are tied to aggregate demand. Upward surges in money wages in competitive industries can be attributed not to technical progress and improvements in productivity, but rather to inflation.

The inseparable link between productivity and wages in monopolistic industries and the bifurcation in the process of wage-price determination in the monopolistic and competitive sectors are attributable to a political-economic agreement established between Big Capital and Big Labor in the monopolistic sector after World War II, although the origins of this agreement go back to the turn of the century. This agreement is partly embodied in collective bargaining contracts and partly a matter of mutual understanding between corporation and union leaders. The agreement contains three basic provisions. First, Big Capital agrees to grant wage increases commensurate with increases in productivity. In other words, the corporations agree to pass on productivity gains to workers in the monopolistic sector in the form of higher wages, rather than to the work force as a whole in the form of lower prices. The result is not only the bifurcation of the work force but also the tendency toward permanent inflation.

Second, in return for wage scales pegged to productivity changes, Big Labor not only abstains from fighting technical progress, but also actively collaborates with employers when major innovations require large-scale reorganization of the work process (although there have been exceptions, notably railroading).[9] A central function of unions in monopolistic industries is to guard against spontaneous rank-and-file activity such as wildcat strikes and agitation around the general issue of "managerial prerogatives" and to maintain labor discipline in general. At times, union leaders have discovered that this is a difficult task because increases in productivity normally depend on labor-saving technological changes,[10] and, as a

9. Workers and unions also fight for reductions in work time, since World War II chiefly in the form of more paid vacations and holidays and earlier retirement. Reduced work time (like higher wages) depends on increases in productivity, in particular, lower unit-wage costs. This factor has provided additional incentives to unions to ally with Big Capital in expanding productivity.

10. It should be added that the relation between productivity and technological

result, the number of jobs (and employed workers) in monopolistic industries tends to rise slowly, and in many cases decreases absolutely. In effect, unions are the agents of technical progress and rational manpower planning by monopoly capital.

But this agreement is *not* an arrangement made between equals. Unions exercise no control over prices, which are flexible only in an upward direction in monopolistic industries. Thus, the third provision of the agreement (closely related to the first), is in effect forced on the unions: this is the need for cost-of-living clauses to keep inflation that is attributable to monopolistic pricing from eroding the purchasing power of wages of union members. The decisive moment was the 1948 United Auto Workers contract which included a cost-of-living escalator. A more or less standard cost-of-living clause then spread to other industries and union contracts. The result is that the burden of inflation is shifted to workers in the unorganized industries and competitive sector.

STATE INDUSTRIES

The state industries, the third major sector of the economy, may be divided into two major groups: production organized by the state itself, and production organized by industries under contract with the state. Examples of the first kind of activity are postal, education, public health, welfare, and other services, and the military effort (excluding the production of arms). Examples of the second type of activity are military equipment, capital construction in education, and highway construction (in Europe, many manufacturing activities fall into this group, as well). In the American economy, about one-eighth of the civilian labor force is engaged in the first type of

change is complex: ". . . increases in labor productivity may arise because of economies of scale or increases in the extent to which productive capacity is used. In addition, since there is often a considerable gap between labor productivity with best-practice techniques and labor productivity with the existing mix of techniques, the rate of growth of labor productivity depends on the rate of diffusion of the best practices. Finally, the rate of growth of labor productivity depends on the nature, as well as on the rate of technological change. . . ." Edwin Mansfield, *The Economics of Technological Change* (New York: Norton, 1968), p. 22.

activity, and perhaps as much as one-third of the total work force is employed in both activities combined.[11]

In the activities organized by the state itself, the ratio of capital to labor and productivity is relatively low (and increases relatively slowly), and the growth of production depends mainly on the growth of employment.

In the second group of activities, the ratio of capital to labor is relatively high, and the growth of production depends on capital investment and technical progress, as well as on the number of workers employed. Nevertheless, productivity in these activities also tends to be relatively low and to increase sluggishly. The reason is twofold: first, the outputs of many military contractors and other state contractors are original or distinct, one-of-a-kind products such as new weapons systems, research and development, and airbases on unfamiliar terrain. This means that it is difficult to make sectoral or temporal comparisons of the physical productivity of labor, and that it is difficult to regularize production planning and coordination and other aspects of the work process. Second, neither the market nor the drive for profit maximization disciplines state contractors because they are producing under government contract (this is particularly true under cost-plus contracts). Production in state industries in both groups of activities depends on the state's budgetary priorities and its ability to mobilize tax revenues for state production. Costs in both sets of activities (including profits flowing to the contractors) are borne by taxpayers, or the work force as a whole.

The demand for labor in the state sector is relatively stable, excepting shifts in political forces that cause changes in budgetary

11. According to a Brookings Institution study by Victor K. Heyman (cited in John R. Bunting, *The Hidden Face of Free Enterprise* [New York: McGraw-Hill, 1964], pp. 145–46), over one-fourth of the labor force was directly or indirectly supported by state payrolls and contracts a decade ago. The proportion of the working class employed by the state sector undoubtedly has increased since then, perhaps to one-third. Whatever the case, we will assume that the competitive, monopolistic, and state sectors of the economy are all of equal size, each employing one-third of the labor force. This convention will simplify arithmetic calculations made in the course of the analysis below.

priorities. The reason is that production is subsidized by the state. The management of demand reduces or eliminates the unpredictable ups and downs that characterize competitive markets. As a result, workers in search of employment security and relatively high wages (see below) who belong to the dominant social group tend to monopolize the better-paid occupations in the state sector. On the other hand, the political norms that govern hiring, promotion, transfer, and other personnel decisions in government activities (e.g., equality of opportunity, equal pay for equal work, etc.) compel state enterprises and contractors to open doors and career ladders to oppressed minorities and women workers. Consequently, the social composition of the work force in state industries tends to be heterogeneous, even though white males practically monopolize the middle and higher positions.

Stability of employment, labor immobility, and the large size of production units are the chief factors favoring the organization and growth of labor unions in state industries. On the other side, the social heterogeneity of the work force—in particular, the concentration of large numbers of women workers in elementary school teaching, nursing, social work, and other sex-typed jobs—inhibits the growth of labor unions. Professionalism, part-time work, and status distinction also play a role. More important, it is difficult for state administrators and contractors to raise labor productivity, and wage increases tend to force up unit labor costs. For this reason among others, government agencies normally attempt to discourage the growth of strong, independent unions in state industries. The state sector is better organized than the competitive sector, but more poorly organized than the monopolistic sector.

Interrelationships Between the Three Sectors

In capitalist economies, the creative powers of the producing class are harnessed to private profit. In the absence of actual or expected profit, production is cut back or halted. Since state industries are not organized for direct profit, the private sector is the leading factor in economic expansion. Within the private sector, the monopolistic industries comprise the "engine" of capital accumulation and economic growth.

The growth of physical capital (which almost invariably is accompanied by technical progress) is the springboard of economic growth within the monopolistic sector. Production expands on the basis of output-increasing, labor-saving innovations in plant and equipment, the organization of work, including the planning and control of production, and in the distribution system. However, in contrast with competitive industries, declines in unit labor costs attributable to the growth of productivity are not reflected in lower product prices. The reason for this is twofold: first, as we have seen, monopolistic firms normally pass productivity increases along to workers in the form of higher wages, thus placing a floor on money costs and prices. Second, the fear of price competition in all monopolistic industries is allayed by "live-and-let-live" agreements by corporations that are able to reduce or eliminate competition by administering prices.

Because monopolistic firms normally do not lower prices when unit labor costs are reduced, profits tend to grow in step with productivity and production. Fresh sources of profits are used to finance new capital investments, technical innovations, and product development, which ultimately lower costs (or expand demand) and raise profits still more. Productivity, prices, profits, and production thus tend to advance together.

Nevertheless, in the long run, the growth of production in the monopolistic sector requires the expansion of the state sector. Over time, production becomes more interdependent and the division of labor more specialized. Technical progress and the growth of profits and wages in the monopolistic sector increasingly depend on the growth of "human capital" (that is, the availability of masses of technical and administrative workers needed to research, develop, plan, execute, coordinate, and control modern production), research and development facilities, and social overhead investments such as highways, airports, urban transit systems, and so on. Moreover, the greatest part of state health and welfare spending is needed to preserve the peaceful relations between capital and labor, especially between Big Labor and Big Capital, required for the uninterrupted accumulation of capital. Further, large-scale, government-financed social-consumption expenditures, particularly in the area of suburban development, are needed to keep up the level of spending for housing, house furnishings, appliances, autos, and so on. Finally, federal government military spending is required to maintain the level of *aggregate* demand and thus preserve profitable markets at home, as well as to create and protect markets abroad. Hence, the growth of the monopolistic sector depends on the expansion of higher education, military-financed research and development and technical training, highway construction, suburban development and urban renewal, general warfare—welfare spending, and other activities that are *indirectly* productive from the standpoint of monopolistic industries and the economy as a whole.[12]

A crucial feature of the economy is that production in the monopolistic sector normally does not expand fast enough to maintain "full employment" in this sector. The reason is that markets in the monopolistic sector do not grow in step with wage income in the monopolistic sector alone, but with increases in wage income in the economy as a whole. An example may be used to illustrate: Suppose that the rate of growth of productivity, wages, and profits in the monopolistic sector is 3 percent per year. Suppose further that other things being equal the rate of growth of productivity and wages in the competitive sector and state sector is 1 percent annually.

---

12. It should be stressed that "indirectly productive" only means that productivity and production in the *monopolistic sector* depend socioeconomically on state spending. The effect of state spending on production as a whole is another question. To take an extreme example, the economy (and society) obviously could not reproduce itself year in and year out in the event that all resources were devoted to military production. On the other hand, although the immediate effect of an expansion of the state sector is to reduce productivity in the economy as a whole (because average productivity in the former is less than in the latter), in the long run increased state activity may *accelerate* productivity in the private sector, and thus *improve* productivity in the economy as a whole.

Given that roughly one-third of the work force is employed in the monopolistic sector, the annual rise in average wages in the economy as a whole (commensurate with the rise in average productivity in the economy as a whole) is only 1.66 percent. Clearly, the growth of wages (and consumption demand) falls below the growth of productive capacity in monopolistic industries. The result is that employment in the monopolistic sector does not grow as fast as productivity and production. For example, only four of thirty-six major American industries had employment gains averaging over 4 percent from 1957 to 1969; by contrast, productivity rose by more than 4 percent in seventeen industries. In thirteen industries, especially coal mining, railroads, petroleum refining, and flour milling, where small output increases were associated with large productivity increases, employment actually declined (there was no decline in productivity in any of the thirty-six industries).[13] The result is that more and more workers who have been employed in monopolistic industries (together with new entries into the work force who seek employment in this sector) are "technologically unemployed," and they are compelled to seek work in the competitive and state sectors. In fact, these two sectors have taken up most of the "slack" in employment in the monopolistic industries during the past twenty years. The state sector alone accounts for 25 percent of the total growth of employment between 1950 and 1966. New York City has added seventy thousand workers to the city payroll during the past five years.

The increase in the supply of labor tends to reduce wages in the competitive sector or at least keeps wages from rising so fast as they otherwise would. As we saw, the absence of effective unions means that workers in competitive industries cannot peg their wages to

13. *Indexes of Output per Man-Hour, Selected Industries, 1939 and 1957–1969*, Bureau of Labor Statistics, U.S. Department of Labor, Bulletin No. 1680 (Washington, D.C.: Government Printing Office, 1970), pp. 1–2. As we have seen, the relationship between productivity and technological progress is more complex than we have assumed in our basic description of the economy. Thus, the positive correlation between increases in productivity and decreases in employment, on the one hand, and the degree of monopoly, on the other hand, is weak.

rising pay scales in the monopolistic sector. Further, the availability of relatively cheap labor in the competitive sector tends to discourage labor-saving technical innovations and productivity increases, which also keeps wages low.

One result of this process is a growing disparity between wages in the monopolistic sector and pay in the competitive sector. This disparity normally is not offset by movements of workers from low-paid competitive industries to relatively high-paid monopolistic industries. For one thing, as we know, the demand for labor in the monopolistic sector is inelastic in the short run. For another, the fact that productivity tends to grow faster than product demand means that the demand for labor increases relatively slowly in the long run as well. A number of studies have shown that the allocation of labor is sensitive to job vacancies rather than to movements in wages.[14] The expansion of productivity and production in the monopolistic sector thus tends to increase employment in the competitive sector, discourage technical progress (by expanding the supply of labor), and depress wages and worker incomes. As a consequence, unemployed, underemployed, *and* fully employed workers in competitive industries increasingly depend on the state to supplement their incomes, either directly in the form of minimum wage laws or indirectly in the form of social services, subsidized housing, welfare, and the like.

A second result of the process of accumulation in the monopolistic sector is the tendency for profits in competitive industries to become depressed. One reason is the expansion of monopoly capital into traditional competitive enclaves such as trade and construction. In addition, the expansion of labor supply in competitive industries makes it easier to set up new businesses, thus increasing competition and depressing profits. The relative (or absolute) decline in wages in competitive industries that have resisted union organization tends to reduce prices, and under certain circumstances may reduce profits.[15]

14. Livernash, "Wages," p. 106.
15. In Marxist theory, surplus value (i.e., surplus labor) is pumped out of the competitive sector and into the monopolistic sector. Because the money value of output per labor hour is relatively low, the market transmits surplus labor from competitive to monopolistic industries via the price mechanism. Because it is difficult for competitive

The consequence of the economically depressed condition of the competitive sector is that small businessmen (as well as workers in this sector) are compelled to depend on the state, indirectly in the form of fair trade laws and directly in the form of loan guarantees, subsidies, etc.

Next let us turn to the relationship between the monopolistic sector and the state sector. As we know, wages are pegged to productivity in monopolistic industries. This fact has important consequences for wages, costs, and production in state industries. Although increases in wages in monopolistic industries are not passed on to workers in competitive industries (putting aside the construction industry and other well-organized industries), wages in state industries are positively affected. The general tendency is for wages in the state sector to be driven up to the level prevailing in the monopolistic sector. The reason for this is threefold: First, one "provision" of the general agreement between Big Labor and Big Capital is that workers employed by state contractors receive union pay scales. Second, the political power of many state and local government employee associations is considerable, and the market power of many state employee labor unions is also growing. Associations and unions of state workers attempt to enforce wage and salary scales in the state sector commensurate with those prevailing in the monopolistic sector, with some success. Third, while the supply of labor in the state sector is highly elastic (for the same reasons that the supply of labor in the competitive sector is elastic), unlike the competitive sector, market forces do not determine wages. Wages are determined politically, or by the forces mentioned directly above, thus placing a floor on average pay scales that is absent in the competitive sector.

The effect of linking wages in state industries to productivity in monopolistic industries is to drive up the costs of production in the

---

industries to pass taxes on to workers or other capitalists (and relatively easy for monopolistic firms to do so), more surplus is transmitted to the state, and hence to monopoly capital.

state sector (it is interesting to note that national income accountants treat salary gains by public employees as price increases). In the words of William Baumol, ". . . the very progress of the technologically progressive sectors inevitably adds to the costs of the technologically unchanging sectors of the economy, unless somehow the labor markets in these areas can be sealed off and wages held absolutely constant." [16]

The Fiscal Crisis of the State

At this point we need to pull together some of the themes introduced above. Our general conclusion is that the growth of capitalist production places increasing stresses and strains on the state budget. On the one hand, at least 25 percent and perhaps as much as one-third of the work force is directly or indirectly employed by the state. Further, tens of thousands of doctors, welfare workers, and other self-employed and privately employed professionals and technicians use facilities provided by the state and are dependent in whole or in part on government budgets. Finally, tens of millions of men and women are dependent on the state budget as clients and recipients of state services. On the other hand, the state continues to rely on taxes—even though traditional state functions have been greatly expanded and many new functions added. In other words, private capital, at times alone and at times allied with labor, has socialized many costs and expenses of production, but has not socialized profits. In modern capitalism, state expenditures tend to outrun taxes; what people need from the state exceeds what they are willing to pay to the state.

The underlying reason for the fiscal crisis is the basic relation

16. William J. Baumol, "Macroeconomics of Unbalanced Growth: The Anatomy of Urban Crisis," in *Is Economics Relevant: A Reader in Political Economics*, ed. Robert L. Heilbroner and Arthur M. Ford (Pacific Palisades, Calif.: Goodyear, 1971), p. 111.

between Big Capital and Big Labor, who, in effect, "export" their conflicts to the competitive and state sectors of the economy. This happens in a number of different ways: first, labor and capital in the monopolistic sector support the growth of state-financed higher education, research and development activities, transportation and communications facilities, and other indirectly productive state investments. From the standpoint of Big Labor, the more costs of production are socialized, the higher will be productivity and wages in the monopolistic sector.

Second, unions and management in monopolistic industries collaborate in the introduction of labor-saving technology, which leads to an expansion of employment in both the competitive and state sectors. Labor income in state industries tends to be determined by productivity and wages in monopolistic industries. Thus, when the state "takes up the slack" by expanding state employment (as opposed to increasing welfare), costs in state industries tend to increase. More, there is a steady upward pressure on unit labor costs attributable to the growth of wages in the monopolistic sector.

Third, Big Labor and Big Capital combine to socialize the *social* costs of production, the costs of ameliorating urban decay, reducing pollution and other environmental damage, and so on. Shifting these costs to taxpayers as a whole permits profits *and* wages in monopolistic industries to expand more rapidly. Fourth, reproduction costs such as medical expenses and retirement income of workers in monopolistic industries also tend to be socialized. Both Big Labor and Big Capital presently support national health insurance, the expansion of old age and survivors insurance, and similar social outlays. Monopolistic industries burdened with expensive health and medical insurance programs that labor unions have won through collective bargaining seek to shift this burden to the state. Normally, they can count on the willing collaboration of unions sensitive to membership demands for better and more comprehensive health care. Last but not least, both Big Capital and Big Labor are ardent supporters of the military budget.[17]

17. We have confined our analysis to the relationships within and between the three sectors of the economy producing and distributing goods and services. There is

There is one crucial difference between the attitudes of Big Capital and Big Labor toward economic activity organized by the state. Capital normally opposes the establishment of state industry that competes with private capital. Put another way, capital opposes any program that socializes profits. Thus big business supports national health insurance and opposes socialized medicine; favors federal highway programs and opposes state-managed construction firms; agitates for enormous military budgets and the sale of state armories and other production facilities to private capital. Not only are costs of production socialized but also profits are guaranteed. In the field of health and medicine and in the system of military contracting, in particular, these guaranteed profits can reach astronomical heights, placing additional drains on the state budget.

Role of Taxation and Inflation

In the advanced capitalist countries, state expenditures in relation to gross national product have risen more or less steadily from the last decade of the nineteenth century to the present. This has been the result of the socialization of many of the costs and expenses of production and the subsidization of profits. By and large, state expenditures have contributed to the growth of total production. Thus, the state and private sectors have expanded simultaneously. State spending has increased taxable incomes and the tax base and hence has been self-financing in whole or in part. But as the costs of the state sector continue to rise out of proportion to productivity in the state sector, it becomes less and less possible to finance state

another sector which is normally organized by private capital and which engages in financial activities (or circulation of capital). In America, the same families and interest groups which dominate the monopolistic industries also control the major financial institutions. The cooperation of the banks is indispensable to both the private and state sectors of the economy. For example, when the state takes over unprofitable private activities such as urban transit or puts up new infrastructure (e.g., downtown urban renewal projects), bonds must be floated to finance the purchase of investment. Amortizing these bonds over a long span of time is a very expensive proposition (as in the cases of the Chicago and New York City rapid transit systems)—expensive from the standpoint of taxpayers as a whole.

activities from the "growth dividend." Within the framework of capitalist property relations, there are only three ways for the state to cover these rising costs: higher tax rates, inflation, or increases in productivity in state activities. In this section, we take up tax and inflationary finance.

Whatever the particular combination of tax and inflationary finance used by the state, the effect is to reduce the real wages of the work force as a whole. A hypothetical example will illustrate this process. Suppose that productivity and money wages in state industries and competitive industries are growing by 3 percent and 1 percent per year, respectively. Next, let us assume that inflation or taxes or both reduce money wages in all three sectors by two percentage points (under the conditions that inflation and the tax load fall proportionately on working class income). The effect will be to confine the rise in real wages in monopolistic and state industries to one percent annually, and to *lower* real wages in competitive industries. Now let us bring in our familiar assumption that the work force is divided evenly between the three sectors, and that productivity in the state and competitive sectors rises by 1 percent per year. Real wages in monopolistic and state industries thus rise slightly more than the increase in average productivity in the economy as a whole, while real wages in the competitive sector fall below average productivity increases.

In the last analysis, competitive workers are materially impoverished because they are socially oppressed, the victims of racism and sexism. But the casual relationship between oppression and impoverishment runs both ways. The relative or absolute decline in real wages has the effect of reducing material standards of life, and lowering opportunities for upward mobility within the work force as a whole. Simultaneously, declining material standards force the competitive work force to rely on state services for bare survival (thus increasing costs within the state sector, and stimulating the entire mechanism again). The absence of opportunities for upward mobility and increasing dependency on the state reinforce racist and sexist attitudes and race-typing and sex-typing of jobs. As a result, bitterness and antagonism between "mainstream" workers in the monopolistic and state sectors and "peripheral" workers in the competitive sector increase. Finally, the issue of taxes and budgetary priorities becomes a central issue dividing the work force as a whole: monopolistic and state workers call for budgetary priorities in their favor. The only possible way for the work force as a whole to get what it wants is to establish an alliance against capital as a whole. But this is impractical because of the agreement between Big Capital and Big Labor that guarantees workers in the monopolistic sector their "fair share" of productivity gains in return for more than a modicum of labor peace.

Relations of Production in the Monopolistic Industries

At this point, we can see that the fiscal crisis of the state (the tendency for expenditures to outrace revenues) is at root a social crisis in the form of economic and political antagonisms that divide not only labor and capital but also the work force as a whole. The social crisis (bitterness and conflicts between blacks and whites, women's liberation, welfare rights struggles, and the fiscal crisis that mirrors and enlarges the social crisis sooner or later work their way back into the arena where the big battles between labor and capital are fought—the monopolistic industries.

Despite the steady advance of money wages, real wages tend to fall behind productivity gains in the monopolistic sector. In the United States, between 1965 and 1970 productivity in manufacturing industries increased by about 13 percent, while real wages remained the same. This fact has potentially stupendous effects on the functioning of capitalist society as a whole. On the one hand, union leaders increasingly become unable to discipline rank-and-file workers whose standard of life is threatened by inflation and taxation. On the other hand, union leaders increasingly become *unwilling* to discipline the rank and file. They are no longer willing to sit back and watch union membership stagnate or decline (while collaborating actively with employers in the introduction of labor-saving innovations) because they are no longer confident that the wages of union members who retain their jobs will rise in step with productivity, or even maintain themselves at an even level. In this way, inflation and heavy taxation encourage militancy on the part of both union leaders and rank and file.

The result is that the unions organize defensive strikes to keep *real* wages in line with productivity. If these strikes are successful (as many of them were in 1970–71), money wages increase more rapidly than physical productivity. This has the effect of pushing up unit labor costs, which forces monopolistic industries to raise prices to protect profit margins. Across-the-board increases in prices in the absence of commensurate rises in productivity and production are inflationary. They are especially (at least in the short run) inflationary to the degree that there is an expansion of employment and production in the competitive and state sectors, where productivity is relatively low, hence pulling down average productivity in the economy as a whole. In one sense, the "cost-push" theory of inflation is correct: the erosion of living standards by inflation forces workers to defend these standards, which in turn causes more inflation.

The entire mechanism described above is perpetuated in this way. Wage increases in the monopolistic sector spread to the state sector, increasing unit labor costs in state industries. If monopolistic industries protect profit margins by introducing more labor-saving methods of production, workers are "pushed" into the competitive sector where labor income is low. More and more workers thus come to depend on the state budget to maintain their living standards. If monopoly capital depends solely on price increases to maintain profits, inflation worsens, burdening the state with more costs and encouraging workers to demand higher money wages. In either case, taxes or inflation or both will rise, and the social crisis will deepen.

Three Options Open to the State

Sooner or later, monopoly capital must face a critical dilemma. On the one hand, monopoly capital is compelled to grant increases in money wages to avoid a rupture in relations with unions and workers, even though unit labor costs and prices rise continuously. On the other hand, domestic inflation reduces foreign demand for United States products, cutting into exports and worsening the balance of trade. This is particularly serious as time goes on because foreign sales constitute a rising portion of total sales of many of the largest corporations.[18] Further, inflation pushes up interest rates, which in turn chokes off mortgage and credit-financed spending on housing and consumer durables—the two mainstays of the private economy. If prices are kept firm, rising costs cut into profit margins; if prices are raised, falling demand reduces sales and profits (demand will fall particularly low if inflation is accompanied by growing unemployment).

There are three possible ways out of this dilemma—managed recession, wage-price controls, and increased productivity in the private and state sectors, which would in turn require a remodeling of the relations of production throughout the society.[19] Let us consider the practicality of each of these ways in turn.

The first option is to use fiscal and monetary policy to reduce aggregate demand, increase unemployment, and weaken the bargaining power of unions in the monopolistic and state industries. The positive effect is to reduce the rate of increase of money wages, unit labor costs, and interest rates, and to slow down the growth of price inflation. One negative effect is the reduction of aggregate demand and sales. Another negative effect is the increase in the number of

18. "The War and Its Impact on the Economy," *Review of the Union for Radical Political Economics*, Special Issue, August 1970.

19. Until now, monopoly capital has been able to export some of its inflation to Western Europe by establishing the dollar as the world's reserve currency. This has been very important in "solving" the dilemma outlined above. There is still another possibility, to which President Nixon gives only lip service—namely, breaking up industrial and "labor" monopolies with the aim of making the economy more competitive.

unemployed and underemployed workers and therefore the number of people dependent on the state. At the same time, managed recession reduces aggregate wage and profit income, lowers the tax base, cuts into tax receipts, and squeezes the budget from the revenue side. On the other hand, unemployment of labor and underutilization of productive capacity mean that state spending raises not only aggregate demand but also real output and income, and finally, the tax base and tax receipts. In other words, in a recession state expenditures help to pay for themselves and in terms of the real resources used can be virtually costless. Nevertheless, recessions create demands on the state budget at precisely the time when the ability of the state to meet these demands without recourse to large-scale deficit financing is weakened. More important, serious recession is a threat to the harmonious relations between Big Labor and Big Capital. For these reasons, no modern government could long retain power in the event that it choose to depend exclusively or mainly on the option of managed recession.

The second option is to impose wage-price controls on the monopolistic sector.[20] From the standpoint of capital in the monopolistic sector, wage and price controls have the same advantage as a managed recession: responsibility for keeping money wages down is shifted from the industries themselves to the government. A lid is placed on wages, but it is difficult for the unions to blame management. Wage-price controls have the additional advantage of reducing the risk of a downward spiral of employment, income, demand, production, and profits—a risk that is always latent in managed recessions. If the state decides on a particular volume of investment (and thus savings) needed for high employment or balance-of-payments equilibrium, and establishes wages and prices such that this volume of investment and savings is forthcoming, the state effectively controls the distributive shares of income and guarantees a certain level of profits. On the other hand, from the

20. Actually, controls have to be placed on any sector in which money wages advance significantly more rapidly than productivity—e.g., in the construction industry in the United States.

standpoint of labor in the monopolistic industries, wage and price controls are anathema. The reason is that the unions are forced to bargain away their right to improve labor's share of income in return for policies designed to maintain high employment. Labor and capital in the monopolistic sector are also reluctant to agree to controls because they represent a conscious choice to give up their privileged status vis-à-vis labor and capital in the competitive sector. During the 1960s, "economists and others who have been closest to union-management negotiations tend to regard guidepost wage restraints as nonexistent or very minimal." [21]

In addition, there are two serious disadvantages of wage and price controls from the standpoint of monopoly capital. First, controls introduce an element of inflexibility in the ability of management in the monopolistic sector to mobilize and allocate capital profitably. Second, as we have suggested, wage and price controls transform antagonisms between labor and capital into conflicts between labor and the state. Controls thus open objective possibilities for alliances between workers in monopolistic and competitive industries. The real danger of wage and price controls is the potential growth of a class-conscious and unified working class.[22] How dangerous this can be for the stability of the capitalist system was illustrated by the May 1968 general strike in France, where state management of the economy in peacetime has reached unprecedented levels. Finally, from the point of view of the state administration, wage and price controls are extremely difficult to enforce: for one thing, thousands of wage rates are not determined by collective bargaining at the national level but rather at the base by local management; for another, it is difficult to win agreement on how to measure productivity; moreover, fringe costs are not subject to controls.

The third and in the long run the only practical option available

21. Livernash, "Wages," p. 102.
22. Wage and price controls or incomes policies "tend to bring the crisis in the trade union movement to a head, rather than integrating it further into the State and eliminating conflict" (Ernest Mandel, "A Socialist Strategy for Western Europe," *International Socialist Journal* 2, no. 10 [August 1965]: 433.

to the state is to encourage the growth of productivity in both the monopolistic and state industries (raising productivity in competitive industries is highly impractical because of the great number of firms, their small scale, and the relative absence of economic integration). As a result, the state is forced to put its own house in order by increasing efficiency in state industries (including facilities owned by state contractors). Immediately, a seemingly insurmountable problem confronts the state administration: goods production in the state sector is not destined for the market but rather is contracted for by state agencies. Most tangible goods produced by or for the state are unique outputs, one-of-a-kind products. Policies to increase efficiency in state industries boil down to the use of modern management techniques such as systems analysis and program budgeting. Since World War II, and particularly since 1960, the federal government in the United States has been increasingly preoccupied with the "efficiency" and "economic rationality" of its various programs, especially the military program. In the Department of Defense, "a buyer-seller scheme [attempts] to impose on a sprawling network of military units a coordination and constraint that controls economic units under private property in the market." [23] And the use of "cost-benefit" analyses of government programs is widespread in all of the federal departments.

These techniques are able to cut some of the fat from the budget, but not very much. For one thing, the very meaning of "efficiency" outside of the marketplace, where there are no independent buyers and sellers, continues to be debated by economists and government officials. Moreover, as we know, in the provision of services it is difficult to raise productivity, whether the services are provided by private or state capital. Conflicting private interests also limit the ability of the state to develop programs characterized by *overall* efficiency; for example, river-valley development and transportation programs must satisfy the conflicting claims of different

23. The economics of this arrangement are discussed in Norman V. Breckner, "Government Efficiency and the Military 'Buyer-Seller' Device," *Journal of Political Economy* 68, no. 5 (October 1960).

kinds of private interests. In industries supplying military goods, the state underwrites capital investments, guarantees orders, provides needed technical help and frees private capital from economic risk and uncertainty, thus eliminating the traditional "entrepreneurial function" and virtually guaranteeing a high level of inefficiency. Government programs that aim to stabilize the social order by providing regular employment for unskilled or underemployed workers are also inefficient from the standpoint of minimizing costs and maximizing output.

Finally, in the absence of a firm détente with the Soviet Union with regard to the "permissible" type, number, and deployment of weapons, the Department of Defense must concentrate mainly on new weapons development, rather than on improving the efficiency of traditional weapons production and distribution. All in all, it would appear that the prospect of improving productivity in established state activities is relatively dim.

"Increased productivity" in the state sector therefore has a very special meaning. It will be recalled that the importance of state activities is that they can be indirectly productive from the standpoint of the private sector, especially monopolistic industries. State investments of various kinds provide valuable infrastructure for private capital. It follows that "increased productivity" means less increasing efficiency in current state activities than it does *changing budgetary priorities as a whole.* Options to reduce unit labor costs in the state sector are few, but options to lower labor costs in the monopolistic sector are many, and to a degree untried. An obvious example is education and manpower development. Education and job-training programs can be designed to tap more fully available manpower reserves, and to create fresh reserves, inhibiting upward pressures on wages and supplying more skilled labor to industry. Existing education programs in colleges and universities can be "rationalized" by gearing degree programs to "career goals." More "inefficiency" can be cut from highway and other transportation programs by eliminating duplication of facilities and by locating new housing and industrial developments on the periphery of metropolitan areas where land and construction costs are relatively small. Still more savings could be made by developing a vast "halfway house" program for mental patients and criminal offenders. The list of new budgetary priorities is potentially endless.

Programs such as these hold out many advantages to monopoly capital (and to a lesser degree state contractors).

Education, training, housing, and other social programs geared to expanding productivity and financed by the state would provide fresh fields of investment for monopolistic industries. Social tensions arising from the material impoverishment of workers in competitive industries might be reduced by creating jobs for those presently unemployed and underemployed. And to the degree that social investments were organized directly under the auspices of monopolistic industries (such as new corporate-organized teaching systems sold to local school districts), the fiscal crisis of the state might be in part relieved directly.

By contrast, private capital in the competitive sector has everything to lose and little to gain from the growth of a social-industrial complex. Competitive capital in goods-producing industries requires cheap labor and a flexible, often transient labor force. Competitive capital in distribution thrives on slum housing, high rents, and high retail prices. Competitive activities in the sphere of circulation—in particular, small and exploitive credit and loan companies—also have a strong interest in maintaining the status quo. Consequently, the precondition for the success of a program of social reconstruction based on the needs and priorities of monopoly capital is the elimination of the power of small-scale capital, not only in the marketplace, but also in the arenas of local and state politics where local and regional capital in competitive industries has much influence and power.

Moreover, labor unions in the monopolistic sector potentially have a great deal to lose from the development of a social-industrial complex. The main reason is that the surplus generated within monopolistic industries that is presently distributed to workers in the form of money wages commensurate with (or in excess of) productivity would have to be appropriated by the state and plowed into programs for social reconstruction. And although social investments geared to expanding productivity in the monopolistic sector would raise productivity in the long run, during the transition period, the rate of growth of productivity would no doubt decline, affording a relatively narrow basis for wage increases in the monopolistic sector.[24] Thus radical shifts in budgetary priorities require deep-going changes in the relations of production as a whole. And radical shifts in the structure of the tax system in favor of monopoly capital and impoverished workers in the competitive sector (for example, via the negative income tax) and against workers in monopolistic and state industries also require profound changes in the relationships between and within social classes in America.

24. The situation is actually more complicated than this. To stop inflationary wage demands, the state must stop inflation, thus keeping money wages in line with productivity. If the state tried to siphon off enough surplus to finance a social-industrial complex (that is, subsidize monopoly capital and workers in the competitive sector) without halting the present decline in real wages, the alliance between Big Labor and Big Capital would explode. On the other hand, stopping inflation means slowing down the rate of growth of aggregate demand. As we have seen, wages in the competitive sector depend closely on the growth of aggregate demand and inflation. Thus with one hand the state might have to take away from competitive workers what it gives with the other hand.

Global Corporations: Their Quest for Legitimacy

Richard J. Barnet
Ronald E. Müller
with Joseph Collins

The managers of the world corporate giants proclaim their faith that where conquest, religion, and diplomacy have failed, business can succeed in unifying the world. "In the 1940s Wendell Willkie spoke about 'One World,'" says IBM's Jacques Maisonrouge. "In the 1970s we are inexorably pushed toward it." Aurelio Peccei, a director of Fiat and organizer of the Club of Rome, states flatly that the global corporation "is the most powerful agent for the internationalization of human society." "Working through great corporations that straddle the earth," says George Ball, "men are able for the first time to utilize world resources with an efficiency dictated by the objective logic of profit." The global corporation is ushering in a genuine world economy, or what business consultant Peter Drucker calls a "global shopping center," and it is accomplishing this, according to Jacques Maisonrouge, "simply by doing its 'thing'; by doing what came naturally in the pursuit of its legitimate business objectives." By making ordinary business decisions, the managers of such firms as GM—and IBM, Pepsico, GE, Pfizer, Shell, Volkswagen, Caterpillar, CPC, Exxon—now have more power than most sovereign governments of the world to determine where people live; what work, if any, they will do; what they will eat, drink, and wear; what sorts of knowledge schools and universities will encourage; and what kind of society their children will inherit.

The rise of the planetary enterprise is producing an organizational revolution as profound in its implications for modern man as the industrial revolution and the rise of the nation-state itself. This revolution is producing four key structural changes in global relationships. First, the rise of the global corporation is the culmination of a process of concentration and internationalization which has put the world economy under the substantial control of fewer than five hundred business enterprises which do not compete with one another according to the traditional rules of the market. Total sales of global corporations exceed the gross national product of every country of the world except that of the United States and the USSR. The value of goods and services produced and distributed by the global corporations exceeds the gross national product of all but the biggest powers. Power to influence the direction of national economies is now being concentrated in what are, legally and politically speaking, private hands.

Second, the rise of the global corporation is producing new sets of loyalties which transcend and often conflict with national loyalties. The efficiency of the world company, which is its primary justification, is based on its capacity for global profit maximization. The decisive interest of top management is the world balance sheet. It is increasingly necessary, for global profit maximization, to minimize profits in particular countries. Because of their incentive and their ability to shift profits and jobs from one country to another, global corporations are exacerbating some fundamental conflicts. Tax-avoidance practices, currency transactions, pricing arrangements, and job-relocation policies that are optimal from the corporation's viewpoint have highly unfavorable effects on the majority of people who, unlike the corporations, cannot escape the territory in which they live.

Third, the global corporations are instrumental in bringing about a process in which the poor nations of Asia, Latin America, and, soon, Africa—long the hewers of wood and carriers of water for the international economy—are becoming the principal sites of new production. The center of "hardware" production is being shifted from the northern to the southern hemisphere. The move to fourteen-cents-an-hour labor in South Korea is changing employment patterns in the United States. The capacity of the poor countries to exact higher prices for raw materials, particularly energy, and their growing power over the manufacturing process itself means that to maintain profits, global corporations must raise their prices to the consumer in the rich countries.

Fourth, concentration of power in the hands of the global corporations results increasingly from control of technology. Global corporations dominate the technology of production, i.e., how to make, package, and transport goods; the technology of accounting, i.e., how to create their own private global economy insulated from the vicissitudes of national economies by means of shifting profits, avoiding taxes, and transfer pricing; the technology of marketing, i.e., how to create and satisfy a demand for their goods by marketing a consumption ideology through the control of advertising, mass media, and popular culture.

The most revolutionary aspect of the planetary enterprise is not its size but its political pretension. The managers of the global corporations are seeking a role in shaping the contemporary world which will profoundly alter the nation-state system around which human society has been organized for over four hundred years. What they are demanding in essence is the right to transcend the nation-state, and in the process, to transform it. "I have long dreamed of buying an island owned by no nation," says Carl A. Gerstacker, chairman of the Dow Chemical Company, "and of establishing the World Headquarters of the Dow company on the truly neutral ground of such an island, beholden to no nation or society. If we were located on such truly neutral ground we could then really operate in the United States as U.S. citizens, in Japan as Japanese citizens, and in Brazil as Brazilians rather than being governed in prime by the laws of the United States. . . . We could even pay any natives handsomely to move elsewhere." [1]

A company spokesman for a principal competitor of Dow, Union Carbide, agrees: "It is not proper for an international corporation to put the welfare of any country in which it does business above that of any other." As Charles P. Kindleberger, one of the leading U.S. authorities on the economics of international business puts it, "The international corporation has no country to which it owes more loyalty than any other, nor any country where it feels completely at home." The global interests of the world company are, as the British financial writer and M.P. Christopher Tugendhat has pointed out, separate and distinct from the interests of every government, including its own government of origin. It is a measure of the great gulf between natural persons and the artificial persons we call corporations that statelessness should represent tragedy for the one and liberation for the other.

It is not hard to understand, however, why American corporate giants, even those whose presidents must still make do with an office in a Park Avenue skyscraper instead of a Caribbean island, feel that they have outgrown the American dream. Some of the largest and most famous U.S. corporations now derive over 50 percent of their profits outside the United States: IBM, Uniroyal, Squibb, Coca-Cola, Mobil, Pfizer, Gillette, Woolworth, and Reynolds, to name only a few. A recent study by Business International Corporation, a service organization for global corporations, shows that of the top 178 U.S.-based multinational corporations, 122 of them had a higher rate of profits from abroad than from domestic operations. In the office-equipment field, for example, the overseas profit for 1971 was 25.6 percent compared to domestic profits of 9.2 percent. The

1. Carl A. Gerstacker, "The Structure of the Corporation" (Paper delivered at the White House Conference on the Industrial World Ahead, February 7, 1972), pp. 9f.

average reported profit of the pharmaceutical industry from foreign operations was 22.4 percent as against 15.5 percent from operations in the United States. The food industry reported profits from overseas of 16.7 percent as compared with U.S. profits of 11.5 percent.

The Business International survey shows that dependence of the leading U.S.-based corporations on foreign profits has been growing steadily since 1964. In the last ten years it has been substantially easier to make profits abroad than in the U.S. economy. The result has been that U.S. corporations have been shifting more and more of their total assets abroad: about one-third of the total assets of the chemical industry, about 40 percent of the total assets of the consumer goods industry, about 75 percent of the electrical industry, about one-third of the assets of the pharmaceutical industry are now located outside the United States. Of the $40 billion invested worldwide by the U.S petroleum industry, roughly half is to be found beyond American shores. Almost 60 percent of U.S. manufacturing exports are sold by America's MNCs to their own foreign subsidiaries. It is estimated by the British financial analyst Hugh Stephenson that by the mid 1970s, 90 percent of exports of U.S.-based corporations "will be manufactured abroad by American-owned and controlled subsidiaries." "Investment abroad is investment in America" is the new slogan of the global corporations.

The popular term for the planetary enterprise is "multinational corporation." This article seeks to avoid it because it suggests a degree of internationalization of management, to say nothing of stock ownership, that does not exist. A study of the 1,851 top managers of the leading U.S. companies with large overseas payrolls and foreign sales conducted two years ago by Kenneth Simmonds reveals that only 1.6 percent of these high-level executives were non-Americans.[2] Similarly, Raymond Vernon of Harvard, after a six-year study of U.S.-based multinational corporations, concludes that non-Americans

2. Kenneth Simmonds, "Multinational? Well, Not Quite," in *World Business*, ed. Courtney C. Brown (New York: Macmillan, 1970), p. 48.

have no more than 2 to 3 percent of the stock of these enterprises.

More important, however, we find the term inadequate because it fails to capture the very aspect of contemporary world business that is most revolutionary. Businessmen have been venturing abroad a long time, at least since the Phoenicians started selling glass to their Mediterranean neighbors. Some of the great trading companies, such as the sixteenth-century British Muscovy Company, antedated the modern nation-state. Each of the great nineteenth-century empires— the British, the French, the Dutch, and even the Danes—served as protectors for private trading organizations that roamed the earth looking for the markets and raw-material sources on which the unprecedented comforts of the Victorian age depended. Nor could it be said that doing business abroad is a new departure for Americans. At the turn of the century, American firms, such as Singer Sewing Machine Company, were already playing so important a role in the British economy that the book *The American Invaders* was assured an apoplectic reception in the City when a London publisher brought it out in 1902. General Motors and Ford have had assembly plants in Europe since the 1920s, and the great oil companies have been operating on a near-global scale since the early days of the century.

What makes the global corporation unique is that it is the first enterprise in human history with the practical potential to operate on a planetary scale. Unlike the earlier era of international business, when corporations were primarily interested in adding new markets and, later, new productive facilities in different parts of the world, the global corporation no longer looks at these as extensions of its home operations but rather, in the words of Jacques Maisonrouge, chairman of IBM World Trade Corp., views the entire world as "one economic unit." Basic to this large view, he points out, "is a need to plan, organize, and manage on a global scale." [3] It is this holistic vision of the earth, in comparison to which "internationalism" or "multinationalism" seem parochial indeed, that sets the men who have designed the planetary corporation apart from the generations

3. Jacques G. Maisonrouge, "After the American Challenge—The American Model" (Graduate School of Business, University of Chicago, November 5, 1969).

of traders and international entrepreneurs who proceded them. A new entrepreneurial class that aspires to become the first Earth Managers has appeared on the scene. Its rise is a consequence of the post-World War II technological explosion. The global corporation is a child of the computer, the communications satellite, and the jet airplane. It is the product of the intellectual revolution wrought by twentieth-century technology which has transformed man's view of time, space, and scale.

The new world economy rests upon the international control of four fundamental elements of economic life: technology, finance, labor, and marketplace ideology. The internationalization of production means simply that more and more of the world's goods and services (gross world product) are being produced in more than one country, and that the production process increasingly ignores national frontiers. In practical terms, companies with operations in more than one country are taking over a greater and greater share of the gross world product. Some observers, such as Professor Howard Perlmutter of the Wharton School, estimate that by 1985, 200 to 300 global corporations will control 80 percent of all productive assets of the noncommunist world. Others, such as Louis Turner of Salford University, dispute this prediction on the ground that the giants are going to encounter increasing competition from smaller global firms, but all agree that some number of global companies will take over a radically increased share of world production. Karl P. Savant of the University of Pennsylvania, for example, calculates that by the turn of the century global companies will own productive assets amounting to $4,200 billion, or about 54 percent of the world's total.

Industry has transcended geography. One clear indication of this is that many of the largest U.S. corporations have 30 to 50 percent of their payroll outside the United States. It is important to understand, however, that the rise of the global corporation is far more than the overseas expansion of U.S. corporations. Even the U.S.-owned and managed global corporations are, because of their interests and outlooks, something more than American companies operating abroad. But the global corporation is not an American invention nor is it an exclusively American phenomenon. Although U.S.-based global corporations are still preeminent, the growth rate of their Japanese and European-based competitors is higher.

The revolutionary aspect of international production is that widely dispersed productive facilities can be integrated into what is, conceptually, a global factory without geographical ties. A global factory produces components in many parts of the world. Before its product reaches the consumer, it will bear the stamp of many lands, the capital of one, the resources of another, and the labor of a third. Thus, to take one example, Massey-Ferguson, a Canadian-based global company, assembles French-made transmissions, Mexican-made axles, and British-made engines in a Detroit plant for the Canadian market. Ford now supplies the U.S. market from its Canadian and Brazilian plants. Volkswagen has begun to supply the German market from its Mexican plant.

The internationalization of capital is as crucial to the Global Shopping Center as the internationalization of production. Global corporations can borrow money anywhere in the world. Dollars, despite the patriotic slogans on the bills, have no nationality. In the 1960s, the first transnational money market was developed into what quickly became the more than $50 billion Eurodollar pool. During the same period, the international loan syndicate and the international bank consortium appeared on the scene. Typical of these consortiums is Orion Multinational Services, organized in 1971 by Chase Manhattan, National Westminster (UK), Royal Bank of Canada, and Westdeutsche Landesbank Girozentral. At the same time, U.S. banks have increased their overseas operations enormously. In 1972 First National City Bank had foreign dollar deposits in excess of its U.S. domestic deposits. Global industrial corporations are also establishing financial arms. The Dow Bank, started by the global petrochemical firm, is now the sixth-largest bank of Switzerland.

Charles Levinson points out how global corporations are able to hedge against threatened currencies to protect their "vast accumulated investment funds from erosion due to inflation or deflation" by placing "billions of dollars, pounds, or francs on the short-term and 'spot' money markets." Two days before President Nixon announced on August 15, 1971, a totally new monetary policy for the United States, Donald G. Robbins, Jr., the chief financial officer for Singer, exchanged $20 million for Swiss francs and British pounds. Since many of the other four thousand multinational companies were also shifting currencies, they were, *Newsweek* concluded, "the prime force behind the whole currency crisis." James Meigs, economist for the Argus Research Corporation, is more explicit. "If you want to find all those evil speculators, don't look for them on the Orient Express. They're on the five fifteen to Larchmont."

Through the increasing use of centralized, computerized cash-management systems, global corporations are in a unique position to play the world capital market, arranging where possible to have their accounts payable in weak currencies and their accounts receivable in strong currencies. Because of these advantages, they are able to attract local capital, particularly from poor countries. Between 1957 and 1965, U.S.-based global corporations in Latin America financed 83 percent of their investment from local savings, through reinvested earnings and local borrowing. Thus, only about 17 percent of the U.S. investment during this period represented a transfer of capital from rich countries to poor.[4] For an Argentine or Uruguayan businessman, to take two examples of countries where flight of capital is creating a domestic economic and social crisis, it is much more attractive to invest in the Eurodollar market than to take the risks of inflation and revolution by investing at home. The effect, of course, is to add to the critical shortage of local capital needed for development.

The global factory also requires the internationalization of labor. Rapid and relatively cheap transportation now make it possible to draw on a global labor pool in the assembly of such everyday items as radios, TVs, autos, and cameras. Top management continues to be

4. Fernando Fajnzylber, *Estrategia Industrial y Empresas Internacionales: Posicion relativa de America y Brazil* (Rio de Janeiro: Naciones Unidas, CEPAL, November 1970), p. 65.

recruited from rich countries; workers increasingly come from low-wage areas. For a world corporation, it is an ideal combination. While automation continues to reduce the total labor costs in the manufacturing process, wage differentials are becoming more critical in maintaining competitive profit margins for the global corporations themselves. Thus, a few years ago only the most labor-intensive industries would go abroad looking for cheap help. Today Fairchild Camera, Texas Instruments, and Motorola have settled in Hong Kong to take advantage of the dollar-a-day, seven-day workweek conditions there. Timex and Bulova make an increasing share of their watches in Taiwan where they share a union-free labor pool with RCA, Admiral, Zenith, and IBM, among many others. Kodak imports its top seller, the "Instamatic," from Germany. Indeed, Polaroid is now the only major camera being manufactured in the United States. European companies are also moving to Southeast Asia. Rolleiflex, having figured out that wages make up 60 percent of the cost of the modern complex camera, and that wages are six times higher in Germany than in Singapore, is building a huge factory in that "heavenly city of the global corporations," as Singapore's Foreign Minister recently billed his industrious little island. (It is heavenly in large part because the government guarantees freedom from union trouble for a given number of years in return for a minimum dollar investment.) U.S. companies are licensing produc- tion of the Video Recorder, the next potential consumer best-seller in the electronics field, to Europe and the Far East, and it is unlikely that this innovation developed by CBS and other U.S. companies will ever be manufactured in commercial quantities on American soil. Having found that what were once highly skilled jobs can now be routinized and subcontracted to low-wage areas, U.S. companies are now making components in Mexico, sometimes within a mile of the border, and importing the finished product into the U.S. market. The ability of global companies to shift production from one facility to another perhaps thousands of miles away is already having a crucial impact on organized labor around the world.

The fourth requirement of the global shopping center is a

planetary marketing ideology. To develop a world market, it is essential to create what Ernest Dichter, the architect of Exxon's "put a tiger in your tank" campaign, calls "the world customer." Writing in the *Harvard Business Review*, he observes that companies with "foresight to capitalize on international opportunities" must understand that "cultural anthropology will be an important tool of competitive marketing." The advertising firm McCann Erickson recently sent a detailed questionnaire to professors of Latin American studies seeking for their clients such useful information as the eating habits of *campesinos* and the consumption patterns of the new urban middle-class family. Only when the corporate manager is aware of the similarities and differences in the hopes, fears, and desires of human beings in different parts of the world can he tailor his product and his sales pitch to take advantage of the "world revolution of human expectations." The development of new markets, Dichter points out, depends upon knowing that "only one Frenchman out of three brushes his teeth" or "four out of five Germans change their shirts but once a week." It is equally vital to know enough of the local culture to be able to take advantage of or to shape local tastes and customs. Dichter reports that a toothpaste company tried unsuccessfully to adapt its U.S. advertising campaign to France, but "threatening Frenchmen that if they didn't brush their teeth regularly, they would develop cavities or would not find a lover, failed to impress." A more permissive approach, emphasizing that brushing teeth is "chic" and "modern," succeeded after company anthropologists decided that Frenchmen feel immoral about "overindulging in bathing or toiletries." U.S. toilet-tissue manufacturers have also found a way to overcome cultural resistance to their product. For example, in West Germany many families, despite rising affluence, still think newspapers will do. "The advertising approach, then," says Dichter, "has to deal much more with providing absolution and selling the concept that good quality toilet tissue is a part of modern life." Thus it is, as Pfizer's John J. Powers puts it, that global corporations are "agents of change, socially, economically and culturally."

Lee S. Bickmore, chairman of National Biscuit Company, believes the key to the global market is "the tendency for people all over the world to adopt the same tastes and same consumption habits," and he has some ideas to help that process along. Some time ago he told *Forbes*: "Why we plan someday to advertise all over the world. We might spend, say, $8 million for an advertisement on a communications satellite system. It might reach 359 million people. So what we are doing now is establishing the availability of our products in retail outlets all over the world." When we ourselves interviewed him four years later,[5] he was talking of reaching 4 billion potential munchers. In projecting the Ritz cracker box on TV screens around the world, he emphasized he is selling more than crackers. "We are selling a concept."

Time's 24 million readers are apt to have more in common with each other than with many of their own countrymen. High income, good education, responsible positions in business, government, and the professions. The readers constitute an international community of the affluent and the influential. . . .

The world's leading corporate managers now see the nation-state, once the midwife of the industrial revolution, as the chief obstacle to national planetary development. "The political boundaries of nation-states," declares William I. Spencer, president of First National City Corporation, which does business in ninety countries, "are too narrow and constricted to define the scope and sweep of modern business." For George Ball, former undersecretary of state and chairman of Lehmann Brothers International, the world corporation "is planning and acting well in advance of the world's political ideas" because it is "a modern concept, designed to meet modern requirements." The nation-state, unfortunately, "is a very old-fashioned idea and badly adapted to our present complex world."[6] A true world economy, says John J. Powers, president of Pfizer, echoing

5. Interview with authors, December 5, 1972.
6. George Ball, Speech delivered before New York Chamber of Commerce, May 5, 1967, p. 10.

Ball, "is no idealistic pipe dream but a hard-headed prediction; it is a role into which we are being pushed by the imperatives of our own technology." Even more blunt an attack on the nation-state comes from Jacques G. Maisonrouge of IBM, a Frenchman, who is number-one manager in a vast hierarchy with headquarters in the United States that presides over employees in other countries. "The world's political structures are completely obsolete. They have not changed in at least one hundred years and are woefully out of tune with technological progress." The "critical issue of our time," says Maisonrouge, is the "conceptual conflict between the search for global optimization of resources and the independence of nation-states." [7] Business International warns its clients in a 1967 Research Report: ". . . the nation state is becoming obsolete: tomorrow . . . it will in any meaningful sense be dead—and so will the corporation that remains essentially national."

Thus, a little more than a generation after the withering of the wartime dream of world brotherhood—"Globaloney" was Clare Booth Luce's epitaph for Wendell Willkie's "One World"—a new breed of globalists have launched an attack on the nation-state more radical than anything proposed by World Federalists, UN enthusiasts, or other apostles of "woolly-headed internationalism" who traditionally cause dismay in boardrooms and country clubs. The men who run the global corporations, aware that ideologies, like crackers, travel well only if skillfully packaged, are putting great energy into marketing a new gospel of peace and plenty, which has more potential to change the face of the earth than even the merchandizing miracles that have brought Holiday Inns and Pepsi-Cola bottling plants to Moscow and Pollo Frito Kentucky to Latin America. Jacques Maisonrouge likes to point out that "Down With Borders," a revolutionary student slogan of the 1968 Paris university uprising, in which, incidentally, some of his own children were involved, is also a company slogan at IBM.

The new generation of planetary visionaries, unlike globalists of

7. Jacques G. Maisonrouge, Address to the American Foreign Service Association, Washington, D.C., May 29, 1969, p. 11. Mimeographed.

earlier days, come to their prophetic calling not by way of poetic imagination, transcendental philosophy, or Oriental mysticism but by way of solid careers in electrical circuitry, soap, mayonnaise, and aspirin. But they proclaim the heavenly city of the global corporation with something approaching the zeal of Savanarola. For Roy Ash, the former head of Litton Industries and now Nixon's budget director and chief consultant in matters managerial, the world corporation represents a "transcendental unity." It is the wave of the future, "for nothing can stop an idea whose time has come." Men like Ash know that their vision of a world without borders is the most important product they have to sell, for the extraordinary role they are proposing to play in human affairs challenges what Arnold Toynbee calls "mankind's major religion, the cult of sovereignty." What we need, Pfizer's president, John J. Powers, told a business gathering some years ago, are "philosophers in action" to explain "the promise of the world corporation." David Rockefeller calls for a massive public relations campaign to dispel the dangerous "suspicions" about the corporate giants that lurk in minds not yet able to grasp an idea whose time has come.

The rhapsodic tone which the new globalists have developed in their celebration of the world corporation as "the instrument of world development," "the only force for peace," "the most powerful agent for the internationalization of human society," or, in the words of Dean Courtney Brown of Columbia Business School, the "prologue to a new world symphony," is no doubt attributable in part to the salesman's traditional weakness for puffing. But, more important, the hard-sell of the world corporation, now being promoted in hundreds of industry speeches and industry-sponsored studies, and by elaborate lobbying activities such as the Emergency Committee for Foreign Trade, is a reflection of deep and growing customer resistance.

The managers of the global corporations keep telling one another that there can be no integrated world economy without radical transformations in the "obsolete" nation-state, but, however progressive a notion this may be, those who depend on the old-fashioned structures for their careers, livelihood, or inspiration are not easily convinced. The executives who run the world corporations have persuaded themselves that they are far ahead of politicians in global planning. The men who manage political units are, as these executives see them, prisoners of geography. As much as the mayors of Minneapolis or Milan or Sao Paulo may aspire to a planetary vision, their careers depend upon what happens within the territorial domain they are paid to manage. Rulers of nations exhibit the same parochialism for the same reasons. They are jealous of their sovereign prerogatives and do not like to share, much less abdicate, decision-making power over what happens in their territory.

The new globalists are well aware of this problem. "Corporations that buy, sell, and produce abroad," says George Ball, "do have the power to affect the lives of people and nations in a manner that necessarily challenges the prerogatives and responsibilities of political authority. How can a national government make an economic plan with any confidence if a board of directors meeting five thousand miles away can by altering its pattern of purchasing and production affect in a major way the country's economic life?" [8] But the Earth Manager's answer to the charge of being a political usurper is not to deny the extraordinary power he seeks to exercise in human affairs but to rationalize it.

David Rockefeller is calling for a "crusade of understanding" [9] to explain why global corporations should have freer rein to move goods, capital, and technology around the world without the interference of nation-states, but this will no doubt prove to be the public relations challenge of the century. Perhaps the logic of One World has never been so apparent to so many, but the twentieth century is above all the age of nationalism. There has been no idea in history for which greater numbers of human beings have died, and most of the corpses have been added to the heap in this century. The

8. George Ball, "Cosmocorp: The Importance of Being Stateless," in *World Business*, ed. Courtney C. Brown (New York: Macmillan, 1970), p. 334.
9. David Rockefeller, Speech delivered at Detroit Economic Club, May 1, 1972.

continuing struggle for national identity is the unifying political theme of our time. The imperial architects of greater Germany, Italy, and Japan, the guerrilla leaders of liberation movements, Tito, Ho, Castro, and those who are still fighting to free Africa from colonial rule have all been sustained by the power of nationalism. "The nation-state will not wither away," the chairman of Unilever, one of the earliest and largest world corporations, has declared. A "positive role," he concludes reluctantly, will have to be found for it in the remaining third of the twentieth century.

Any enterprise with a global appetite is bound to gather a global collection of enemies. Basically, they fall into three distinct groups. The first includes those whose economic interests are adversely affected by the rise of the world corporation. In the United States the most vocal member of this group is organized labor. To the UAW and the AFL-CIO the "prologue to a new world symphony" looks like nothing more than an updated version of the "runaway shop." Singer Sewing Machine, one of the earliest international companies, has in recent years reduced its main U.S. plant in New Jersey from 10,000 employees to 2,000. General Instruments recently cut its New England labor force by 3,000 and increased its force in Taiwan by almost 5,000. The examples are endless. The global corporations claim that the effect of internationalization of production is a net increase in jobs, because the stimulation of new industry is greater than the job displacement in older industry. Whether one reads union studies or industry studies, the fact is indisputable that thousands of U.S. workers are losing jobs because of plant relocation. Whether other workers in other places may be getting jobs in the process is small comfort to the unemployed.

The discomfort is sufficiently acute that organized labor has mounted a campaign to pass frankly punitive legislation, such as the Hartke-Burke bill designed to discourage foreign investment. Organized labor is hostile to the world corporation not only because it employs cheap labor under what can only be described as sweatshop conditions (60 percent of the male workers of Hong Kong work seven days a week for about a dollar a day) but also because the mobility of the global enterprise robs labor of its traditional bargaining weapons. (Companies now deliberately duplicate production facilities so that they can shift from one to another in the event of labor trouble.)

Older domestic industries, such as shoes, textiles, and steel, are less than enthusiastic about a world without borders because they are dependent upon such borders to protect them from the devastating competition of places like Hong Kong and Taiwan, indeed to keep them in business. The motto of the growing band of neo-protectionists is *Up With Borders*, exactly the opposite of the one that supposedly unites revolutionary students and IBM executives. National industry in poor countries, threatened with either absorption by the global giants or lethal competition, also form part of the protectionist coalition that has marked the global corporation as its number-one enemy.

But the torrent of articles, exposés, and impassioned speeches on the global companies, particularly in the Third World countries, are a reflection of a second group of enemies, who are motivated more by political feelings than economic interest. The sensational disclosures of ITT's efforts to bring down the Allende government in Chile have confirmed widespread fears in many places that the world corporations have too much power. There is increasing concern around the world that global corporations are in a position to dominate governments, dislocate national economies, and upset world currency flows. The fact that the Senate Foreign Relations Committee in the United States and the Social and Economic Council of the United Nations are holding hearings and sponsoring studies on these questions is an indication of how deep these fears are. Sir Frederick Catherwood, director general of Britain's National Economic Development Office, poses the political problem created by the global corporations this way: "The British citizen does not have votes in the U.S. Congress and does not like decisions which affect his destiny to be completely removed from his control." It is a sentiment that is widely shared, particularly in poor countries where

weakness and inefficiency of local governments are easily translated
into corporate advantages. Whether the global corporation should be
welcomed, barred, or fitted with a legal straitjacket is shaping up as a
prime political issue in virtually all developing countries and
increasingly in the more industrialized nations as well.

Potential members of the second group include officials and
bureaucrats in the larger developed countries who are beginning to
see the worldwide corporate attack on "irrational nationalism" as a
direct challenge to their own power. It is one thing when the U.S.
government bureaucrats are against "irrational nationalism" in
Guatemala, where, presumably, what is meant by the term is
expropriation of bananas. It is something else again when the same
epithet is being applied to the U.S. State Department, Justice
Department, or the Pentagon.

The third group of antagonists is somewhat undefined, but
ultimately it could be the most lasting. Men such as David
Rockefeller and Jacques Maisonrouge are convinced that there is a
dangerous surge of antibusiness sentiment throughout the world, and
they are especially alarmed about its impact in the United States. The
Council of the Americas, an organization of the major U.S.
corporations doing business in Latin America, devoted its 1972
annual meeting to the theme of anticorporatism and how business
must "explain itself" better. A similar concern pervaded the 1972
White House Conference on the Industrial World Ahead 1990.
David Rockefeller shocked bankers at the Detroit Economic Club by
pointing out that three out of five students believe, according to a
recent poll, that "big business has taken the reins of government
away from the Congress and Administration." Rockefeller's poll is
corroborated by a University of Michigan survey which reveals that
59 percent of all Americans think that "the government is run by a
few big interests looking out for themselves." Opinion Research
Corporation reports that "53 percent of the people feel business is
doing very little in pollution control while only 10 percent think it is
doing a great deal."

The attitude of young people around the world to the global corporation is a cause of particular concern. "If I were asked to describe the current stereotype of the corporation held by the young," says Jacques Maisonrouge in a speech[10] he has delivered on more than one occasion, "I would be compelled to say:

> A corporation is a business structure whose sole reason for existence is the earning of profits by manufacturing products for as little as possible and selling them for as much as possible. It does not matter whether the product does good or evil; what counts is that it be consumed—in ever-increasing quantities. Since everything the corporation does has, as its ultimate goal, the creation of profit, it offers its workers no deep personal satisfactions, no feeling of contributing anything worthwhile to society, no true meaning to their activities. Go to work for a corporation and you are, through good salaries and various fringe benefits, installed as a faceless link in the lengthening chain—completing the circle by becoming one more consumer of all that junk. And, like all circles, the whole structure signifies nothing.

"America's Growing Anti-Business Mood," as *Business Week* calls it, threatens what the Earth Managers seek above all: public acceptance of the global corporation as the most effective and rational force to develop and distribute the resources of the world. In short, political legitimacy.

The confrontation between the global corporation and the odd assortment of enemies just now beginning to surface promises to influence the shape of human society in the last third of the century more than any other political drama of our time. To survive and to grow, certainly to fulfill its promise to create a rational, integrated world economy, the global corporation must forge a new global consensus on the most fundamental questions of political life: What kind of social and economic development meets the needs of

10. Jacques G. Maisonrouge, "Youth and the Business World" (Paper delivered at Second International Personnel Conference, November 13, 1969), p. 8.

twentieth-century man? What is a just social order? What is "freedom," "justice," or "need" in a world in which 4 billion inhabitants are struggling for food, water, and air? What does "efficiency" or "growth" or "rationality" mean in such a world?

Money Crises and the Operation of Multinational Firms

The following is an excerpt from a Report on multinational firms, prepared by the United States Tariff Commission for the U.S. Senate Committee on Finance. While the report was generally laudatory of multinational corporations, this chapter in the report outlined the relationship between multinational corporations and financial institutions (banks) and the international monetary "crises" which have occurred repeatedly since 1967.*

Some Definitions

Throughout the chapter, several technical terms recur. These are defined below.

CAPITAL MARKETS

Capital markets are markets for long-term investment funds. The instruments used in them may be debt securities (bonds and notes), or equity securities (stocks), or combinations of the two—such as bond issues which are partly or wholly "convertible" into

* U.S. Senate, Committee on Finance, "Implications of Multinational Firms for World Trade and Investment and for U.S. Trade and Labor," 93rd Cong., 1st Sess. (Washington, D.C.: 1973).

equities. By convention, capital funds usually are thought of as those having maturities longer than a year. "Medium-term" generally denotes periods of from one to five years; medium-term loans of fairly short maturities often can look more like "money" transactions than "capital" ones. "Long-term" issues usually are those whose maturities run beyond five years. Any sort of capital market issue can be either "publicly placed" (on securities exchanges or through consortia of underwriting concerns) or "privately placed" (sold to one or a small group of institutional buyers with no public offering or notice taking place).

MONEY MARKETS

Money markets are markets for short-term funds, usually at maturities of a year or less. Instruments traded in the money markets can be bank deposits (demand or time), treasury bills, and similar types of short-term government paper, commercial paper (public or privately issued notes of nonbank concerns), or trade bills (which can become "acceptances" when they bear proper bank endorsements). A "certificate of deposit" or CD is merely a piece of paper which denotes the negotiability of a time deposit at a commercial bank. Ordinary short-term bank loans, too, are money market instruments. In general, the capital markets finance fixed investment; the money markets finance working capital needs.

EUROCURRENCIES

Eurocurrencies—including Eurodollars—are bank deposits, usually time deposits, denominated in currencies other than that of the country in which they are held. A Eurodollar deposit is identical with a dollar deposit in New York, except that it is held outside the United States.

EUROBONDS

Eurobonds, capital market instruments, are debt securities. They are issued through international underwriting syndicates and sold mainly in countries which have currencies different from those in which the issues are denominated. "Foreign bonds" also are sold outside the country of the borrower, but they traditionally have been issued by foreigners in some key financial center, in the currency of that center, and sold through underwriters of that center, chiefly to buyers of that country. "Eurobonds" and "foreign bonds," when discussed together without distinction between the two, are termed "international bonds." An "international bond," therefore, is simply any issue sold outside the borrower's country. Because of the U.S. Interest Equalization Tax, international bond issues are sold in the United States only in small amounts.

FOREIGN EXCHANGE MARKETS

Foreign exchange markets are used whenever it becomes necessary to make or receive payments in a currency other than one's own. Ordinary purchases or sales of foreign exchange for current use are "spot transactions." If a person owing a debt to a foreigner can persuade the foreigner to accept his, rather than the foreigner's currency, no exchange transaction takes place and there is no effect on the spot rate. This happens, especially in the case of the dollar, which is widely used as a "vehicle" currency for transactions outside the United States. Going further, if the foreigner accepts this arrangement, he can accept a deposit of foreign exchange in the country of the original debtor—say, a dollar deposit in a New York bank. However, if he then places that dollar deposit in a bank of his own country—say, London—the deposit becomes a Eurodollar deposit. The chain of dollar claims now runs backward from the original foreigner to the foreign bank in which he has placed the deposit, to the U.S. bank which always did owe the money—first to the original U.S. citizen who dealt with the foreigner, then to the foreigner himself, and lastly to the foreigner's London bank. As this dollar deposit is lent and relent outside the United States, the chain can lengthen ad infinitum—but there will be no effect on the foreign exchange market unless or until someone "converts" those dollars into another currency.

The foreign exchange markets obviously must be able to handle more than current or spot transactions. They also must accommodate transactions which involve credits, debts, and the dimension of time. Such transactions are *forward exchange* transactions, which merely are contracts—like futures contracts in commodities—to deliver specified amounts of currency to a buyer at a given future date, in return for specified amounts of foreign currency. Forward exchange rates depend on two things: (1) spot rates, or the market's expectation of where spot rates will be at maturity of a contract; and (2) because time is involved, money market interest rates in the countries of both buyer and seller for obligations with maturities the same as that of the forward contract. A forward transaction is a way of transferring the exchange risk onto someone else. The decision to undertake such a contract depends on the tradeoff between the possibility of earning a return on one's money abroad in the meanwhile (by buying spot exchange now and investing it abroad until the debt is due) and the possibility of a rate change (which would have to be risked if one invested at home and bought exchange three months hence). The "going" forward exchange rate for that maturity is the market's judgment about this tradeoff. If one agrees with it—or if he disagrees by thinking that forward exchange is available "cheap"—he will enter a forward contract. If he disagrees, thinking that the market overestimates the forward risk, he will sit tight and enter the spot market when his debt is due.

The Growth of Multinational Banking

The progressive integration of the world's major money and capital markets during the past decade or so may be interpreted as an economic phenomenon. It has its institutional counterpart in the rapid expansion not only of multinational business, which has been a major force in the stimulation of truly "international" finance, but also of multinational banking. . . . The simultaneous, parallel growth of both business and financial firms into international "space" has important symbiotic elements, of course. The one serves the other.

The overseas movement of U.S. banks and U.S. firms, both of which proceeded at a pace that quickened notably in the second half of the 1960s, exemplify this symbiosis best. A key reason for the widening of the international branch networks of the major U.S. banks has been to serve the banking needs of similarly expanding U.S. business firms, especially those in the manufacturing sector.

As recently as 1960, overseas branching was *not* a predominant characteristic of the international business conducted by most of even the largest U.S. banks. At that time, only two large banks—the Bank of America and the First National City Bank of New York—had decisively moved in the direction of setting up foreign branch coverage that could accurately be called "networks." Other banks had foreign branches—sometimes multiple ones—but their structure of branch operations did not yet reflect a commitment to use branch operations as the principal path of international expansion. Most banks, even those with enviable reputations in international banking, still preferred to develop their foreign business through widespread correspondent banking that had been developed in a time when most international banking activity was concerned with financing foreign trade of the traditional, arm's length variety. Through correspondents, a bank could process collections, letters of credit, and a certain amount of foreign loan activity with reasonable efficiency.

Two developments changed the background to international banking during the 1960s, however. The first was the increasingly sophisticated development of international business itself. This generated new corporate financial needs which were not best serviced through the correspondent banking system. Companies with coordinated international financial operations needed similarly coordinated banking support. At the same time, multinational business bred a new generation of corporate treasurers who are well informed about international banking. They began to see traditional international banking procedures as unnecessarily time-consuming and costly. They balked at transfer delays. Knowing that a customer—possibly their own affiliate—had paid a debt with "good funds" in London last night, they wanted "good funds" credited to their account in New York tomorrow—not next week—and they did not care to see these balances eroded away in transit by "banking" charges that could aggregate to a sizeable amount relative to a transaction's value. As a result, pressure was put on the banks to streamline their operations. In fairness, it should also be noted that many innovative bankers helped push this process along, often providing the spark which alerted company officials to the possibilities of cutting the costs of international financial transactions.

The second development that altered the international banking climate was the growth of the Eurocurrency market itself. The only way for a bank to obtain a proper piece of that action was to be there. Moreover, as the events of 1969 showed, the ability to use foreign branches as a source of dollar funds when monetary conditions were strongest in the United States led to demonstrable advantages, and set off a boom in branching activity.

These two developments went together. Neither one was primarily causal in the sudden growth of multinational branching by U.S. banks. In fact, the rapid speedup of the branching process itself led to new kinds of business and new developments, so that the entire process of increasing multinationalism on all fronts fed upon itself. In Europe, for example, the U.S. banks were practically the only ones which have had a branch "presence" in nearly all the important countries. As a result of this, they found it much easier than did local banks to move money around the continent to where the needs—and banking profits—were. Thus, when money was tight in Germany and loan rates were high, the Frankfurt branch of Bank A could arrange with its Brussels sister to loan dollars to a German customer direct. Bigger German banks, without Brussels branches, could not match this service.

The result of all these developments has been a vast increase in the number and financial resources of U.S. banks' foreign branches— along with a wholesale shift in American bankers' outlook, toward using branching as the principal device for expansion of their foreign business. Banks joined the other MNCs as heavy direct investors abroad. Data showing the development of foreign branch banking between 1966 and 1970 indicate that the number of branches of U.S. banks abroad more than doubled over the period, from 244 to 536. At the same time, total assets/liabilities of the branches, worldwide, more than quadrupled, from $12.4 billion to $52.6 billion. In 1970, three-quarters of the total asset figure was accounted for by branches in Europe. Also notable was a substantial expansion of branch activity in the Bahamas, which is close to the U.S. geographically, close to Europe technologically and institutionally, and has a minimum of regulations and restrictions. . . .

There are some important differences between the asset and liability structures of U.S. branch banks overseas and those of commercial banks generally in the United States. These differences are attributable mainly to the heavy activity of the branches as intermediaries in the Eurodollar market. In general, such activity leads to heavy reliance on time deposits relative to other deposit liabilities, strong cash positions, and weak loan positions, as Eurodollars may be lent in the interbank market simply as placements of deposits with other banks. Whereas the branches as a group show time deposit liabilities as nearly 90 percent of their total deposits, the comparable figure for commercial banks in the United States is only 48 percent (1970 figures). Similarly, the branches in 1970 held 33 percent of their assets in the form of cash; the comparable figure for U.S. domestic commercial banks was only 19 percent. About 55 percent of the branches' total assets appeared in their loan accounts, a proportion not much different from the 54 percent reported for domestic banks. However, a large proportion of these loans was "captive" in the form of loans to head offices in the United States. Excluding these, the proportion for the branches of loans to total assets drops to under 40 percent. . . .

Taking advantage of relaxed banking laws in some countries and the Edge Act in the United States,[1] the banks have become

1. The Edge Act permits U.S. commercial banks to establish domestic subsidiaries strictly to conduct international business, with considerable relaxation of restrictions on the kinds of activity in which they can engage. Edge Act subsidiaries have proliferated in recent years, although the enabling legislation has been on the books for many decades.

involved in many species of investment banking operations, including both medium- and long-term financing of capital projects. They have led in the development of leasing techniques abroad. Finally, the U.S. banks operating abroad have become major purveyors to customers of economic, financial, and credit information—intelligence organizations of some skill.

Foreign bankers have responded competitively. Including branches, representative offices, subsidiaries and shareholdings in foreign banks, the U.S. banks have a presence in an estimated 2,000 foreign banking offices of one sort or another. British bankers, with the legacy of their own banking system's strong international position, have a similar presence in around 5,000 places. Elsewhere, foreign banking traditions, especially in Europe, put a strong brake on multinational branching or mergers. But tieups of various sorts among foreign banks have begun to increase in recent years. They range across the spectrum from gentlemen's agreements on "close cooperation," to the establishment of new multinationally-owned banks which—notably indeed in light of the development of the Eurocurrency and Eurobond markets as hallmarks of international financial integration—are strongly oriented to medium- and long-term financing as well as investment banking, plus services specifically geared to the requirements of multinational enterprises.

The MNCs' Financial Needs and IMM Practices

So far in this chapter, the MNCs themselves—i.e., U.S. corporations with direct investments abroad—have received scant mention with respect to their activity in the international financial markets. The objective of the discussion so far has been to establish and describe part of the framework within which the MNCs operate—and which they have themselves had a large hand in creating. As indicated, it comprises a steadily more integrated world of international finance, supported by a fast-expanding network of international—not to say multinational—banking institutions. The questions now at hand are, "What kinds of activities do the MNCs engage in, within this framework?" and, "Have they changed the framework itself?"

The large multinational corporation is involved in a multitude of financial activities that transcend national boundaries and involve dealings in both long- and short-term funds. For purposes of exposition, however, it is better to think in terms of a process which begins with planning and ends with involved activity. This process begins with some form of strategic thinking on the part of management. It usually takes place at least once a year, and can vary from "budget" discussions to full-fledged planning of a very sophisticated sort.

For any firm with international production facilities, one fundamental decision—an operating decision with strong financial implications—has to be made and held to for fairly long periods. That decision concerns the firm's locus of profit responsibility. Is final accountability to be placed with the manager or head of each local branch or subsidiary; with a regional headquarters; or with the corporate headquarters in the United States? From a financial point of view, much hangs on this decision. On the one hand, if the firm decides to grant maximum autonomy to its local managers abroad, then it forecloses the possibility of centralized financial management in the interests of the corporation as a whole, except possibly for the most fundamental investment decisions. Obviously, if the local manager's performance is to stand or fall on his contribution to profitability, he will demand—and should get—nearly total control, including financial control, of his operation, lest his position become untenable. On the other hand, the corporation can maximize its control over its farflung financial activities only if it centralizes profit responsibility, so that the performance of the corporate treasurer and his finance department is integrated into the overall profit performance of the firm as a worldwide whole.

Many firms do not yet practice centralized control although the trend is in that direction—as any big bank's IMM consultant staff will quickly point out. Centralization is more or less a matter of corporate maturity and corporate size. Small firms with small headquarters staffs and only a few direct investments usually will prefer to hire a good manager and let him go, with full profit responsibility. The same often is true of very rapidly expanding firms, on a path of fast overseas growth, which have not yet taken the time to reorganize their corporate management structure sufficiently to provide for centralized control.

A large, mature corporation, however, one with a fairly sizable network of overseas branches and/or subsidiaries and with considerable international experience usually begins to think in terms of centralized management. Its objective becomes the profitability of the organization as a whole rather than the individual performances of overseas holdings engaged in unseemly and possibly unprofitable competition with each other. From this viewpoint, centralization becomes a sine qua non for efficient IMM.

Assuming that the decision to centralize has been made, the process of corporate planning typically involves detailed inputs from the foreign subsidiaries, including sales forecasts, related production plans, and investment plans. In very large MNCs, these plans are coordinated and cleared by regional management staffs before being brought to the corporate headquarters in the United States. Finally, however, the process leads to detailed plans which are approved at headquarters and become the operating bible for the firm over the course of the plan period—which usually has linked phases extending from the operating year (for which plans are most complete) out to three-, five- or ten-year horizons.

The financial aspects of the plans are complex, for a large firm, with each subsidiary having an operating budget to which it is expected to conform. One of the primary targets of the firm as a whole concerns capital investment. Investment decisions are taken fairly far in advance, whence they are built into operating goals. Decisions about capital spending obviously are built into the planning process. If investment is to be financed out of internally generated funds, it must be decided where these funds are to be generated within the overall corporate structure, and whether the source is to primarily depreciation charges, retained earnings, or some combination of the two. If retained earnings are involved, the profit remittance policies of the company clearly are affected. Decisions also must be made on how much capital is to be transferred from the parent organization, how much is to be borrowed in the parent country, and how much abroad. Guidelines are required for changing these decisions in the course of the plan period, should capital market conditions change, and systems must be set up to effect such changes. All of these, essentially, are questions about "cash flow" which, in the centrally managed corporation, is planned, watched, and manipulated by the headquarters organization.

In sum, the long-term planning of investment merges with the short-term management of cash flow in the ongoing financial life of the firm—and it is the job of the corporate treasurer's department to watch over it all. It is important to note, however—and this often is overlooked in discussions of IMM practices—that most modern corporations work against fixed plans covering all aspects of the business over a fairly long term. The plans are flexible, and they allow for much reaction to current developments, but they are there, and corporate management generally has a clear notion of where it wants to go.

The financial sides of corporate operations are closely intertwined with the firm's banking relationships. Typically, a large corporation will have a "lead" bank, with which it maintains large balances; and on which it depends for a variety of financial services. It also will have accounts with one or more other banks—each vying with the others and with the lead bank for a larger share of the firm's business—which gives the firm some optional control over the institutions through which transactions will flow. Each of the firm's subsidiaries will have similar banking relationships, and one of them is likely to be with a foreign branch of one or more of the firm's banks at home. It is obvious but often forgotten that, except for some intracompany transactions treated as offsetting bookkeeping entries, any transaction made by a firm or its subsidiaries is made through one or more banks.

At one end of the financial spectrum, the firm borrows capital funds, to the extent that it has decided not to finance expansion out of internally generated funds. There is a choice here, among three options: (1) to use the parent's domestic capital markets, thence transferring direct investment capital to desired locations abroad; (2) to use one or more of the local capital markets in which the existing subsidiaries are based; or (3) to borrow in the international market, perhaps through a "finance subsidiary" created by the firm specifically to float such issues. The actual route taken depends in the first instance on relative interest costs, net of any applicable taxes and underwriting costs. It always makes sense to borrow in the cheapest market. However, other factors enter. Regulations, such as capital controls at home, may put a physical limit on the amount of capital that can be transferred abroad to a given location. Local capital markets may be too narrow to support a large borrowing. The international markets may be insisting on sweeteners such as convertible issues, or it may prefer DM issues over dollar issues, which brings up for decision the question of whether the firm wants to risk a long-term debt in a currency that the market thinks is likely to appreciate. It is likely that, in the process of choosing from among these options, the firm will have coordinated closely with an investment banking house that has wide international connections and that, if an international issue is chosen as the path to follow, ultimately will put together a large, multinational underwriting consortium.

Still another factor may be involved. The distinction between "long-term" and "short-term" is not nearly as sharp as described so far. Medium-term financing has risen considerably in popularity. This usually means bank financing, probably abroad, and often with funds related to the Eurocurrency markets. It may involve term loans, or a portfolio of notes spread around to a number of banks (and possibly other financial institutions). It could take the form of simple short-term financing that is rolled over and over until it has that long-term look. It represents another choice for the firm in its financial planning. Often, this kind of financing is "privately placed" with little or no publicity. If so, observers cannot count it when they go about guessing how large the international financial markets really are.

Once a borrowing decision is made, the firm comes into possession of large amounts of funds which it must put somewhere until they are spent for their designated purposes. These now have become, from the firm's point of view, short-term or money market balances, and they thus merge with the other operating cash flows of the firm. What happens from now on essentially becomes the subject matter of IMM.

A distinction should be made here between "stocks" of funds and "flows" of funds. The "stocks" are the balances under the command of the firm at any moment. The "flows" are compounded of the movements of these stocks as well as the patterns by which the stocks are increased or decreased in response to the firm's worldwide operations.

For simplicity, the operational flow-generating mechanisms of the firm—i.e., payrolls, sales, payments for materials and components, interest flows, intracompany payments and all the rest—will be ignored temporarily in order to focus without distraction on what happens to the stocks which exist at any given moment. Since the stocks or balances of the firm are likely to be quite sizable, financial officers are highly unlikely to hold them in idle, noninterest-earning forms, except for the necessary demand deposits needed to support current operations, which have just been assumed for the moment to have fallen to zero.

In deciding where to hold its balances, the firm has at least half a dozen money markets to choose from, as well as a much larger number of forms in which the balances can be held. Three factors will govern decisions about where the stocks will be allocated. First, because the operations of the firm come first (it is not a bank, but a business), the money ought to be put where it is going to be needed for future use, i.e., for future flows. This may not be an especially important factor, because transfers between and among money markets have become both simple and fairly low in cost in the modern world. One real constraint, however, is the element of time—one cannot invest one's balances for six months when he needs to spend them in three, except in the extraordinary case where he can earn more on the investment than it will cost him to borrow at short term to meet the three-month obligation.[2] Second, relative interest rate levels on different kinds of instruments in different money markets will influence both the locations and the forms in which balances are held. Other things being equal, the firm clearly will go for the highest possible interest return on its balances.

Third, however, exchange risks intervene. The high-interest country may have a shaky exchange rate, which not only increases the risk of a loss on moving the funds ultimately into a needed currency, but also increases the risk that, to defend its exchange rate, the country in question may offer inducements for short-term capital to flow in, while placing controls on letting capital flow out again. Conversely, the low-interest country may have an exceedingly strong exchange rate, one so strong that a finance officer who knows the market will see clearly that "speculative" pressures are building up for a possible revaluation on which a profit might be made—a profit possibly bigger than the interest earnings foregone.

In both these cases—high-interest-plus-weak-exchange-rate, as well as low-interest-plus-strong-exchange-rate—the final decision about where to place funds depends in the end on a weighing of risks against potential gains. It is subjective. Most corporate finance officers "go with the market" which is the ostensibly safe thing to do, unless the market is wrong, which usually is not the case. The more courageous but less numerous ones will follow their subjective instincts.

Financial decisions sometimes are easy to make. Weak-currency countries with low interest rates repel funds, while strong-currency countries with high interest rates attract them, and objectives do not

2. Exchange risks have a bearing here. If one expects soon to make a payment denominated in a presently weak currency, it makes sense to hold off on that payment as long as possible in order to take advantage of any exchange depreciation that might occur. On the other hand, buying a strong currency now avoids having to pay more for it on the exchange market later.

conflict. The latter situation applied to West Germany in 1970–71. In retrospect, it seems hard to understand why anyone with available funds would *not* have placed them with the Germans in that period.

One reason for ignoring operational flows for the moment in this analysis has been to make the obvious point that decisions about where to put stocks of funds lead automatically to flows which can be significant, even before one begins to consider the effects of flows generated by the firm's day-to-day operations. The simplified analysis also serves to reveal the basic principles which govern the movements of the firm's funds: (1) the need to get funds to where they are needed, when they are needed; (2) considerations of interest returns available; and (3) foreign exchange market risks and opportunities.

These principles do not disappear when operational flows are reintroduced into the analysis. They continue to function because they govern where the firm will be holding its balances at any given moment, this structure of balances being determined ultimately by all the flows which have taken place up to that moment. Thus, the discussion almost could end here, except that there are some important side issues to explore.

The flows generated by the firm's operational activities—as opposed to the flows produced by its IMM-oriented financial managers—may not necessarily be oriented in directions dictated by IMM requirements. IMM is overlaid upon these operational flows. In some cases, the firm is able to direct or redirect the flows as they occur—a customer can be asked to direct his payments to any of the firm's locations, for example, provided that no additional costs for him are incurred. Similarly, all intracompany payments can be controlled as desired, with offsetting bookkeeping entries. In other cases, however, when operational flows give rise to balances in one spot, IMM-induced flows may well move these balances to other spots. The result is an increase in the overall rate of turnover of the firm's fund balances, so that the volume of transactions which passes through the national and international money markets is increased.

It can be taken for granted that the MNCs operate in the international financial markets—the money markets, the capital markets, and the foreign exchange markets—with much the same techniques that all firms with international business employ. In this sense, the MNC behaves no differently from the ordinary trader, for example, except that it probably has bigger balances to play with. Thus, it reacts to market developments in the same way as the "small fellow," but with greater speed and with a heavier quantitative impact on the system. It moves more money faster.

In addition to these "normal" sorts of transaction techniques, however, the MNC (or a multinational bank), because of its unique presence in a number of countries on a continuing basis, has certain other powerful options available. With its farflung operations, it is continually generating payments into and out of different markets and currencies, building up debt, liquidating it, and granting credits. The range of its financial interests is large and, most important, a considerable part of this range of transactions is internal to the firm as a whole—or subject to some control through internal firm decisions.

"Leads and Lags" are a case in point. A non-MNC firm dealing with foreigners has some opportunity to play this game, but it is limited. He can delay his payments to a weak-currency country and speed his payments to a strong-currency one for a time; but he cannot do so indefinitely unless he can find someone—with whom he must deal at arm's length—to lend him the necessary resources as his debts fall due. The MNC, on the other hand, can instruct its subsidiaries to go on leading and lagging in their *intracompany* payments for a very long time. When the subsidiary in the weak-currency country runs short, it can be told to borrow in its own domestic money market, which helps the firm as a whole to inflate its debt position in the weak currency, which is just what is wanted. Similarly, the strong-currency subsidiary may shortly be swimming in funds, which it can place in its local money market, thus building up the entire firm's assets in the strong currency, which also is to be coveted.

Variations on the basic theme of altering the timing of

intracompany payments can be used across the whole spectrum of a firm's dealings. Intrafirm trade payments are only part of the picture. Interest and dividend remittances, royalties and fees, and even capital flows can be affected. Moreover, as the above description of "leads and lags" suggested, the manipulation of timing in intracompany transactions can affect the firm's net positions vis-à-vis outsiders by changing the patterns of subsidiary borrowing and lending in different markets. Again, however, no mystery attaches to the reasons for such behavior. They result from the decisions taken by the firm to minimize interest costs, maximize returns, and avoid exchange risk. These are the basic motivations behind the behavior of any person or entity with balances denominated in currencies other than his own. If the MNCs make a difference for the system, therefore, it is a difference of degree rather than kind. All the rest—the entire field of dazzling IMM techniques and rituals—turns out to be mere technical embellishment which increases the efficiency of the international financial system but does not alter its character.

The Role of the MNCs in Generating Liquid Short-Term Capital Flows and International Monetary Crises

Since 1967, the international monetary system has been subjected to a series of shocks that have threatened its foundations, called into question the utility of the Bretton Woods Agreements of 1944 on which it is based, and, finally, forced the abandonment of the parity of its lynchpin, the United States dollar. The only comparable period of such strain on the system within living memory was that of the hectic international monetary history of the 1920s and 1930s. Indeed, the threat of a return to the disordered conditions of those two decades—and the fear of it—lend urgency and fire to the current debate about just what is wrong with the present system. It should be clearly underlined, however, that despite the recurrence of severe international *financial* crises in recent years (especially since 1967), the economic troubles which beset the major countries in the 1920s and 1930s have been absent. Despite disruptions in the monetary sphere, world economic growth, world trade, and international investment have reached record levels.

THE TYPICAL "CRISIS"

The international monetary crises of recent years have been more alike than different. They have so many characteristics in common that it is an easy matter to describe the "typical" financial crisis, which begins with a balance of payments disequilibrium between one country with a relatively large deficit and one or more countries with large surpluses, the counterparts of that deficit. National policies are applied with greater or lesser enthusiasm in order to correct this disequilibrium. Generally, they are applied more severely in the deficit country than in the surplus ones, and sometimes the policies applied by the surplus countries turn out to be perverse, from the balance of payments point of view. That is, they find themselves, depite payments surpluses, in inflationary situations which they attempt to combat with tight money and high interest rates. These kinds of policies work to increase rather than decrease payments disequilibria.

In any case, exchange rates begin to reflect the payments problems. The deficit country's rate becomes "weak" and the surplus countries' rates become "strong." Under a par value system of the Bretton Woods type, exchange rates are fixed within the short run; in practice, the monetary authorities of the developed countries have attempted to keep them fixed in the long run too. Central banks have bent every effort to defend existing rates. In this process, the deficit country must sell off its reserves, while the surplus countries accumulate them.

In fairly short order, this process has led to huge and heavily disequilibrating flows of liquid short-term capital. Funds move away from the weak currency and toward the strong ones. The deficit country loses its reserves at a rapid rate; the surplus countries gain them equally fast. The deficits get bigger, and so do the surpluses.

Soon, the question of the appropriateness of policies to rectify balance of payments problems in the long run—or even the extended short run—becomes academic. Capital flows have depleted the deficit country's reserves and swelled the surplus countries' holdings to the point of unwelcomeness.

THE ACCUSATION AGAINST THE MNCS

Opponents of the MNCs argue that they play a crucial, destructive role in international monetary crises. The argument sometimes includes an accusation that they bear responsibility for at least part of the balance-of-payments problems that originally generate the crises, but this accusation is not central to the argument. Rather, the central point is that the MNCs are a source of the large flows of liquid short-term capital that are the proximate cause of the wreckage. Moreover, it is argued that these flows arise because the MNCs are predilected toward sustained, unstoppable "speculative" attacks upon exchange rates. Thus, it is held, speculators, with the MNCs in the van, can cause enough havoc within the system to produce the threat of devaluation or revaluations of exchange rates *even if* underlying national economic policies are appropriate and severely enough applied to rectify the balance-of-payments disequilibria—if only the speculators would give them the necessary time, which they do not.[3]

THE EVIDENCE

An evaluation of the allegations made against the MNCs should involve an analysis of flows of liquid, short-term capital as they show up in the balance of payments, isolating and measuring those flows that are attributable specifically to the MNCs. Unfortunately, this is

3. Defenders of the MNCs are sensitive to these accusations and hasten to deny them. See, for example, *The Economist*, 31 October 1970, pp. 54–55; *Business Week*, 25 September 1971, pp. 82–107 (especially pp. 101–2), and *Newsweek*, 20 November 1972, pp. 96–104. For a statement of the problem that is not necessarily accusing in tone, see *Foreign Trade, A Survey of Current Issues to Be Studied by the Subcommittee in International Trade of the Committee on Finance, U.S. Senate* (Washington, D.C.: USGPO, 14 May 1971, p. 4.

not possible. Data for the flows attributable to the MNCs are not available. In this respect, central banks and governments are technologically inferior to the MNCs which, in their own operations, are able to gather, analyze, and act upon the information necessary to them.

There is a useful alternative, however. This approach, the one taken in the following analysis, involves, first, an identification of all those kinds of institutions—banks and business firms—which have dealings in the international money markets, as opposed to strictly domestic ones. Once this identification is made, the next step is to add together, as accurately as possible, the total resources—assets and liabilities vis-à-vis each other—which these institutions have at their command. Essentially, this procedure estimates the amounts of short-term funds that *can* flow in a crisis situation. If the numbers turn out to be small, then it can be concluded that these institutions' financial muscle is overrated by the critics. If they are large, then it can be concluded at least that the possibility of disequilibrating behavior is speculative. That is, do the MNCs speculate aggessively (by risking assets for financial gain), or do they merely react protectively, to guard their assets against possible loss in value due to an exchange rate change brought on by the underlying balance-of-payments disequilibrium?

In sum, therefore, while it is not appropriate to judge that speculative behavior characterizes the international financial dealings of the great majority of MNCs, it is appropriate to stress that they have been a primary creative force in the growth of the international money and capital markets. This is the sense in which the MNCs indeed have altered the international realities around which policies of governments—and the international monetary "system" in general—are framed. Indeed, if the large amount of privately held liquidity which now characterizes the international markets had not been generated as it was by the MNCs, then the last decade's upsurge in world economic growth, trade, and investment might have been more restricted in the absence of some cooperative international effort to act in the MNCs' place.

The size of the international money market which the MNCs have helped to create would not, by itself, necessarily represent an effective change in the realities of international finance, were it not for the parallel and complementary development of new institutions —especially the Eurocurrency markets—which give the market flexibility and an ability to generate almost instant flows of funds among national money markets. In an earlier time, central banks and governments had more freedom to work out appropriate monetary policies because the institutions of international finance were sufficiently underdeveloped that national money markets remained partially isolated from one another. The development of a strong, flexible international money market has taken away that advantage, allowing the international financial community to focus its flows quickly and directly—a focus which, as the recent international monetary crises have shown, has caused serious problems for the world's central banks.

Basic Facts: Distribution of Personal Income and Wealth in the United States

Letitia Upton
Nancy Lyons

This report describes the distribution of personal income and wealth in the United States. Simply stated, income is money that people receive from various sources; wealth is the value of their possessions and property. We have attempted to clarify and consolidate the existing, and sometimes conflicting, studies that show the allocation of income and wealth to families ranked from rich to poor; the changes that have occurred over time; and the impact of taxes and welfare programs on the overall distribution.

No single source provides adequate information on personal income and wealth distribution in this country. The Census Bureau surveys, based on interviews of sample households, receive more complete information about earnings than about nonearned income and thus tend to underestimate the income of the top and bottom brackets; less information is received from the rich than from the rest of the population on wealth holdings. The Internal Revenue Service, the other major source of information, excludes incomes too meager to be taxed. Income classifications published by the IRS also underestimate the before-tax income of the higher income brackets by excluding, for instance, half of the net profits from the sale of stocks and other investment assets (capital gains). In addition, some studies drawn from these sources omit such important issues as the effect of taxes and nonmoney income on distribution.

The result is that estimates of distribution based on different sources of information and on varying concepts of income and wealth are difficult to compare. In spite of the differences in details between studies, however, they all present a similar picture of income and wealth distribution that may help to explain some of the social, economic, and political dilemmas that confront America today.

Income[1]

There are limits to the contrasts of poverty and affluence that people will tolerate when they believe the credo of a society that proclaims that all men are equal and that none are prescribed by birth to low status or high. Today there is reason to believe that this country has transgressed those limits.

—James Tobin[2]

1. We have stressed the income distribution since World War II. Researchers disagree about earlier trends. Some believe there was a decisive reduction in inequality in the early 1940s compared to earlier years (see, for instance, Edward C. Budd, ed. *Inequality and Poverty* [New York: Norton, 1967], p. xx). Others maintain that there has been essentially no change since 1910 (see Gabriel Kolko, *Wealth and Power in America* [New York: Praeger, 1962], p. 13). Joseph Pechman speculates that recent distributions may not be very different from the distribution of the early 1920s, but acknowledges that "the available data for those [earlier] years are simply not good enough to say much more" ("The Rich, the Poor, and the Taxes They Pay," *Public Interest*, no. 17 [Fall 1969]: 22).

Another point of controversy concerns the reduced income share of the top 5 percent and its effect on redistribution. Whatever the exact amount of the decline, which depends on the concept of income that is used, it does not seem to result in any significant change in overall income shares (see table 1, for example). See Selma Goldsmith, "Changes in the Size Distribution of Income," *Inequality and Poverty*, ed. Edward C. Budd (New York: Norton, 1967), pp. 65–79.

2. J. Tobin and W. A Wallis, *Welfare Programs: An Economic Appraisal* (Washington, D.C.: American Enterprise Institute for Public Policy Research, 1968), p. 27.

There is a startling and continuing inequality in the distribution of income in the United States, and the overall pattern has remained virtually unchanged since World War II. By the most conservative estimates, the income of the richest 20 percent of families has been more than all the income received by the bottom 60 percent for the entire period. Depending on the concept of income that is used, each family in the highest fifth has had on the average between 7 and 9 times the income of each family in the bottom fifth.

The most up-to-date information about the distribution of income is Census Bureau data. Families[3] are ranked by money income before taxes and the percent of income received by each fifth is given for several years (table 1). The approximate income ranges for each fifth in 1970 were: poorest fifth, under $5,000; second fifth, $5,000–$8,000; middle fifth, $8,000–$11,000; fourth fifth, $11,000–$14,000; richest fifth, $14,000 and over; top 5 percent, $24,000 and over.

If incomes were divided equally among families, each fifth would receive 20 percent of the total. In fact, however, the census data shows that since World War II, the poorest fifth of families has received less than 6 percent of money income; the richest fifth has received over 40 percent. Put another way, the average income of the 10.4 million families in the bottom fifth in 1970 was $3,054; the average income of the 10.4 million families in the top fifth was $23,100. If money income had been divided equally among families in 1970, the average income for each family would have been over $11,000.[4]

If the country's total income (based on net national product which includes governments and corporations as well as individuals) had been distributed to families in 1970, the average income would

3. "Family income" is the total received by two or more people residing together who are related by blood, marriage, or adoption.
4. U.S. Bureau of the Census, *Current Population Reports*, Series P-60, No. 80, "Income in 1970 of Families and Persons in the United States" (Washington, D.C.: Government Printing Office, 1971), pp. 1, 17. There were 51.9 million families with a mean income of $11,106 in 1970. The mean of the lowest fifth was 27.5 percent of the national mean; the mean of the highest fifth was 208 percent of the national mean.

Table 1 Percentage Share of Before-tax Money Income of Families by Fifths and Top 5 Percent, Selected Years, 1947–70

Families Ranked from Lowest to Highest Income	1970	1968	1962	1960	1958	1950	1947
Poorest fifth	5.5	5.7	5.1	4.9	5.1	4.5	5.0
Second fifth	12.0	12.4	12.0	12.0	12.4	12.0	11.8
Middle fifth	17.4	17.7	17.5	17.6	17.9	17.4	17.0
Fourth fifth	23.5	23.7	23.7	23.6	23.7	23.5	23.1
Richest fifth	41.6	40.6	41.7	42.0	40.9	42.6	43.0
Total [a]	100.0	100.0	100.0	100.0	100.0	100.0	100.0
Top 5 percent	14.4	14.0	16.3	16.8	15.8	17.0	17.2

[a] May not add to 100 due to rounding.

Source: U.S. Bureau of the Census, Current Population Reports, Series P-60, no. 80 (4 October 1971), table 14, p. 28.

Notes: 1. Money income (before deductions for federal and state income taxes, social security contributions, and other taxes) includes: wages or salary; net income from nonfarm and farm self-employment; social security, dividends, interest on savings and bonds, income from estates or trusts, net rental income; public assistance or welfare payments, unemployment compensation, government employee pensions, veterans payments; private pensions, annuities, alimony, regular contributions from persons not living in the household, and other periodic income.
2. Family income is the total received by two or more people residing together who are related by blood, marriage, or adoption.

Table 2 Comparison of Shares of Money Income of Families by Fifths, Top 5 Percent and Top 1 Percent Before and After Adjustment for Nonreporting and Underreporting of Income, 1966

Families Ranked from Lowest to Highest Income	Before Adjustment		After Adjustment	
	Income Range (dollars)	Percent of Income Received	Income Range (dollars)	Percent of Income Received
Lowest fifth	2,760	4.1	3,070	3.2
Second fifth	2,760–5,380	10.9	3,070–5,890	10.5
Middle fifth	5,380–7,850	17.5	5,890–8,620	17.0
Fourth fifth	7,850–10,980	24.9	8,620–12,260	23.9
Highest fifth	10,980 and over	42.7	12,260 and over	45.8
Top 5 percent	17,840 and over	15.8	19,920 and over	19.1
Top 1 percent	33,330 and over	4.8	44,560 and over	6.8

Source: Joseph A. Pechman, "Distribution of Federal and State Income Taxes by Income Classes" (Presidential Address, American Finance Association Annual Meetings, New Orleans, Louisiana, December 28, 1971), p. 6. Mimeographed.

Notes: 1. The income concept used is "money income" as defined by the U.S. Census Bureau. It includes money factor income and transfer payments, and excludes capital gains.

Table 3 Comparison of Shares of Money Income and Total Income by Fifths, Top 5 Percent and Top 1 Percent, 1968

Families and Individuals Ranked From Lowest to Highest Income	Money Income (Unadjusted)[a]		Total Income Before Tax and Transfer Payments[b]	
	Money Income Range	Percent of Income Received	Total Income Range	Percent of Income Received
Lowest Fifth	Under $3,150	3.7	Under $3,800	3.0
Second Fifth	Between $3,150 and $6,100	11.1	Between $3,800 and $8,200	9.5
Middle Fifth	Between $6,100 and $8,800	16.5	Between $8,200 and $12,100	16.5
Fourth Fifth	Between $8,800 and $12,500	26.2	Between $12,100 and $17,500	23.0
Highest Fifth	Over $12,500	42.5	Over $17,500	48.0
Top 5 Percent	Over $19,700	16.8	Over $29,700	22.0
Top 1 Percent	Over $32,000	4.9	Over $60,000	9.3

Source: Roger A. Herriot, and Herman P. Miller, "Who Paid the Taxes in 1968?" (U.S. Bureau of the Census Paper prepared for the National Industrial Conference Board meeting in New York, March 18, 1971), p. 3.

[a] Money income as published by the Bureau of the Census.

[b] Total income includes before-tax money income as published by the Bureau of the Census; $76 billion in underreported money income; $67 billion of imputed income (which includes, for example, wages in kind, value of food and fuel produced and consumed on farms, net imputed rental value of owner occupied homes); $18 billion in realized capital gains; $27 billion in retained corporate earnings; $74 billion in indirect taxes (taxes either shifted back on wages and dividends or forward onto consumers) less transfer payments.

Table 4 Composition of 1962 Before-tax Money Income

Specific Source of Income as Percentage Share of Total Income	Total Income[a]	Wages and Salaries	Business[b]	Property[c]	Pensions and Annuities[d]	Other Income[e]
(Percent distribution of mean amounts)	100%	75%	12%	6%	5%	2%
Percentage share of specific sources of income received by income fifths (Percent of total dollars)						
Poorest fifth	4%	1%	0%	4%	30%	20%
Second fifth	10	8	7	8	33	37
Middle fifth	16	18	13	10	13	13
Fourth fifth	24	28	17	11	11	16
Richest fifth	46	45	62	65	12	14
All units[f]	100	100	100	100	100	100
Top 5 percent	20	15	42	47	6	1

Consumer units ranked from lowest to highest income

Source: D. Projector, "Composition of Income as Shown by Survey of Financial Characteristics of Consumers," Paper No. 4 in Six Papers on Size Distribution of Wealth and Income, ed. L. Soltow (New York: National Bureau of Economic Research, 1969), no. 33, tables 1, 4; pp. 122, 128.

a Income is total money income received by all members of consumer units (families and unrelated individuals) before payroll or income tax deductions.

b Business income is net income from unincorporated businesses and professions (sole proprietorships and partnerships, farm and nonfarm) and dividends from incorporated businesses in which family member was actively engaged in managing.

c Property income is dividends from publicly traded stock, interest income, dividends from closely held corporations, net income from rents and royalties, trusts and estates.

d Pensions and annuities, including social security payments.

e Other income is public and private transfer payments, excluding old age pensions, such as welfare payments, veterans payments, unemployment compensation, alimony and interfamily transfers.

f May not add to 100 due to rounding.

have been close to $16,000.[5] Most studies of income distribution use a concept of income that falls somewhere between the "money income" of the census surveys and the "total income" of Net National Product. Studies based on broader definitions of income than the census data consistently show not only a larger amount of income, but also a greater degree of inequality (see, e.g., tables 2 and 3).

The distribution of income, of course, merely reflects the distribution of the major income sources. In 1962, for example, wages and salaries were 75 percent of personal money income. Nearly half of all wages and salaries, 45 percent, went to the top fifth of consumer units (families and unrelated individuals). Business and property income, the next largest source of income, was 18 percent of personal money income in 1962 and was even more heavily concentrated at the top. Over 60 percent of business and property income went to the richest fifth (table 4).

The Impact of Government Expenditure on Redistribution

We have not taxed the rich to give to the poor; we have taxed both the rich and the poor, and at least since 1940, contributed only a small fraction of the proceeds to the welfare of the poor.
—Gabriel Kolko[6]

GOVERNMENT EXPENDITURES

Government programs have had only a marginal impact on the overall distribution of income. Cash welfare payments to raise the income of people in certain categories, such as the blind, the unemployed, the aged, etc., are called "transfer payments." These payments do, of course, make a vital difference to the very

5. U.S. Bureau of the Census, *Statistical Abstract of the United States* (92nd ed.; Washington, D.C.: Government Printing Office, 1971), pp. 308, 309. Net national product, which is gross national product less capital consumption allowances, was $892.2 billion in 1970. Per capita net national product was calculated to be $4,344. The average family size in 1970 was 3.62.

6. Gabriel Kolko, *Wealth and Power in America* (New York: Praeger, 1962), p. 38.

poor—they were 56 percent of income for those with less than
$2,000 in 1965.[7] But transfer payments amount to only 7–8 percent
of personal income, not a large share compared to the 92–93 percent
in wages, salaries, and business and property income (table 5). The
effect of transfer payments on redistribution of income is thus
necessarily limited by their being a small share of total income.

Table 5 Transfer Payments, 1968

Cash Income-support Programs and Selected
Income-in-kind Programs

State and federal cash payments for categorical aid (AFDC, etc.)	$ 5.2 billion
Medicaid	4.6
Food stamps and surplus commodities	.4
Veterans pensions (nonservice-connected health care, death, or disability)	3.0

Social Insurance: Major Programs
Including Some Vendor Payments

Old Age, Survivors and Disability Insurance	24.9
Medicare	5.0
Unemployment Insurance	2.2
Workmen's Compensation	1.6
Railroad Retirement	1.5
Transfer Payments, 1968	$ 48.4 billion
Personal Income, 1968	688.7 billion
National Income, 1968	712.7 billion

Notes: 1. Transfer payments are from "Poverty Amid Plenty," *Report of the President's Commission on Income Maintenance Programs* (Washington, D.C.: Government Printing Office, November 1969). Sects. 3, 4, 5, Supplementary Statements.

2. Personal Income and National Income are from *Statistical Abstract of the United States 1971.* U.S. Bureau of the Census. Washington, D.C., 1971, p. 310.

7. Pechman, "The Rich, The Poor, and the Taxes They Pay," p. 33.

Social security payments (Old Age, Survivors, and Disability Insurance) account for over half of total transfer payments. Eligibility and benefits are determined by prior tax contributions and earnings, not by need, and payments are made throughout the income scale. Thus, the largest category of transfer payments is not confined to low-income groups. Indeed, social security is distributed in such a way that the highest payments usually go to those who have the most money from other sources, such as savings and investments.

In spite of these limitations, it is still surprising that increases in total transfer payments over the years have not resulted in some small improvement in the relative income position of the bottom fifth. Apparently, the poor are receiving less from the private economy so that "increases in government transfer payments [are] needed to prevent a gradual erosion of their income shares." [8]

Closely related to transfer payments are government subsidies for goods and services, such as funds for education, housing, highways, and so forth. Since most of these services are available to a broad spectrum of income groups, it is difficult to measure precisely their effect on inequality. A common assumption is expressed by Herman Miller of the Census Bureau, who wrote that "the extension of government services benefits low-income families more than those who have higher incomes by providing better housing, more adequate medical care, and improved educational facilities." [9] This is very much open to question. For instance, according to the report of the President's Commission on Income Maintenance Programs, the very poor are excluded not only from rent supplement programs but from public housing because they lack sufficient income to meet the minimum rent requirements.[10] A California study shows that state-supported higher education, although legally available to all, is

8. Ibid., p. 25.

9. Herman P. Miller, *Rich Man, Poor Man* (New York: Crowell, 1971), p. 51.

10. "Poverty Amid Plenty," *Report of the President's Commission on Income Maintenance Programs* (Washington, D.C.: Government Printing Office, November 1969), pp. 129–130.

of use primarily to the more affluent.[11] Similar conclusions can be drawn about the large subsidies involved in other public services, like highways and airports.

Taxation

The effect of the federal individual income tax on income redistribution is very modest and has been roughly constant during the post-World War II period.[12] In 1962, for example, the income share of the top fifth declined from a pretax 45.5 percent to 43.7 percent after taxes. The bottom three-fifths increased their combined share by only 1.4 percent, moving from 31.8 percent to 33.2 percent. The smallest gain went to the poorest fifth who moved from 4.6 percent to 4.9 percent, so that after taxes they were even further behind the families in the next three-fifths.

The tax, in effect since 1913, was for many years levied on high incomes only. The redistributive potential was greatly weakened in the 1940s when the majority of middle- and low-income families began to be taxed to meet increased revenue needs (particularly military spending). The tax is nominally progressive. This means that tax rates are higher as incomes increase. The progressive intent of the tax has been weakened considerably, however, because the *effective* tax rates (actual taxes paid) have been declining since World War II; and the reduction has been greatest for the higher income groups who can take advantage of preferential treatment of capital gains, percentage depletion allowances, depreciation allowances, exclusion of interest on state and local bonds, etc. Although the nominal tax rate for top income brackets ranges from 50 percent to 70 percent, "the effective rate of tax paid in 1967 by the top 1% was

11. W. L. Hansen and B. A. Weisbrod, "The Distribution of Costs and Direct Benefits of Public Higher Education—The Case of California." *Journal of Human Resources* 4 (1969): 176. Cited in Leonard Ross, "The Myth That Things Are Getting Better," *New York Review of Books* 17, no. 2 (12 August 1971): 8.

12. Pechman, "The Rich, the Poor, and the Taxes They Pay," p. 28.

only 26% of their total reported income, including all of their realized capital gains." [13]

The reality of the American capitalist system is that tax legislation, whatever its progressive intent or the country's need for revenue, is designed to protect and encourage private investment. Thus, earned income (wages and salaries) which most families depend on, is subject to much higher effective tax rates than property income (dividends, interest, rent, etc.). For example, in the

Table 6   Social Security and State and Local Taxes as Percent of Total Income, by Income Level, 1968

Adjusted Money Income Levels[a]	Social Security Tax	State and Local Taxes		
		Total [b]	Property	Sales
Under $2,000	7.6%	27.2%	16.2%	6.6%
2,000–4,000	6.5	15.7	7.5	4.9
4,000–6,000	6.7	12.1	4.8	4.1
6,000–8,000	6.8	10.7	3.8	3.6
8,000–10,000	6.2	10.1	3.6	3.3
10,000–15,000	5.8	9.9	3.6	2.9
15,000–25,000	4.6	9.4	3.6	2.4
25,000–50,000	2.5	7.8	2.7	1.8
50,000 and over	1.0	6.7	2.0	1.1

Source: Roger A. Herriot and Herman P. Miller, "Who Paid the Taxes in 1968?" U.S. Bureau of the Census. Paper prepared for the National Industrial Conference Board meeting in New York on March 18, 1971. Table 7.

a Transfer payments are not included in adjusted money income.

b Total is *all* state and local taxes, including property and sales.

$25,000–$50,000 income class, earners pay 47 percent more tax on their income than do property income recipients. As one tax expert concludes, "aside from the modest degree of progression by income classes, the major weakness of the federal individual income tax is its

13. Ibid., p. 27.

uneven impact on persons with the same total income but different income sources." [14]

More important than the federal individual income tax in the overall tax picture are social security payroll taxes and state and local taxes. To begin with, they are regressive taxes. This means that low-income families pay a greater percentage of their income in these taxes than high-income families (Table 6). Second, these regressive taxes provide more public revenue. In 1969, for example, the social security tax, together with state and local sales and property taxes, provided $91.4 billion in revenue compared to $87.2 billion from the federal individual income tax.[15] In addition, these regressive taxes are rapidly increasing. "The payroll tax has been the fastest growing major tax in the postwar United States. The maximum tax per employee for Old Age, Survivors, Disability and Hospital Insurance alone rose from $60 in 1949 to $749 in 1970 and is scheduled to reach $1,017 in 1973. . . . The yield from this taxation of labor income substantially exceeded corporate income taxes in 1969." [16] Similarly, "the states and local governments must have increased rates by 68 percent in these 17 years [1951–68] to push up their tax yields to current levels. The net result is, of course, that a greater degree of regression is being built into the national tax system by the states and local governments as they continue to seek for more revenues." [17]

In any single year there is some redistribution of personal income through transfer payments and federal individual income taxes, but the effect on overall inequality is modest. Taking into account both the federal individual income tax and transfer pay-

14. Joseph A. Pechman, "Distribution of Federal and State Income Tax by Income Classes" (Presidential Address), American Finance Association Annual Meetings, New Orleans, December 28, 1971, p. 14. Mimeographed.

15. *Economic Report of the President*, February 1971, pp. 273, 281.

16. John A. Brittain, "The Incidence of Social Security Payroll Taxes," *American Economic Review*, 61 (1971): 111.

17. Pechman, "The Rich, the Poor, and the Taxes They Pay," p. 31.

ments, income shares have remained essentially the same during the entire post-World War II period. Although comprehensive trend data is not available, it seems likely that when state, local and social security payroll taxes are considered, disposable income shares have become more unequal.

Wealth

Concentrated asset-wealth not only brings in larger personal incomes, but confers on the owners and their deputies a disproportionately large voice in economic, political and cultural affairs.

—Ferdinand Lundberg[18]

Income studies are concerned with who gets what; wealth studies estimate who has what. Just as most families receive some income, so, too, most families have some wealth. But the distribution of wealth shows a far greater degree of inequality than the distribution of income. For instance, in 1962 the top fifth, ranked by income size, received 41.7 percent of personal income; the top fifth, ranked by wealth size, owned 77 percent of personal wealth (table 7). The total wealth of the top 20 percent of families was three times greater than the entire wealth of the bottom 80 percent. The top 1 percent of families and unrelated individuals receives at the most 9 percent of personal income; the top 1 percent of individual wealthholders owns between 20 percent and 30 percent of all personally held wealth and has done so for decades. The concentration of income-producing wealth is even greater. The top fifth owned 97 percent of the corporate stock in 1962. The top 1.6 percent of adults in 1953 owned 82 percent of the corporate stock in the personal sector, 90 percent of the corporate bonds, and virtually all the state and municipal bonds.[19]

18. Ferdinand Lundberg, *The Rich and the Super-Rich* (New York: Bantam, 1968), p. 30.
19. Robert J. Lampman, *Changes in the Share of Wealth Held by Top*

Combining information from the nineteenth century, which is admittedly sketchy, with the best current data available discloses a striking long-term concentration of wealth at the top.

Percent of Personal Wealth Held By:

Top 1 Percent of Families[a]

1810	1860	1900
21%	24%	31%

Top 1 Percent of Adults (Age 20 and over)[b]

1922	1939	1949	1956
31.6%	30.6%	20.8%	26%

Sources:
[a] Robert Gallman, *Six Papers on Size Distribution of Wealth and Income*, ed. L. Soltow (New York: National Bureau of Economic Research, 1969), 23:6.
[b] Robert Lampman, *Changes in the Share of Wealth Held by Top Wealth-Holders 1922–1956* (New York: National Bureau of Economic Research, 1960), Occasional Paper 71, p. 21.

Table 7   Percentage Share of Wealth Held by Fifths, Top 5 Percent and Top 1 Percent, 1962

Consumer Units Ranked from Lowest to Highest Wealth	Total Wealth	Corporate Stock
Poorest fifth	a	a
Second through fourth fifth	23	3
Richest fifth	77	97
Top 5 percent	53	86
Top 1 percent	33	62

Source: Edward C. Budd, ed., *Inequality and Poverty* (New York: Norton, 1967), p. xxii.
[a] Less than ½ of 1%.

Wealth-Holders, 1922–1956 (New York: National Bureau of Economic Research, 1960), Occasional Paper 71, p. 30.

There have, of course, been fluctuations. "It appears . . . that the degree of inequality in wealth holding increased from 1922 to 1929, fell to below the pre-1929 level in the 1930s, fell still more during the war and to 1949 and increased from 1949 to 1956." [20] As is true with income distribution, apparently the country has not moved toward equality in wealth distribution since World War II. In fact, although current data are not available, the figures from the late 1940s to mid-1950s suggest a trend toward greater inequality. In 1949 the top 1 percent owned 20.8 percent of personal wealth; its share had increased to 26 percent by 1956.

There is very little information about trends in wealth distribution for the whole population, but estimates for one year, 1953, give a good indication of the overall distribution (table 8). If total gross estates (all tangible and financial assets technically belonging to individuals, including stocks, bonds, real estate, mortgages, and the like) had been distributed equally, each American adult would have

Table 8 Estimated Distribution of Total Adult Population by Percentage Share and Average Size of Gross Estate, 1953

Percentage of Persons Aged 20 and Over	Percentage of Total Gross Estate	Average Gross Estate Size
50.0	8.3	$ 1,800
18.4	10.2	6,000
21.2	29.3	15,000
5.8	13.4	25,000
1.9	6.3	35,000
.8	3.2	45,000
.3	1.7	55,000
.1	.9	61,000
1.6	27.6	186,265
100.0 [a]	100.0 [a]	$10,800

Source: Robert J. Lampman, *The Share of Top Wealth-Holders in National Wealth, 1922–1956* (Princeton, N.J.: Princeton University Press, 1962), p. 213.

[a] May not add to 100 due to rounding.

20. Lampman, *Changes in the Share of Wealth*, p. 30.

had a gross estate of $10,800. But in 1953, the average gross estate for the bottom 50 percent of adults was $1,800; the average gross estate for the top 1.6 percent was $186,000. The lower 90 percent of adults altogether owned less than half, 47.8 percent, of the total gross estate wealth in 1953.

According to a 1962 survey, some components of wealth are fairly widely owned throughout the population: 57 percent of consumer units owned or had equity in homes; 73 percent in automobiles; 79 percent had liquid assets (checking accounts and savings). Homes, automobiles, and liquid assets accounted for 92 percent of total wealth for the bottom 16 percent of consumer units, and had an average value of $364. (This excludes the 10 percent of consumer units who had no wealth or were in debt.) These same three assets were only 8 percent of total wealth for the less than 1 percent of consumer units at the top, and had an average value of $105,005.[21]

Homes, automobiles, and liquid assets, which differed greatly in their value from one wealth level to another in 1962, comprised most of the wealth (75 percent and over) of the bottom 74 percent of wealth-holding consumer units. Yet taken altogether, these three assets were only 43 percent of total personal wealth. Thus, homes, automobiles, and liquid assets, however important they may be to well-being, are not in any sense an adequate measure of the country's wealth distribution.

The most influential form of wealth—wealth which also produces income for its owners—accounted for 51 percent of total consumer wealth in 1962, and was heavily concentrated at the top. Investment assets and equity in businesses and professions made up 73 percent of the wealth of the top 1 percent of consumer units, compared to 6 percent of total wealth for the bottom 16 percent.[22]

21. Dorothy S. Projector and Gertrude S. Weiss, *Survey of Financial Characteristics of Consumers* (Washington, D.C.: Board of Governors of Federal Reserve System, August 1966), p. 110.
22. We have not included home ownership in the category of investment wealth for several reasons. It is true that the federal individual income tax favors the

Investment assets were 33 percent of consumer wealth in 1962, the largest single source of wealth. Less than 7 percent of consumer units (those whose wealth was $50,000 and over) owned 80 percent of these assets. In particular there is heavy concentration in the ownership of corporate stock at the top. In 1922, the top 1 percent of adults owned 61.5 percent of the corporate stock in the personal sector. By 1953 the share owned by the top 1 percent of adults had increased to 76 percent even though their holdings of total personal wealth had decreased slightly.[23]

The number of individual investors has increased dramatically from between 8 and 9 million in 1956 to 31 million in 1970.[24] This has led some analysts to conclude that a redistribution of stock ownership is underway. To be sure, many more people do own a few

Table 9   Percentage Share of Top 1 Percent of Wealth Holders in National Balance Sheet Accounts, Mid-year

	1953	1958	1962
Corporate stock	85.7	69.5	71.6
Bonds	47.6	34.3	47.5
Notes and mortgages	30.7	35.9	24.4
Real estate[a]	15.8	14.8	15.8
Insurance equity	13.2	14.2	11.2
Other assets, trusts, and pension fund res.	15.0	13.0	11.9
Total Net Wealth (total wealth less debts)	27.3	26.4	28.0

Source: James D. Smith, Unpublished paper prepared for report on expanded ownership, pt. III-B, table 12, p. 186. September 1971. To be published by the Sabre Foundation.

a Includes residences.

homeowner over the renter by deductions for property tax and mortgage payments. It is equally true, however, that the regressive property tax weakens overall tax advantages for lower-income families. More important, however, is a qualitative difference: people do need shelter. Thus, the purchase and sale of a home for a profit is by its very nature quite different from the buying and selling of corporate stocks or real estate holdings for profit.

23. Lampman, *Changes in the Share of Wealth*, p. 26.
24. *New York Times*, 3 January 1971.

shares, but there is no evidence that this has lessened the concentration at the top. On the contrary, the portion of corporate stock owned by the wealthiest 1 percent of the population *increased* from 69.5 percent in 1958 to 71.6 percent in 1962 (table 9).

TAXATION

Taxing the property an individual leaves to his heirs is a much older form of taxation than the income tax and grew naturally out of the state's function to protect property and supervise its transition from one generation to another. The nominal tax rates on estates are sharply progressive, ranging from 3 percent on the first $5,000 in excess of $60,000 (the allowable deduction) to 77 percent of taxable estate in excess of $10 million. As with the federal individual income tax, however, the impact of these ascending rates is virtually nullified by a variety of loopholes. "The effective rate of estate taxes on wealth passed each year from one generation to the next must be less than 10 percent." [25]

For example, the marital deduction in the estate tax allows a person to leave one-half of his estate to his spouse. This lessens, or even removes, the tax liability on estates of $300,000 or less. Generous exemptions for gifts to children made during the lifetime of wealth-holders also result in considerable tax savings.

For those with net estates worth $1 million or more, the most frequent and successful device for tax avoidance is the personal trust. The significance of the trust is that a large family fortune can be protected from the estate tax for two or three generations so that it is neither diminished nor redistributed for sixty years or more. In fact, because of the nature of this wealth, a family fortune is most apt to increase during these years.

In view of these tax-avoidance mechanisms, it is not surprising that the estate and gift taxes play a very small role in providing federal revenue (1.7 percent in 1969) and have little, if any, effect on the distribution of wealth.[26] According to Joseph Pechman, "about 3 percent of the estates of adult decedents and less than one-fourth of

25. Pechman, "The Rich, the Poor, and the Taxes They Pay," p. 30.
26. Ibid.

the wealth owned by the decedents in any one year are subject to estate or gift taxes." [27]

While only 5 percent of all consumer units in the 1962 survey inherited a *substantial* portion of their wealth, 34 percent of those with wealth of $500,000-and-over reported that a substantial portion of their wealth had been inherited.[28]

Conclusion

We have examined the long-standing inequality in personal income and wealth distribution in the United States. Not only are most of the investment assets held by the top wealth-holders; even the most widely distributed income, wages and salaries, is heavily concentrated at the top.

The basic facts point out that traditional political reforms have not prevented the continuing maldistribution of income and wealth. While the government wages a "war on poverty," increases public welfare programs, and the country experiences a general rise in income, the absolute dollar difference between the families at the bottom and those at the top grows wider each year. It seems clear that if change is to occur, more fundamental approaches are necessary.

27. Joseph A. Pechman, *Federal Tax Policy* (Washington, D.C.: Brookings Institution, 1966), p. 182.

28. Dorothy S. Projector and Gertrude S. Weiss, *Survey of Financial Characteristics of Consumers,* p. 148.

Character
and
Work in
America*

Michael Maccoby
Katherine A. Terzi

W hat is the relationship between our work and the kind of people we are becoming? How can work be reconstructed to further healthy character development in America today?

Theory and Concepts

Work, as experienced by the worker, is not merely a specific task or set of tasks, nor is it merely a role to be acted out. Both task and role help define, constrain, and stimulate the worker's participa-

* This report is part of the Project on Technology, Work, and Character of the Harvard Seminar on Science, Technology and Public Policy, currently aided by grants from the Andrew W. Mellon Foundation and Harman International Industries. The division of work of the report was that Maccoby formulated the main hypotheses and proposals while Terzi had the main responsibility for the research on the work force. We are grateful to David Riesman and Jody Palmour for helpful suggestions.

tion in the work-place subculture, with its particular traditions, rules, and rights. In the cultural system of each work place, work must be described in terms of the worker's relationship to technology, authority, coworkers, capital, profit, and product. These relationships are mainly influenced by the nature of the social system and the market in which the work culture is embedded, and by the type of product made.

At one extreme of work cultures is the hierarchically and mechanically organized factory or office where the work system has been constructed to maximize job simplicity and minimize the worker's freedom to make decisions, thus making him a replaceable standardized part in a machine. Furthermore, his rights to free speech and privacy are limited and in a dispute with management, he is considered guilty until proved innocent. In this cultural system, authority commands and subordinates are expected to obey. Even the work pace may be so controlled that workers must obey the dictates of machines. Relations to coworkers are largely determined by technical demands programmed into the division of labor. Typically, on the lower levels a worker does not control or own any part of the capital; only on the managerial levels do some workers own stock and share in the profits and decisions affecting their work. Few, if any, workers have a say in how profits will be used and for what purpose, and the workers have no influence in determining the kinds of products they make.

At the other extreme of American work cultures is the self-employed craftsman or professional owning his own time and with greater freedom to develop his own projects within the limitations set by the market on the one hand, and his talents and entrepreneurial skills on the other. The self-employed worker must relate to others—buyers, sellers, subcontractors, etc.—in ways that require shrewdness and skill and cannot be programmed. He typically owns his own capital (tools, equipment, etc.) although he may also rent and have to shoulder debts. If there are profits, he decides how they will be used and to what end. He can decide what products he will or will not make and what services he will or will not perform. Thus, while the self-employed individual might perform some of the same tasks as the employee of an organization, in the larger sense of the work culture, his work is different.

These differences are particularly important for individual psychology, or *character*, which refers to emotional attitudes or deep-rooted impulses that determine what deeply satisfies or annoys an individual; what he finds attractive, exciting, or frustrating; and how he relates to himself and to others. Character is expressed in behavior; however, very similar behavior may be rooted in different character traits. For example, two individuals refuse to work at a certain mechanized job. On the surface, they seem alike, but underneath they are very different. One person may be passive and self-indulgent; he lacks interest in work in general. The second is a craftsman and an independent person. His refusal to work comes from a deep resentment at being forced into a mold and treated as a machine part. To the outside observer, the behavior of both men may seem the same. But the similarity of their behavior conceals the underlying difference in the character systems of the two men, a difference which is significant for analyzing and responding to problems of work in America.

In considering questions of work and character in terms of large groups rather than individuals, we use the concept of *social character*, that is, the character structure common to most members of groups or even classes in a given society.[1] Social character does not refer to the complete, and highly individualized, in fact, unique, character structure as it exists in an *individual*, but to a "character matrix," a syndrome of character traits shared by a particular group and usually adapted to their common economic, social, and cultural conditions.[2] Indeed, some idea of social character has long been pointed to in the popular American belief about farmers, that the organization of the family and the work that is done on family farms tends to develop a

1. The concept of *social character* was developed by Erich Fromm in a number of books. See, for example, *The Sane Society* (New York: Holt, Rinehart & Winston, 1955).

2. The social character may not be adaptive when conditions change rapidly, causing a "character lag."

rooted, responsible, and craftsmanlike character who is not afraid to stand up for his convictions. However, it is not so commonly understood that *all* types of work stimulate or reinforce character traits and often play a decisive role in molding individual and social character, for better or worse.[3]

To understand how the modern work place with its complicated division of labor selects and molds character, we use the concept of *psychostructure*. Psychostructural analysis focuses on the interrelationship between work and character in an organization. It describes the character types required on different levels by a particular work structure, for example, what kind of people make it to the top and what kind stay on the bottom. Thus, large organizations or bureaucracies tend to select and develop different character types for lower-level workers, middle managers, and top executives.[4] The psychostructure itself may be either pyramidal and authoritarian, or more egalitarian and participative; its shape is determined by a combination of factors, particularly the type of product produced, the method of production, and the kinds of rights and responsibilities built into the structure.

The kind of work a person does may fit his character and thus be satisfying or it may clash with character, thus causing dissatisfaction and suffering.[5] What happens when character is *maladapted* to

3. Of course, the mode of work is not the only important cultural influence in character formation. History, climate, ideals, traditions, schooling, current prestigious models as shown in the media, and family all play important roles. Still, several factors point to modes of work as the decisive influence on character development even before individuals enter the work force. For a discussion of these factors, see Erich Fromm and Michael Maccoby, *Social Character in a Mexican Village* (Englewood Cliffs, N.J.: Prentice-Hall, 1970).

4. For example, see M. Maccoby's description of the different roles for "craftsmen," "company men," "gamesmen," and "jungle fighters" in electronics corporations (" 'Winning' and 'Losing' at Work," *Spectrum*, July 1973).

5. While some individuals may be satisfied merely by earning a decent income at work, for others work must fulfill the need for the exercise of special abilities or the realization of a vocation, and it must contribute to maintaining and/or enhancing life in the community. Thus "job satisfaction" occurs when the worker's character fits the requirements of his work. "Satisfaction," therefore, says nothing either about the intrinsic nature of the work nor its long-term effects on the worker's health and emotional development.

work? There is abundant evidence that the loss of "satisfying" work may result in emotional and/or physical symptoms of illness, particularly depression. This phenomenon can occur on the level of a whole society, when many people lose satisfying work.[6] How many Americans with the character of craftsmen, farmers, or small shopkeepers suffer such a fate today, lacking a fit between their needs and the available work? Although there is no census data to answer this question, many workers testify to the depressing loss of farm and craft work and the forced acceptance of more mechanized work.

This conceptual framework prepares us to ask more specific questions about work and character in America.

1. What kinds of character traits are being selected and developed by the work people do in America today? How are the economy and job market changing? What are the dominant psychostructures, and what character types are they developing?

2. Is the character of the work force in tune with the requirements of the available work; that is, do the workers want to do what they have to do to keep the institutions of work running smoothly? Or does their character conflict with the requirements of work as it is now organized in many companies? To put it another way, given the prevalent work structures, does the psychology of the workers constitute social cement or social dynamite?

To study these questions fully would require detailed strategic research on social character and social organization in a number of key industries.[7] Lacking such knowledge, we must depend on

6. Erik Erikson has described how the Sioux Indian lost his sense of identity and dignity as first a hunter and then a rancher. He writes that once the Sioux' cattle were taken from him, "He could become a sedentary farmer, only at the price of being a sick man, on bad land" (Erik A. Erikson, *Childhood and Society* [2nd ed.; New York: Norton, 1963], p. 154). Having lost the chance for work that he was raised to do and which fit his character, the result was illness and deep resentment against the society which deprived him of work which he could do wholeheartedly. The will to work also disappeared in the East African Bemba when they were forbidden by the British to continue hunting and warfare. See Audrey I. Richards, *Land, Labor, and Diet in Northern Rhodesia* (London, Oxford Press, 1939).

7. Such studies might be based on the social psychoanalytic theory of character as developed by Erich Fromm and methods of understanding social character as developed by Fromm and Maccoby (*Social Character in a Mexican Village*, Englewood

observations, reports, census data, and other statistics for useful information on certain trends in the workforce that are likely to have a direct relationship to the character traits required by work.

The Independent Character

The relation of work and character in America also offers rich possibilities for studying many different character types, focusing on regional and cultural differences. Given requirements of space, we have chosen to limit our discussion and to concentrate first on the character trait of independence. Since any character trait is fully understood only in its structural relationships, a discussion of independence also requires consideration of other character traits. Even so, there are three reasons why we choose to concentrate on independence. First, independence of mind and heart is a sign of general health and activeness. Second, the majority of Americans have long valued independence, at least in part because the colonists and pioneers had to be relatively independent people, to tear up their roots and face the unknown, and start new settlements in the frontier.[8] Third, we believe that a just society requires people who are both cooperative and independent, and we are concerned that present-day work institutions tend to form egocentric and dependent people who are neither emotionally healthy nor good citizens.

Americans like to think of themselves as an independent people, self-reliant, individualistic, and to a degree anarchistic. The republic was founded by farmers, craftsmen, proprietors, and professionals, and our form of democracy is rooted in the belief that there are

Cliffs, N.J.: Prentice-Hall, 1970). A group of us, directed by Maccoby, are now doing a study of work in corporations at the forefront of advanced technology, and of workers in an auto parts factory, developing methods of understanding workplace psychostructures that can then be applied to other industries and occupational sectors. See Michael Maccoby et al., *The Corporate Individual* (in preparation); see also his " 'Winning' and 'Losing' at Work," *Spectrum*, July 1973.

8. This was not the case for blacks brought to this country as slaves.

enough independent Americans to stand up against demagogues and would-be dictators. Even though this belief has been battered by recent social psychology, from *White Collar* and *The Sane Society* to *The Lonely Crowd* and *The Organization Man*,[9] and shaken by increasing submissiveness by Americans to the state and large corporations, the value is so strong that it sometimes spurs us to reaffirm our independence.

Before analyzing the social basis of independence, we should stop and consider the various meanings of the concept in the American past and present. Like any character trait, the meanings of "independence" may vary according to the total character structure of an individual, and these meanings imply different social outcomes. For the crusty farmer or backwoodsman, independence meant obstinacy, suspiciousness, and uncooperativeness as well as self-reliance. For the promoters and hustlers, "independence" meant being a lone wolf with the freedom to exploit others. As David Riesman points out in *The Lonely Crowd*, many Americans of the nineteenth century were independent of pressure from others because they obeyed the internalized dictates of idealized parents. Such individuals were likely to be emotionally childish and rigidly authoritarian. Thus, their independence was bought at the expense of compulsive submission to the past and resulted in limiting the independence of others under them. Moving to the present, "independence" for the organizational careerist means absence of loyalty and willingness to sell oneself to the highest bidder, but it seldom means critical thought or courage in opposing irrational power. The careerist is likely to ingratiate himself with the boss or hide from moral questions by stressing that his knowledge is limited to technical questions, or that he is not responsible for the policies of his organization or superiors, which he is bound to follow.

9. See David Riesman, *The Lonely Crowd: A Study of the Changing American Character* (New Haven: Yale University Press, 1950); Fromm, *The Sane Society*; William H. Whyte, *The Organization Man* (New York: Simon & Schuster, 1956); and C. W. Mills, *White Collar: The American Middle Classes* (New York: Oxford University Press, 1951).

In contrast, there were more attractive types of American "individualists": the responsible businessmen-entrepreneurs who created new industry on the basis of ingenuity and paternalistic principles; the craftsmen who struggled against the growing power of large industry as late as the 1880s, so that they could continue to organize their own work, promotions, wages, and contracts;[10] and the naturalists like Thoreau and Rachel Carson whose nonconforming independence was combined with a reverence for life.

Today, longings for an ideal of independence persist in fantasies, movies, and fiction, and may emotionally support jungle-fighting careerism rather than healthier forms of independence. For example, many detectives on TV—such as Mannix, Cannon and Banacek—express the public's longing for independence as private operatives rather than employees of an agency. The desire for independence is also projected in the image of the astronaut, the newest model for the young. In an attempt to assimilate him to the old heroic mold, schoolteachers often compare the spaceman to earlier explorers such as Columbus and Magellan. Although both twentieth-century astronaut and fifteenth-century seafarer share traits of competence and courage, structurally they are poles apart. The early explorers were rugged individualists who overcame superstition, setting out in largely untested craft to confront unforeseen weather conditions and unknown cultures. There was no Mission Control back in Madrid. The astronauts are parts of a highly technological, intricate, and centrally controlled machine. The fewer the unknowns and the less decisions they have to make, the more successful the project for the team as a whole.

The popularity of the best-selling *Jonathan Livingston Seagull*[11] also attests to the American longing for independence. In this story, the nonconformist seagull gives up the flock's philosophy of life—that

10. See David Montgomery, "Trade Union Practice and the Origins of Syndicalist Theory in the United States" (unpublished paper, Columbia University seminar on American civilization, 1972).

11. Richard Bach, *Jonathan Livingston Seagull, a Story* (New York: Macmillan, 1970). This book also appeals to a longing for more spiritual development, but in fact supports the illusion that technical proficiency leads to a greater capacity for love.

life and flight serve only to find food—in favor of perfecting his ability to fly. His flight is a symbol of freedom for many people, although ironically, the model of virtue presented by the book, that is, to develop one's technical abilities to the fullest and then teach others, is a philosophy most appropriate not to the self-employed, but to professors in large universities and managers of high-technology corporations.

Psychological independence in all but the most exceptional cases requires roots in one's way of making a living. The traditional material basis of independence in America has been ownership of property or of skills that made a person self-supporting. The farmer, small shopkeeper, or craftsman could speak his mind, hold his ground, and even choose dignity over profit because he had no boss to threaten him.[12] So attractive is the ideal of self-employment as a basis for independence that many Americans cling to the belief that the hardworking individual, if he has a little capital or a craft, can always make a go of it in business by himself. According to this view, if one feels locked into an organization it is due to his lack of get-up-and-go. This belief soothes the conscience of those who see no need to improve the quality of work in organizations, and it also sustains workers who accept unfulfilling work because they hope someday to set up their own shops.

Do people really enjoy their independence, or is it merely the idea that is attractive? To answer this question, we examined a detailed analysis of the 1969 national *Survey of Working Conditions* in terms of the relationship between self-employment and job satisfaction. Here we found that self-employed individuals were much more satisfied with their work than were wage-and-salary workers, in

12. Many small shopkeepers seek profit as the first priority, but this may in part be due to the extreme competition from chain stores, so that the small businessman must struggle to stay solvent. In less industrialized countries, such as Mexico, where there is less of such pressure, small shopkeepers sometimes take pleasure in refusing to sell their goods to rude or overbearing clients. Sometimes this attitude is abused, by its justification of racial discrimination. However, it contrasts sharply with the employee of a large chain—such as Sears or Safeway—who is paid to maximize profit, not to exercise his sense of dignity.

terms of four factors: the opportunity to develop their special abilities; the freedom to decide how to do their work; the opportunity to see the results of their work; and the chance to do work they found interesting.[13]

In view of the value placed on independence and the greater work satisfaction of the self-employed, it is important to examine the prevalent belief in the possibility of self-employment and determine whether it is based on reality or wish-fulfillment. How possible *is* it for people to be self-employed in America today?

Statistics on the Work Force and the Economy

What do the statistics tell us about the possibilities for independence in work in America today? [14] The available data shed light on this question in two ways: First, there are figures on *self-employment* vs. wage-and-salary employment. These data will

13. It might be argued that such satisfaction is really the result of higher income, since the self-employed tend to be richer than wage and salary workers, and we know that income is positively correlated with job satisfaction. To test this hypothesis, we statistically separated the factor of income from employment status. The results of this analysis, done for us by the Survey Research Center at the University of Michigan, showed that job satisfaction, in terms of the four items mentioned above, is almost as much a result of self-employment as it is of income. The small independent plumber or storekeeper is thus more likely to be satisfied with his work than the corporate manager or government employee making the same amount of money.

A dramatic example of men who prefer self-employment to increased income is a group of southwestern ranchers who refuse to sell out to rich businessmen looking for an attractive tax loss. Even when these ranchers are offered sums that could earn them annual interest higher than their average income, they still turn down the deal. See Thomas J. Mahoney, "The Past as Future, or The View from Marlboro Country" (Paper presented at CIDOC, Cuernevaca, Mexico, 1972. mimeographed).

14. When we began, we thought that statistics would be available from the census and other sources to study how much independence and autonomy is generally possible in work for Americans today and how this has changed over the years. To study this we hoped to compare various occupations in terms of whether people in these occupations work mainly in small or in large establishments. Unfortunately, such precise statistics do not yet exist. We have, therefore, had to use less exact figures, which in some cases are more suggestive than conclusive, but which nonetheless indicate certain tendencies.

tell us something about the degree of autonomy and independence available today because a self-employed person has no boss to account to, and is in that sense free to work when and how he sees fit, and he cannot be fired. Second, there are figures on the employee *size of establishment* in various industry sectors. These data show more directly the degree of bureaucratization likely in the work place, since a large enterprise has more need for coordination and tends to develop standardized procedures and paperwork, which can often restrict individual autonomy and initiative.

Looking at the figures on self-employment, we see that by 1950 only 18 percent of all employed persons were self-employed. This shrunk to 14 percent in 1960 and to 9 percent in 1970. In contrast, considering persons receiving a wage or salary from all sources, private or governmental, we find that in 1950, 80 percent of all employed persons were wage-and-salary workers. By 1960 that proportion increased to 84 percent and in 1970 to 90 percent.[15] In the early nineteenth century, it was only about 20 percent.[16]

Considering the work force from the point of view of different occupational categories,[17] we can see the same trend operating for 1950 and 1960. Self-employed farmers and farm managers dropped from 7.7 percent of employed persons in 1950 to only 3.9 percent in 1960, as farming has become a high-technology business. Managers, officials, and proprietors, the only other large occupational group that was predominantly self-employed in 1950, declined in its percentage of self-employed persons,[18] from 50 percent self-employed in 1950 to only 37 percent self-employed in 1960. These two groups, self-employed farmers and proprietors, in the recent past stood at the center of our economic and social life, and provided leadership for the

15. "Employment and Earnings," U.S. Department of Labor, Bureau of Labor Statistics, vol. 18, no. 8 (February 1972): 48, 150, 162–64.

16. These trends began in the 1800s and were documented and discussed by Mills in *White Collar.*

17. Figures in this section are taken from the Census of Population, "Occupational Characteristics," 1950 and 1960.

18. This shift from self-employed to salaried managers also indicates the increase in bureaucratic and corporate institutions that employ managers.

nation. Today we see them declining as a proportion of the labor force and increasingly becoming employees. It is also striking to note that by 1950, *84 percent* of the nation's "craftsmen, foremen and kindred workers" were wage-and-salary workers. Together with the independent farmers and proprietors, the independent craftsmen were at the foundation of this country.

Thus, the numbers of small entrepreneurs, farmers, and independent professionals have been shrinking over the decades. More and more people have become salaried employees dependent on available jobs for their living and subject to their employers for the quality of their working life. This is a very discouraging trend if self-employment is a necessary condition for independence in work.[19] What replaces self-employment? In general, the answer is increasingly: the large organization.

Industry Sectors

It is a popular conception that work in large organizations does not allow much independence and autonomy, although this is not necessarily the case. Before considering the relation between corporate size and independence, however, we need some idea of the extent of employment in large vs. small organizations.

Census of Business figures show that in the larger sectors of the work force there has been a trend toward domination of the market by an increasing number of larger establishments, corporations, and chains.

The retail trades provide an example of this trend, which is also operating in the service, wholesale, and manufacturing sectors. In retailing, the majority of establishments are still small (with 0–3 paid

19. It is becoming apparent to young people that medicine is one field in which a gifted person can still be independent, make a good living, and feel one is helping other people. Between 1961 and 1971, the number of applicants to U.S. medical schools doubled, while places for medical students increased only 50 percent. Of 29,172 candidates in 1971, only 12,361 were admitted to a medical school. David Cohen, "Pre-Med," *Harvard Alumni Bulletin*, May 1973.

employees); however, the trend is toward larger businesses.[20] This means that small businesses become less secure. To document the degree of financial insecurity of small businesses, we tried to find exact statistics on the percentage of small businesses each year which succeed or fail. These precise figures are not available, but the Office for Planning, Research and Analysis at the Small Business Administration reports that for every nine or ten businesses that open each year, about eight go out of business. This is a discontinuance rate of about 80–90 percent and includes *small* businesses almost exclusively. One source attributed this high failure rate largely to mismanagement and inexperience in business.[21] However, another source at the SBA reported that many proprietors go out of business in order to earn better livings as salaried employees. This seems to us the more likely reason to close down shop because today, even with experience and good management, a small retail business will succeed against the competition of chain stores only if it is particularly favored in location or if the entrepreneur is exceptionally innovative. Even then, he may be stymied by other factors.[22]

20. The smallest retail businesses (1–19 paid employees) hired a lower percentage of the retail-trade work force in 1967 than it did in 1963, 1958, or 1954, while larger establishments (with 20 or more paid employees) increased in the percentage they employed, from about 44 percent in 1954 to about 51 percent in 1967. The largest establishments (50 or more paid employees) also increased in the percentage of retail trade workers they employed, from 26 percent in 1954 to 29 percent in 1967. *1963 Census of Business, Retail Trade, Summary Statistics*, vol. 1, pt. 1, table 1, pp. 3-1–3-9; and *1967 Census of Business, Retail Trade, Subect Reports*, vol. 1, table 1, pp. xxii, 3-1.

21. Dun & Bradstreet cites similar causes for failures of businesses in general, regardless of size. Dun & Bradstreet, Inc., *The Failure Record Through 1970* (New York: Dun & Bradstreet, 1971), pp. 11–12.

22. In "Main Street Goes Private," *The Nation*, 18 December 1972, Rose De Wolf describes these factors:

"First, center location is more expensive—particularly in an enclosed mall, where the merchants not only pay the costs of maintaining their own property, but share the cost of the parking lot, the clean-up, the security, the decorations, the care of the foliage, etc., for the mall.

"Further, most mall managements charge independent merchants higher rents—sometimes twice as much per square foot—as the chain stores pay. Managements prefer the chains because they advertise heavily and are thought to attract customers just by their names."

Census figures document this growing domination of the retail trade market by corporations and chain stores.[23] Other statistics indicate that *larger* businesses are increasing their share of the retail market.[24] And data on multiunits (chains) and single units reflect a similar trend, showing that a very small group of large chains takes a large and growing share of the retail trade market.[25]

This trend implies that it is harder and harder for an individual entrepreneur to prosper. Although some opportunities still remain, such as in advanced technology, special services, or the leisure industries, the competition is tough. The scientist-engineer must have a brilliant idea, be able to raise enough capital, and learn how to market his product; the restaurant owner needs a special attraction or elegance, since new "greasy spoons" cannot compete with the Marriot Corporation's "Hot Shoppes."

Furthermore, character traits that used to serve a certain type of independent small businessman in the market are no longer so adaptive when he has to compete with large corporations. The willingness to work long hours and keep the store open on Sundays and holidays used to contribute to success. But what is the use of such sacrifice and durability when large chains such as Safeway decide to remain open on Sundays? In this market, self-employment becomes a realistic possibility only for the very brilliant, lucky, or entrepreneurial person, not for the average American whose work future more often centers in a large organization.

23. Between 1958 and 1963 the percentage of retail trade establishments classified as "individual proprietorships" decreased by about 3.5 percent, while "corporations" increased by about 5.5 percent. Moreover, receipts from sales of corporations were in 1963 almost 2.3 times greater than those from individual proprietorships. *1963 Census of Business, Retail Trade Summary Statistics*, pt. 1.

24. Although establishments with 50 or more paid employees comprised only .8 percent of retail establishments in 1958 and 1.2 percent in 1967, these large establishments earned 18.4 percent of retail sales in 1958 and 25.2 percent in 1967. Establishments with 100 or more paid employees comprised only .2 percent of retail trade establishments in 1958 and .36 percent in 1967, but earned 10.3 percent of total retail sales in 1958 and 13.9 percent in 1967. *1967 Census of Business, Retail Trade Subject Reports*, vol. 1, p. XXI.

25. *1963 Census of Business, Retail Trade Summary Statistics*, vol. 1, pt. 1, p. 4–246; and *1967 Census of Business, Retail Trade Subject Reports*, vol. 1, p. 4–257.

The statistics testify to a domination of the market by a growing number of large corporations and fading opportunities for self-employment. If we are concerned about preserving or developing the independent character, we must face the fact that its basis in self-employment is fast disappearing, forcing many people who would prefer to be their own boss into large corporations or government bureaucracies.

These findings suggest a number of questions.

1. Presumably, people raised in families of independent farmers or craftsmen will have difficulty adapting to the organizational world. What happens when they are forced into large organizations? Is there a clash between character and work for these people?

2. Since self-employment has been disappearing for over a century, has the character of Americans been changing gradually? If so, what character type or types are being formed? Is there any hope for an independent character in a large organization?

To answer these questions, it is useful to consider the dominant types of organization in terms of their effect on character.

Character Requirements of Corporations

Modern students of organizations are paying increasing attention to objective variables that describe aspects of work structures and worker satisfaction. These variables, such as "complexity," "centralization," "span of control," "mechanization," as well as sheer size, are useful to distinguish elements of a psychostructure, but taken together they do not add up to a cultural system. To understand more fully the demands made on personality by a work organization, we must begin with more global typologies based on sociopolitical concepts.

Some of the earliest work organizations, such as galley ships, were run on the basis of naked coercion, and the earliest factories were not much better. In such organizations, an independent attitude was a liability, and the bosses tried to break the spirit of independent workers. Even today, for many workers, factory work is coercive, experienced as the only alternative to make a decent living. Like conscripts in the army, as opposed to career soldiers, work for many workers is close to a prisonlike existence, and results in a broken spirit or alternatively, a detached attitude that helps to freeze impotent rage.

This is not the case for all workers, nor for all work organizations. One type of work organization which has been most successful in attracting a certain type of worker and gaining his loyalty is the *paternalistic* firm run by the founder or his family. In this type of firm, authority is personalized in owners who want the workers to consider themselves part of a "family" where they will be taken care of as long as they work responsibly. This type of organization appeals to character types in which the need for security is greater than the need for independence. Two subtypes of paternalism can be distinguished, positive paternalism which is relatively benevolent, and exploitative paternalism, which is not. The latter includes plantations, mines, or industries where the company provides housing and owns the store, and where the worker becomes locked in by his indebtedness.[26] In such organizations, little or no concern is shown for the workers' well-being, although there may be an ideology stressing the patron's interest in them. Such a psycho-structure requires authoritarian and exploitative bosses and submissive, spiritually broken workers. It is noteworthy that some unions in the United States developed to protect the worker against such exploitative paternalism, one of the most recent being Cesar Chavez's United Farm Workers.

Positive paternalism requires managers with a responsible and more productive character such as Robert Owen in England and P. B. Noyes in the United States. Such a psychostructure has aspects of neofeudalism. The top managers are paternalistic and responsibly

26. For an account of such a company and the workers' reaction to it, see Leon Stein and Philip Taft, *Massacre at Ludlow: Four Reports, 1914–1915* (New York: Arno Press, 1971).

concerned about the material well-being of the workers. Some of their practices are in large part determined by religious convictions.[27] Relationships are often personal between management and workers; the manager will listen sympathetically to the worker's problems, personally reward him for successes and punish him for "misdeeds." In contrast, the structure requires workers to be submissive and receptive, to seek security in the corporation at the expense of individual rights and personal development. Nevertheless, such security can be extremely comforting when, in times of recession or depression, paternalistic managers make every effort to keep employees on the payroll and sometimes cut their own salaries to make this possible.

While the paternalistic model is today denigrated because it maintains traditional authority and the infantilization of the many by the few, its positive aspects, contrasted to impersonal bureaucracies, are often overlooked.[28] For some workers as well as managers, the neofeudal roles are satisfying, since authority is personalized rather than anonymous; someone takes responsibility for decisions and their effects on people, rather than blaming the rules or the system. Furthermore, some semipaternalistic companies more than other types have been able to give a greater say in decision making to the

27. Of course, religious convictions also justified oppression of workers, meddling in their lives, firing them for smoking or drinking, even off the job.

28. For example, a Pittsburgh factory employing six hundred women in the beginning of the twentieth century was described as follows: "clean, well-ventilated, well-constructed. The stairways are marble, and on the walls are engravings of action and battle and plunging horses. . . . The girls are often summoned to the auditorium at noon to hear an address by some visitor or to sing; in this case they have an hour's recess, instead of half an hour. [Other amenities included a] roof garden for summer use . . . a natatorium, with schedule so arranged that . . . the girls may . . . swim once or twice a week after hours . . . beautifully kept dressing rooms, and a lunch room with pictures on the walls and a piano in one corner" (Elizabeth B. Butler, *Women and the Trades, Pittsburgh, 1907–1908,* The Pittsburgh Survey [New York, 1911], p. 314. Cited in Robert W. Smuts, *Women and Work in America* [New York: Schocken Books, 1971], pp. 78–79).

Another example cited by Smuts is the Willimantic (Connecticut) Thread Company. In the 1880s this company operated a clean, glass-roofed mill planted with flowers. It was set in an attractive mill village with a library for the employees' use, as well as a "mission woman" whose duties included counselling and visiting the sick, while evaluating (in order to report to the President) the condition of the employees' cottages and gardens to see whether they were being kept up to the mill's standards.

workers, because the chief executive is free to act on his humanistic inclinations and can develop a personal sense of trust with workers.[29] In contrast, the chief executive of a less paternalistic company must answer to directors. Since his tenure depends on his performance, personal relationships he has built up last only as long as he does. Since he does not own or control the company, the workers may well question how long that will be.[30]

Although many old-style paternalistic companies are disappearing, some swallowed up by larger corporations and conglomerates, some newer ones still manage to survive and sometimes grow. This is

29. See the description of the American Velvet Company in Fred K. Foulkes, *Creating More Meaningful Work* (New York: American Management Association, 1969). It is notable that in companies like LaPointe and Stromberg, the Scanlon Plan of profit sharing and group decision making only lasted while owner-entrepreneurs remained in charge.

30. An exceptional example of a paternalistic corporation that has endured is Oneida, Ltd. still run by descendants of the leaders of the Oneida Community. The concern of the managers for the workers' well-being (including profit sharing, grants for building their houses, consultative management) was such that the then Metal Polishers, Buffers, Platers Brass and Silver Workers' Union of North America gave up trying to organize the workers in 1916, and the organizer wrote the following report:

"I have investigated the Oneida Community, Limited, Silverware factory with the following results: I find this company is perfectly independent of any affiliation with any of the manufacturers' organizations either in their own line or any other. They work the men short hours, give them good pay, and treat them like human beings. Consequently there is the best of good will between employer and employee. . . .

"The employees seem to be perfectly satisfied with things as they are in the factory. Therefore, I do not believe that any successful organization could be formed among them. . . .

"In fact, the company makes a study of its employees in order to give them every opportunity of having good, clean amusements and all kinds of athletics, picture shows, lectures, bowling, baseball, football, and, in fact, all kinds of outside and inside athletics and amusements that are good for any normal person.

"These are a few of the reasons for the contentment of the employees of this company. I could go on and enumerate many more, but I believe enough has been said to convince you that this company is different from any company you have ever heard of in their treatment of their employees. It is not done for advertising purposes, as a great many of our corporations do, but is simply a business policy carried out by men who put the man and woman ahead of the dollar" (Walter D. Edmonds, *The First Hundred Years, 1848–1948* [Kenwood, N.Y.: Oneida, Ltd., 1958]).

Today, the company is still run according to these principles. In contrast the Hershey Company changed radically when the owner-manager was replaced by professional management.

remarkable in itself, when we consider that for every nine or ten new businesses each year, eight others go out of business. How do a few of these manage to survive and become large corporations? The founders of successful companies are often complex men. They may be a combination of exploitative empire builder and productive builder of new products. What distinguishes them from other entrepreneurs is that they have adopted *principles* which define for themselves and others what they will do and what they will not do. These principles generally have to do with fairness, respect for individual rights, and responsiveness to the needs of those who work for them and are thus part of the "family." (Such concern, of course, does not generally encompass those outside the "family.") Such principles determine conduct in such a way that others can call these men to task if the principles are contradicted by their actions. In contrast to some more modern managers, who treat employees as objects to be used, a principled entrepreneur is able to build up trust with the workers because they can count on his principles. This results in gaining both loyalty and full productive cooperation from the workers and, naturally, it is a key element in developing a successful business.

Such paternalism becomes rarer as the large corporation takes over the market and there are fewer successful entrepreneurs. The dominant type of industrial organization is the *industrial machine,* run on mechanical principles of "efficiency," with the goal of constant growth and increasing profit. Direct authority does not reside in an owner entrepreneur or his family, but in professional managers, bureaucrats, or the representatives of capital who attempt to make the rules of authority as anonymous as possible.[31] Their decisions are mainly based not on their own principles but on professional judgment according to diagnosis of market positions and fixed goals to optimize profit. Frederick W. Taylor's "scientific management" fits neatly into such a culture, where the goal is to so fragment and

31. Some companies are best described as mixed types, e.g., The Polaroid Corporation, built on the principles of an owner-entrepreneur, but increasingly run by professional managers.

simplify the task that the worker becomes an easily replaceable part of the machine.

In some ways, the industrial machine appears to be an advance over paternalism, since it may be more meritocratic, i.e., rules for advancement are laid down on the basis of merit and achievement rather than the favor of the boss. (Indeed, Taylor believed that his rules would be fairer than autocratic management.) On the other hand, the twin goals of efficiency and profit are ruthless to those who do not perform according to this standard, and the principle of the machine is to use up human energy, and replace the tired and the old with younger, smarter, fresher parts. This is as true for white-collar as for blue-collar workers, and the machinelike work place would be unbearable if it were not for the efforts of unions to guarantee some security for older workers and defend all workers from extreme injustice.

In industrial bureaucratic organizations, where over a long period the product does not change appreciably, a relatively static machine can be run by authoritarian autocrats on a more or less military model. The ambitious new managers coming up the ranks are likely to be domineering to subordinates and submissive to superiors. They know their duty and their place. They accept orders and occasional humiliation as the price for eventually gaining command. This role is filled best by individuals with an "authoritarian character," who admire the powerful and are contemptuous of the powerless. As Fromm has described it, the authoritarian feels that he is worthless unless he feels part of and protected by a powerful organization which gives him power over others.

In such a psychostructure, a lower-level worker who is an independent craftsman will fight the system, because it robs him of dignity and authority. (Montgomery notes that in 1905, Taylor called on employers "to wrest control of their factories away from workmen.") The greater the fragmentation achieved through "scientific management," the more the worker was expected to be dull, submissive, and insensitive, if not when he began the job, then certainly after some time on it. Taylor, starting his experiments in scientific management wrote that, "One of the very first requirements for a man who is fit to handle pig iron as a regular occupation is that he shall be so stupid and so phlegmatic that he more nearly resembles an ox than any other type." Earlier, Adam Smith foresaw this effect of the division of labor when he wrote: "The understandings of the greater part of men are necessarily formed by their ordinary employments. The man whose life is spent in performing a few simple operations . . . has no occasion to exert his understanding. . . . He generally becomes as stupid and ignorant as it is possible for a human creature to become." [32] Smith worried about the effects of this process on the body politic. Although this understanding did not move him to oppose the division of labor, he urged semipublic education for the workers as a compensation for such dull work.

Today, industrial jobs require more intelligence and responsibility than Taylor's pig-iron lifting. Even the assembly-line worker studies a computer printout to determine the special, customized spot weld he must make on the next car down the line. But he or she is still a replaceable part in a machine, obeying the computer's orders, unable even to determine one's own rhythm or exercise craftsmanlike concern for the quality of the jobs that go by every minute. Such work does not call for independent, nor even particularly submissive individuals, who obey a boss, but rather, robotlike workers, who fit themselves into the machine.[33]

The division of labor and work is not limited to the production level. Many white-collar jobs have also become mechanized. Designers in the auto industry report that a generation ago they would work on a whole car, but now they're forced to specialize on fenders or grillwork. Accountants who used to organize an office and relate to

32. *The Wealth of Nations* (New York: Modern Library, 1937), quoted by Daniel Bell, *Work and Its Discontents* (Boston: Beacon Press, 1956).

33. For a discussion of the possible emotional effects of mechanized work, see M. Maccoby, "Emotional Attitudes and Political Choices," *Politics and Society* 2, no. 2 (Winter 1972): 209–39. Mechanized work is likely to mold antilife emotional attitudes and political viewpoints.

people and problems are increasingly appendages of the computer.[34] Engineers in aerospace and computer design are limited to highly formatted and specialized tasks that use a small fraction of their knowledge; becoming so specialized, such workers are also left less employable if they lose their jobs.

Some service industries today are similar to the industrial machine in their organization and demands on workers. For example, a few years ago, a private research firm advised AT&T that from the company's point of view, the *successful* employee is "one dependent upon and yielding to authority rather than autonomous; socially unobtrusive rather than exhibitionistic; persistent and enduring in her approach to work; and conservative in her life-style, more conforming than innovative or rebellious." [35]

Other service industries, particularly in the government, have more elements in common with *bureaucracies*. In a bureaucracy, the job requires that the worker perform a role in a hierarchy in which the official work task is but a part. The bureaucrat can get ahead and achieve security, by following the rules and pleasing his superiors.[36] To maintain, much less to develop, independence of character in a

34. In October 1972 Maccoby spoke at the annual meeting of the UAW Technical, Office and Professional workers and took part in workshops on the humanization of work. Members testified to the depressive consequences of these changes in their work.

35. Cited by Harold L. Sheppard in "A Simple Simon's Partial List of Issues About the Current Controversies Surrounding the Quality of Working Life" (Paper presented at the twenty-fifth Meeting of the Industrial Relations Research Association, Toronto, December 28, 1972). Sheppard goes on to quote a statement of Robert Ford of AT&T who said, "We have run out of dumb people to handle those dumb jobs. So we have to rethink what we're doing."

36. "The bureaucrat's official life is planned for him in terms of a graded career through the organizational devices of promotion by seniority, pensions, incremental salaries, etc., all of which are designed to provide incentives for disciplined action and conformity to the official regulations. The official is tacitly expected to and largely does adapt his thoughts, feelings, and action to the prospect of this career. But *these very devices* which increase the probability of conformance also lead to an over-concern with strict adherence to regulations which induces timidity, conservatism, and technicism. Displacement of sentiments from goals onto means is fostered by the tremendous symbolic significance of the means [rules]" (Robert K. Merton, "Bureaucratic Structures and Personality," in Merton et al. *Reader in Bureaucracy* [Glencoe, Ill.: Free Press, 1965], p. 367).

bureaucratic setting requires extraordinary qualities, although some bureaucrats maintain their independence by using the rigid regulations as a protection against demands by superiors on the one hand and the public on the other. Such independence is defensive rather than creative, since it also blocks the bureaucrat from any positive action.[37] Increasingly, however, those who apply, are selected, and get ahead in bureaucracies are the alienated, marketing characters whose only form of independence is their dedication to developing those aspects of the self that are useful for their careers. A number of jobs in large corporations, particularly in sales, marketing, and service, are of this bureaucratic type.

On the level of factory operative and increasingly of service employees, the machine model is preferred to paternalism or bureaucracy when it promises to be most efficient and profitable. However, the machine model of industry is efficient *if and only if* two conditions are met. First, the industry must produce relatively standardized products (like model-T Fords) and second, it must be able to enlist workers with character types to fit this psychostructure; that is, the machine needs human energy. In the modern market of goods and services, there is evidence that both of these conditions are disappearing. Constant model changes and new technology require flexibility and fewer workers will adapt to mechanized work.

A New Social Character?

Is worker discontent due to a change in their social character? The answer to this question is by no means simple. Lacking systematic comparative or longitudinal data, it is hard to *prove* that the social character of workers today, particularly younger workers, has become less submissive and more self-affirmative. Although such a conclusion is strongly suggested both by analysis of trends in the twentieth century and by recent surveys relating to job satisfaction,

37. See Michael Crozier, *The Bureaucratic Phenomenon* (Chicago: University of Chicago Press, 1964).

the truth may be more complicated. Consider the likelihood of two main character types in factories and service jobs. One is the more independent farmer or craftsman, who is forced into the organization because he can no longer make a living working for himself. The second type is the child of employees who is brought up in an "organizational culture" and presumably expects to work in an organization.

Type one, the craftsman or farmer, has never adapted easily to the mechanized organization. When F. W. Taylor started out to mechanize industrial work, he met fierce resistance from many independent craftsmen who understood the threat to their autonomy and dignity.[38] While it was not so easy to find unionized workers or craftsmen willing to fit themselves into a mechanized psycho-structure, industry was able from the turn of the century until the present to recruit workers from immigrant or village backgrounds. In 1946, Peter Drucker wrote that the GM workers in Michigan were "largely first or second generation immigrants from eastern or southern Europe, recent arrivals from the West Virginia and Tennessee hill country, or Negroes," while most managers were "old stock" midwesterners.[39] As we have noted, before 1880, there was a movement to democratize the work place in America. The influx of immigrants combined with the principles of scientific management have up until now muted that movement, although it has never been totally destroyed. Immigrants from Southern and Eastern Europe were forced to accept any decent job they could find, and the traditional, submissive, fatalistic strands of peasant character

38. Samuel Gompers spoke against Taylorism in 1911: "So there you are, wage-workers in general, mere machines—considered industrially, of course. Hence, why should you not be standardized and your motion-power brought up to the highest possible perfection in all respects, including speeds? Not only your length, breadth, and thickness as a machine, but your grade of hardness, malleability, tractability, and general serviceability, can be ascertained, registered, and then employed as desirable. Science would thus get the most out of you before you are sent to the junkpile." Quoted in Sudhir Kakar, *Frederick Taylor: A Study in Personality and Innovation* (Cambridge, Mass.: MIT Press, 1970), p. 183. See also Milton J. Nadworny, *Scientific Management and the Unions* (Cambridge, Mass.: Harvard University Press, 1955).

39. Peter F. Drucker, *The Concept of the Corporation* (New York: New American Library, 1946), p. 150.

eased the transition into the mechanized industrial psychostructure. Furthermore, they were more willing to accept their lot in the factory because there were compensations in the home where the worker was unchallenged head of the family, a respected *pater familias,* and in the community where traditional religion and folk customs enriched his life.

The present generation of workers from working-class and white-collar backgrounds no longer finds its satisfactions in an ethnic subculture. Brought up and educated in the mainstreams of American values and strivings, younger workers are less fatalistic and authoritarian, more ambitious and self-affirmative than their fathers. Not expecting great respect from their children, they are also less willing to sacrifice themselves for them. Unlike workers from self-employed backgrounds, they do not object to organizational work per se, but to the dehumanizing aspects of it. Some of the younger production workers such as those who led the 1972 strike against GMAD at Lordstown are sons of workers who sound no different from young managers in their level of reasoning and their attitude to work.[40]

In part this is the result of education. Critics of schooling have rightly denounced the factorylike organization of schools, the conventionality and abstractification of what is learned, and the boring, nonproductive atmosphere of many schools. These criticisms make sense when the actual is contrasted to the ideal. However, this is not the case for the whole country.[41] For many young Americans, particularly those from blue-collar backgrounds, the atmosphere of local schools is both more stimulating and democratic than either the home or work place.

Harold Sheppard's studies show that for white male blue-collar

40. In contrast, many workers in a southern rural factory we are studying would prefer to work on a farm if they could make a living at it. Their goal is not career advancement but the chance for greater autonomy and craftsmanship.

41. A recent census study reported that the percentage of Americans with a high school diploma has almost doubled from 38 percent in 1940 to 75 percent in 1970. The percent with college degrees has gone from 6 to 16 percent; the proportion of those with one or more years of college has gone from 13 to 31 percent in the same thirty-year period. See Jack Rosenthal, "Census Study Finds an 'Education Gap,' " *New York Times,* 4 February 1971, p. 1.

workers, years of schooling are positively correlated with democratic attitudes, while workers with less schooling tend to be more submissive to authoritarian structures.[42] This finding is consistent with the phenomenon that young workers with high school diplomas are more likely than the older generation to find assembly work oppressive and to rebel against it. When young people compare this mechanized organization of work with their other experiences, the contrast fuels frustration and anger.

Traditional authoritarian submissiveness in the society as a whole has also been undermined by movements of civil rights and war protest. In the 1960s, the twentieth-century challenge to traditional authority reached a crest, and while only a minority of the young believe that all authority should be discredited, a large percent has become more critical of authority based on force rather than competence and leadership. The challenge to traditional authority appears a shared trait of the young throughout the industrialized world. It goes together with new values of self-fulfillment and the disintegration of the extended family.[43] Today, students throughout the United States have begun to question the knowledge of teachers. The pater familias can no longer demand respect, but must earn it. Black Americans have rejected the servile role. Women have opposed inequality and lack of opportunity. These challenges to authority have sometimes been harsh and bitter, expressing resentment and revenge. But they have also reaffirmed the humanistic and democratic principles of the American Revolution submerged during the period of rapid industrial growth and immigration.

Thus, the survey data on worker attitudes may reflect the views of different character types struggling with the organizational society. Since these surveys lack data to distinguish social characters,

42. H. Sheppard and N. Herrick, *Where Have All the Robots Gone?* (New York: Free Press, 1972).

43. For an analysis of survey data supporting this same conclusion in Japan, see Shin-ichi Takezawa, "Changing Worker Values, and Their Policy Implications in Japan" (Paper presented to the International Conference on the Quality of Working Life, Arden House, New York, September 1972).

we cannot explore whether different types give similar responses for different reasons. For example, both type one and type two workers may object to mechanized work, but their dissatisfaction has different meanings. The craftsman longs for self-employment while the modern self-affirmative organization man wants more opportunity to develop himself and further his career. In general, however, surveys indicate growing worker concern for the quality of work, although a large percentage of workers appear to be adapted to the mechanized organization. The latter is not surprising, since if *most* workers were not adapted to the organizations, these could not function at all. From our point of view, one of the basic problems in our society is exactly that so many Americans are adapted to mechanized work at the cost of devitalization.

Notwithstanding, the University of Michigan *Survey of Working Conditions,* sampling workers in all occupations and on all levels, found new priorities in what workers value and want in their work. Of some twenty-five aspects of work (such as pay, working conditions, and relations with coworkers), good pay, considered by conventional wisdom to be the workers' main priority, was ranked fifth by the sample taken as a whole. Above pay, workers placed interesting work, enough help and equipment, enough information, and enough authority to do the job. Opportunity to develop one's special abilities was ranked sixth.[44]

New goals and attitudes to work become clearer when we examine the responses of particular groups of workers, rather than taking the sample as a whole. Looking at occupational groups, clerical workers, service workers, professionals, sales workers, farm workers, and managers and proprietors, all rated interesting work as more important to them than good pay. In addition, six out of eleven occupational groups—clerical workers, service workers, household workers, professionals, operatives, and craftsmen and foremen— expressed considerable dissatisfaction with the *opportunity to develop*

44. For a review of the findings of the Michigan Survey, see Neal Q. Herrick, "Who's Unhappy at Work and Why," *Manpower* 1, no. 1 (January 1972): 2–7.

their special abilities in their work.[45] Lack of *interesting work* is a cause
for discontent among clerical and service workers, as well as laborers
(including farm laborers). And clerical workers, service workers,
operatives, and farm laborers want more *freedom to decide* how to do
their work than they have on their own jobs.

Differences between the young and the old in the work force
also suggest a trend, although one must note that the majority of all
workers are concerned about the quality of work. Thus, 78.5 percent
of workers under thirty years old, as opposed to 70.8 percent of those
thirty and older, say it is "very important" to them to have
interesting work. 68.7 percent of workers under thirty vs. 61 percent
of those thirty and over say it is "very important" for them to have
the opportunity to develop their special abilities at work. The
alternative explanation of age differences is, of course, that the
demands of younger workers do not imply the development of a
different character type in the young, but rather that they will give
up their demands as they get older and adapt to the system. While
this may be true in some instances, where workers are broken by the
organization and lose hope, this explanation is at best a partial one,
since it does not explain all the data nor make sense of the changing
social trends which influence the development of different character
traits.

Surveys conducted by Daniel Yankelovich reveal further evidence of changing attitudes to work on the part of the young. He
found that college students rank "the opportunity to make a
contribution," "job challenge," and "self-expression" at the top of the
list of influences on their career choice.[46] A 1970 survey of high

45. Almost 32 percent of clerical workers and of service workers, 27 percent of
household workers, 19 percent of professionals, and 17 percent of operatives,
craftsmen, and foremen find it is more often "very important" to them to have the
opportunity to develop their special abilities at work than "very true" of their own
jobs. Sales workers also show dissatisfaction, although less, with their ability to develop
themselves at work.

46. Daniel Yankelovich, *The Changing Values on Campus: Political and Personal
Attitudes on Campus* (New York: Washington Square Press, 1972), cited in U.S.
Department of Health, Education, and Welfare, *Work in America* (Cambridge, Mass.:
MIT Press, 1973).

school students found they valued "freedom to make my own
decisions" and "work that seems important to me" much higher than
in the 1960 survey, which stressed job security and opportunity for
promotion.[47] Studies also show that financial success is becoming less
important.[48] For example, one survey of high school students shows a
dramatic shift away from financial considerations as the determining
factors in choosing a career. In this survey, students were asked
whether they would join an all-volunteer army if salaries were
increased. Of 1970–71 students, 43 percent said yes; but by January
1973, only 27 percent said yes.[49] This refusal to join the military
suggests that good pay is less frequently able to compensate for
authoritarian working conditions to young people who are unwilling
to accept such conditions.

Increasingly, such new attitudes toward work mean that people
become dissatisfied with the way work is now organized, suggesting
that it no longer fits their character. The Michigan survey suggests
that American workers taken as a whole are most dissatisfied with
their jobs when they do not provide interesting work, opportunity
for self-development, and resources to carry out the job, as well as the
more traditional problems of inadequate pay, fringe benefits, and job
security.[50]

47. American Institute for Research, "Project Talent: Progress in Education, A
Sample Survey," 1971, cited in *Work in America.*
48. American Council on Education, survey based on interviews with 185,848
college freshmen in the fall of 1967 and on follow-up interviews with 63,570 of them
in July 1971. This survey also sheds light on the effects of education on students'
attitudes, since it polled the same students at the beginning and end of their college
years.
49. Based on nationwide polls conducted by the National Institute of Student
Opinion in 1972–73, 1971–72, and 1970–71, and published in *Senior Scholastic,* 12
March 1973.
50. We arrived at this conclusion by taking the Michigan Survey's list of job
attributes and calculating the discrepancy between what the worker considers
important and desirable job attributes, and what he reports as actually existing on his
job. In this way we found the greatest discrepancies in: interesting work; opportunity
to develop one's special abilities; a chance to do the things one does best; enough time
to get the job done; enough help and equipment to get the job done; good pay; good
job security; and good fringe benefits. Smaller discrepancies were found for: enough
information to get the job done; supervisor competent in doing his job; and the

What are the human consequences if the dissatisfied individual stays at mechanized work? Arthur Kornhauser's study of the mental health of auto workers shows depression and apathy on the part of many who work on the line.[51] Recent factory interviews by Jim Wright expose a direct connection between boring work and alcoholism or drug taking. Workers report taking amphetamines to keep up with the speed of the line and off the line they escape into alcohol or television.

Industrial Responses

One result of work dissatisfaction has been apathy and low productivity. Some industries have recently responded by trying to modify or restructure the machine organization, to make it more satisfying for workers.

Most leaders in this field are companies in a competitive international market which demands innovation and constantly changing products, such as companies developing advanced technology. Continual design and development of new products cannot be achieved in a rigid, hierarchical authoritarian structure, but rather requires a more flexible team where authority is more evenly distributed, particularly for engineers and technicians, but also, in many cases, blue-collar workers.[52]

---

freedom to decide how to do the job. For factory operatives, clerical workers, service workers, sales workers, and farm laborers, there is a more sizable discrepancy in having freedom to decide how to do the job.

51. Arthur Kornhauser, *Mental Health of the Industrial Worker* (New York: John Wiley, 1965).

52. See P. Lawrence and J. Lorsch, *Organization and Environment: Managing Differentiation and Integration* (Homewood, Ill.: Richard D. Irwin, 1969). Also Burns and Stalker, *The Management of Innovation* (London: Tavistock, 1961). This was one reason that Olivetti replaced traditional assembly-line operations to manufacture its office machines with a more flexible team structure. According to *Business Week,* 9 September 1972, the new structure "has given Olivetti great flexibility in a high-technology field that involved frequent changes in the product. Under the traditional assembly-line system it took months to introduce innovations. Partly finished machines were stacked up in warehouses, and workers, accustomed to performing single operations, were difficult to retrain."

In such a technostructure, *motivation* becomes an even more serious problem than in the mechanized hierarchy. It is easier to secure *compliance* for mechanized tasks than to gain *full cooperation* from technical workers so that they are motivated to contribute ideas and criticisms—in other words, their minds as well as their muscles—for developing new products.

One solution has been an appeal to thwarted needs for self-affirmation by allowing more autonomy either to individuals or to flexible teams stressing concepts such as participative management, goal sharing, and an emphasis on rewards rather than controls in the technostructure. A well-known example of such a company is Texas Instruments,[53] where a project-team structure allows engineers freedom in choosing the project they will work on and provides them the opportunity to propose new projects. The idea here is presumably an appeal to the thwarted independent spirit of employees. TI also applies this concept to maintenance crews.[54]

Another solution in the chain-restaurant business appeals more to the ex-proprietor's frustrated yearning for independence. Most chain restaurants are organized on the bureaucratic-machine model, a central unit controlling purchasing, restaurant decor, and the dress and behavior standards of the employees. In these firms, the franchisee is more like a salaried manager in a large company than an independent entrepreneur.[55] In contrast, an article in the *Wall Street*

53. See Charles L. Hughes, *Goal Setting: Key to Individual and Organizational Effectiveness* (New York: American Management Association, 1965).

54. At Texas Instruments, cleaning service teams of 19 people each were set up with the freedom to plan and carry out their jobs according to their own strategies and schedules. Studies were done to find better work methods and the employees received training prior to the formation of the teams, and were taught how to measure their own performance. They were paid more per hour and given better fringe benefits (including profit sharing) than the contracted janitorial crews who had previously done the job. As a result of this restructuring into autonomous teams the cleanliness rating increased from 65 percent to 85 percent; quarterly turnover dropped from 100 percent to 9.8 percent; and cost savings for the entire site averaged $103,000 per annum. See Harold M. F. Rush, *Job Design for Motivation*, Conference Board Report 515 (New York: Conference Board, 1971).

55. Franchisees, who aspire to be small independent businessmen in an era of conglomerates and decreasing self-employment, are now protesting against franchisors such as the founder of International House of Pancakes, who said, "That independent

Journal (May 8, 1972) describes how a group of people forced the Mr. Donut Company to give those individuals with franchises more say in operating their shops and selecting their suppliers. In those few cases where the individual franchisee has more freedom to decide how to do things, satisfaction is reported greater, and the businesses are more profitable.

Even the auto industry, the classic model of hierarchical-machine organization, so suffers from dissatisfied young managers that they have tried to move toward greater sharing of authority. But older, more authoritarian managers struggle to reassert autocratic control. In this, they are aided by the structure of control which keeps continual pressure from the top down. For example, the General Motors Assembly Division includes twenty plants. Each week computers print out the standings of the plants in terms of productivity and efficiency. When a plant falls behind, the screws are tightened all the way down the line. Everyone's primary goal is to be number one, and the only team spirit possible is within an authoritarian context similar to that of a professional football team. In such a situation of constant crisis, increased autonomy for both management and workers is hard to achieve. The Swedish auto companies, Volvo and Saab, seem better able to modify the most mechanized aspects of auto assembly, although their reforms are far from making the work fully autonomous. Greater autonomy is easier to achieve where highly automated factory technology creates interdependent jobs requiring more educated workers. This is the case with continuous process technology in refineries and food or soap processing plants. Also in jobs that involve working with computers or computerized machines where the pace of work is not fully determined by the machine, where workers are expected to make judgments and decisions.[56]

---

businessman idea is misunderstood. Maybe in Samoa you can find one. A man becomes a franchisee because he wants to belong. If he tells me he wants a pancake house because he doesn't like to take orders, I don't care if he's President Nixon's brother in Whittier; I won't sign him on." Charles G. Burck, "Franchising's Troubled Dream World," *Fortune,* March 1970, pp. 116 ff.

56. It may be that the increased demand for educated workers in government, offices, and advanced technology has been a key factor in raising the educational level

One of the most advanced models is the now well-known Pet Food plant in Topeka, Kansas. In an attempt to increase both productivity and work satisfaction, work was designed to maximize autonomy, variety, and possibilities for learning and advancement. Workers are now assigned to groups which set their own schedules and trade-off jobs. Supervision is minimal by "team leaders." Furthermore, the rules for compensation are designed to encourage learning and security. Raises in pay are based on the number of jobs mastered, and workers are guaranteed fifty weeks of work.

The Pet Food plant cannot be easily duplicated in other industries. It was built from scratch and it uses an advanced continuous process technology. It selected an elite group of intelligent workmen to man the factory. And it is nonunion. Despite its limited applicability, the factory is an example of considering the well-being of workers as an important factor in designing work.

So far, we have been considering large corporations where possibilities for worker autonomy can be increased but are constrained by a structure based on centralized control over decision making and planning. Another model which goes far beyond the semiautonomous work group in maximizing worker autonomy and strengthening worker independence is *the cooperative.*

Among the relatively few examples are the plywood cooperatives in the Northwest where the workers own the stock and set company policy.[57] Companies such as Puget Sound Plywood, Inc. and others (for example, the recent worker takeover at the Lipp factory in France) demonstrate that workers can run companies. The

of the workforce as a whole. Since the more educated workers do not function efficiently in mechanical jobs, there is a further pressure to restructure work to fit the needs of these workers.

It may also be the case that the efficiency of workers in mechanized jobs was never very high. (Industrial efficiency is generally overestimated by those outside industry who are unaware of the amount of "goldbricking" and output restriction.) Today, worker demands for higher incomes combined with the increasing pressure of international competition require higher levels of efficiency. If workers are to produce more efficiently, they will require work that is more satisfying as well as financially rewarding.

57. See Daniel Zwerdling, "Where the Workers Run the Show," *Washington Post,* 2 September 1973, pp. D4, D5.

cooperative model is both extremely satisfying and stimulates the highest level of productive activeness among workers. However, the examples are all relatively small firms that function in a competitive market (as contrasted to oligarchic or monopolistic markets). The cooperative model runs up against problems when applied to large corporations and advanced technology, with its large capital needs, centralized hierarchy, and highly technical decisions.

Possibly we may someday arrive at the point where American industry is so decentralized and technically simplified to allow an economy of worker cooperatives. But this unlikely possibility does not negate the need to restructure work at the present, since even a society of smaller firms would require models of restructured technology and organization.

Problems in Restructuring Organizations

The Pet Food factory, together with a number of other examples of designing work to maximize worker satisfaction, were pioneered by exceptionally idealistic and courageous managers who in practically every case had to struggle with their organizations in order to construct the new model. They exemplify cases of independence in large organizations leading to improving conditions of work for others.

Such models are rare, however, even though they generally prove profitable to the company in terms of increased quality, less absenteeism and turnover, and overall increased productivity. These alternatives to the machine model are resisted by management for two reasons: the character of authoritarian managers, and more important, the goals and structures of the machinelike organizations. In regard to the first reason, some managers feel comfortable only in an ordered, hierarchical structure where they can maximize control and predictability. Even when the efficiency of such a system is proved wanting, such a manager feels that any alternative would mean chaos. At least, in the machine structure, he feels he can pinpoint the weak links (workers) and has the power to discipline or replace them. When jobs can no longer be simplified, timed, and otherwise controlled, the worker must be treated more as an independent craftsman. Once the worker has more responsibility and work is shared with semiautonomous groups, each worker becomes more valuable, and it is much harder to replace and control him. Furthermore, as the workers become more aware of alternatives to the technology and organization of work, they tend to become more demanding and often more militant. Other more progressive managers would welcome these changes and would be happier in a more challenging and democratic atmosphere, but such changes clash with a machinelike structure built on the principle of maximal growth and profit. In such a system, each manager must keep running or fall behind. Although progressive managers would support efforts to humanize work, few would take the risk to initiate such programs, and in fact their efforts might be futile, unless systemic organizational changes were made.

One reason why the Pet Food plant can exist within a large modern corporation like General Foods is that it was built from scratch and that it is far enough away from corporate headquarters so that executives do not constantly meddle. In contrast, a very creative program for machinists instituted at Polaroid a decade ago did not survive, exactly because the organization was not prepared to adapt to it. This experimental program restructured machinists' work, so that supervisors were removed and each machinist shared supervisory and quality-control functions. Each worker was also given one hour of classes each day on company time teaching him further skills so that he could move up in the company. From the point of view of both workers and productivity, the experiment was a success, and practically all the workers moved up into higher positions. However, the program was discontinued, and managers at Polaroid have cited two reasons. First, while the program sparked demands for changes in other parts of the organization, there was no one either willing or capable or with a mission to expand the program. Second, the workers involved in the program became more militant and demanded further changes in the direction of greater participation in decision making. This also scared some managers. Indeed, one might say that such projects may stimulate new independence within the organization which is not prepared for it. Some of the Polaroid managers associated with Project 60 (P-60) summarized points to be kept in mind in planning new projects.[58] One of them noted, "Before we continue the education of people, we must understand that the result of education is a freer man and not a more controllable man. Until everyone understands this, we will continue to be surprised by the unexpected actions of the men."

Principles for Reconstruction

Given this all too brief overview of industrial psychostructures, we turn to a final question: How can institutions of work throughout America be reconstructed to stimulate rather than cripple independence? First, we must recognize that the kind of independence that can be developed in a large organization will not be the traditional concept of "individualism" based on the hoarding, obstinate property owner, but it can allow autonomy and individuated development of craftsmanlike abilities in a cooperative framework. This message

58. 1. Any efforts at broadening traditional work will not be readily accepted by the rest of the organization.

2. The whole organization must understand the project or experiment and its meaning, if it is to have any chance for success.

3. To alter traditional thinking in an organization is a big job and it should not be imposed on the part of the organization that is working on product development. It should start with a part of the organization where the work is going to remain more or less the same for a long period of time.

The managers also noted that the educational part of the program was extremely important. Where it worked best, it was because the teachers were particularly effective and took time to help the students. Furthermore, they helped the student integrate his educational experience in terms of the whole job and to develop critical thinking in order to overcome the tendency of being submissive to superiors and being fearful to make a decision by oneself. However, the managers also expressed a caveat that the organization had better expect workers who go through such a program to be different from before.

needs to be made to resentful ex-proprietors and craftsmen who are in no mood to support social welfare programs but do want a greater say in work decisions.[59] We believe that a program to reconstruct the work place, to establish principles allowing greater independence and self-development, could forge a new progressive alliance in America between the old self-employed and the newly self-affirmative. Such a program would sharply contrast to alternatives where the politics of workers are motivated by resentment, or apathetic despair. Today, both the thwarted self-employed and the self-affirmative organization men can start off by recognizing that the only property they have is themselves, and the basic kind of property right to be recognized is the need to protect and develop the self in order to experience one's dignity in an organizational society. For most of us, the old basis of individualism is not possible, nor does the traditional hoarding-independent character fit the requirements of a highly interdependent technological society. What is required are responsible (in the sense of able to respond emotionally as well as intellectually) and cooperative individuals who are secure enough to develop their spiritual capacities, including conscience, so they are not afraid to speak out against organizational practices and products that are harmful to themselves, their coworkers, or the public, and who have the independence necessary to struggle for continued progressive change.

Organizational changes must be conceived in terms of inter-related principles if they are to support a new independence. There are two reasons why this is so. First, it is important to emphasize the fact that many attempts for change are made in the erroneous belief that certain symptoms have a single cause, and if one changes the cause one cures the symptom. This kind of thinking is based on a mechanical model of cause and effect, which does not take into account the fact that individuals live in systems. In a social system each structural principle is related to every other principle. If you change one principle, the others tend to be affected.

59. Data supporting this assertion have been gathered by us and others in factory interviews.

Second, given the fact that the large corporations are increasingly ruled by anonymous authority based on principles of profit and growth alone, human principles that establish human rights are necessary as one counterbalance.[60] Though these principles have elements in common with those of some benevolent paternalists, they go beyond these to establish the rights of free workers who should not be locked in to any organization. In the day of the benevolent paternalist, individual loyalty was established on the basis of personal relationships. In those days, workers might also have trusted that the organization would be loyal to the community as well as to the worker. In the modern world of the multinational corporation, managers move factories when they are not profitable, even though the whole community suffers and such moves are not in the national interest. Workers can no longer depend on the principles of goodwill of an individual or a family who own the business and live in the community. Neofeudalism will not work. The principles that can protect workers today must be established as rights and must be responsive to the social and economic changes that have taken place over the past few decades.

Maccoby and Neal Q. Herrick have proposed four general principles as a basis for constructing a system which will not be destructive to the worker's character, but will create a framework in which he can develop himself productively. They were formulated after studying those models of work organization in both the United States and other countries which have proved workable and have led to positive results for both the worker and productivity.[61] These principles are security, equity, individuation, and democracy (see Appendix).

The first principle is *security*. The worker needs to be free from

60. The other constraint on corporations must be social—laws that place limits on technology, products harmful to health, advertising which manipulates. This important issue is not dealt with here.

61. Neal Q. Herrick and Michael Maccoby, "Humanizing Work: A Priority Goal of the 1970s" (Paper presented at the Quality of Working Life Conference, New York, September 1972. Printed in U.S. Senate Subcommittee on Employment, Manpower and Poverty), *Hearings on the Worker Alienation Act*, 25–26 July 1972, pp. 293–302.

fear and anxiety concerning his health and safety, his income and future employment. One cannot expect workers to cooperate wholeheartedly at work when physical conditions are unhealthy and debilitating. Insecurity about health or economic want naturally provokes fear and anger in workers. Unless security is guaranteed, workers will be suspicious about any changes in the structure of work.

In a society as rich as ours, no individual, particularly one who is willing to work, should have to fear that he will lack the basic necessities of life. Since 1938, the year of the Fair Labor Standards Act, it has been generally accepted that employers should pay no less than a certain minimum wage per hour to their workers. But much has changed since 1938. Our notions of an acceptable standard of living have increased. Changes in the consumer credit structure have made an annual income rather than an hourly wage the measure of security.

Social and historical changes have eroded other guarantees of security. The family no longer meets the needs for insurance against economic hardship, and individuals must turn elsewhere for help in time of need. Mobility and changes in plant location mean that one cannot count on traditional community relationships.

The shift away from self-employment and toward large organizations has had a twofold effect on security. On the one hand, it has lessened the availability of self-employed work, which in the past was more secure than working for someone else because (1) no one could fire you, (2) competition was not so ruthless as it is today against the big chains, and (3) in your old age your children (to whom you passed on your business) provided for you. On the other hand, self-employment itself (what little remains) is today much less secure than in the past. We have seen how hard it is to be self-employed successfully. Some of those who fail at their own businesses end up worse off than those hired employees who have pensions. Indeed, today, with the increase in security for salaried and wage workers (largely due to the efforts of unions), these workers are often better off in terms of security than independent businessmen or craftsmen.

In the organizational society, security must be provided by companies and/or the federal government. To provide this security, it might be possible in some industries to guarantee both work and pensions. While government and large corporations may be the only organizations with the resources to guarantee fifty weeks of work a year, federal insurance could make it possible for smaller companies as well. In a market economy, however, security cannot be solely an employer responsibility. A guaranteed minimal income financed through the tax system would provide the necessary floor.

The worker also needs to be secure about his long-range future. Workmen's compensation to protect the income of those who through accident or illness are unable to work must be adequate. Besides social security, the worker needs protection for his retirement benefits. This means immediate vesting and/or portability so these benefits are not lost if he wants to change his job.

Finally, the worker needs security vis-à-vis the restructuring of work itself and the adoption of new technology. When such changes result in the need for fewer workers, any reduction of jobs should be accomplished on the basis of attrition. Security is the keystone to restructuring work, since any changes which do not protect the worker will rightly be resisted by unions as a new form of exploitation.

The second principle is *equity*. Workers should receive fair compensation commensurate to their contribution to the value of the service or product. Lack of equity (e.g., huge differences in income between bosses and workers and lack of sharing in profits) stimulates envy and resentment leading to hostility. This is particularly a danger when workers are asked to contribute more to the enterprise with changes of technology or job structuring.

It is seldom easy to work out equity, to determine the fair share of each participant in the productive process. In practice, it requires searching for methods of evaluating individual contributions that are considered just by those involved. Because there is no mechanical measure of equity, collective bargaining has proved necessary to approximate it. Nevertheless, once a principle of equity is adopted and directs the process of dialogue and bargaining, increased responsibility and concern for fairness in both work and other relationships will be encouraged.

Serious consideration might also be given to the adoption of national maximum (as well as minimum) wage guidelines. The present gap between the lowest-paid members of the employed labor force and the highest-paid members is too large and cannot be justified in terms of ownership or creation of the enterprise on the part of professional managers. The maximum wage should not be expressed in dollar terms, but in terms of the appropriate ratio between the highest and lowest salaries in an establishment. It could apply to the professional managerial class, but not to entrepreneurs, and could recognize the effect of the size of the corporation upon appropriate maximum salaries. For example, the difference between the lowest-paid person and the highest-paid person at the General Motors Corporation is now about a multiple of 80. In Belgium, the standard difference is 7 to 1, which seems to us more equitable.

The principle of equity should also include profit sharing. Workers in an organization should be contractually assured a specified percentage of the profits (over and above assured salary and benefits) that are based in part on their work. To work, profit sharing and incentive programs require a high level of trust between workers and management, including open books. In some cases of restructured work, a specified share of profits might be divided among democratic work groups, taking into account the contributions of each group toward increased productivity. In some cases, the group might award exceptional individuals. In large corporations, it is often difficult to determine individual contributions, but once the principle is accepted, it has been possible in some companies to develop equitable profit sharing plans with positive results for both the worker and the company.

The third principle is *individuation* (craftsmanship, autonomy, and learning). Work should stimulate the development of the individual's unique abilities and capacity for craftsmanship rather than force him into a mechanized role. It should stimulate learning rather than cause boredom, stagnation, and eventually hopelessness. The principle of individuation, if taken seriously, establishes a nonbureaucratic spirit in which each worker is treated as an individual with different needs and abilities. Eventually this spirit should encourage workers to develop themselves and to learn as much as they wish about the industry as a whole so that they have the knowledge to participate in making complicated decisions.

In contrast, the worker who is denied a job which stimulates craftsmanship, continued learning, and the development of his abilities is likely to become either an automaton or an angry person. Individuation involves reversing scientific management to reestablish craftsmanship at work. It implies that workers should have a maximal autonomy in determining the rhythms of their work and planning how it should be done. The instinct for workmanship, as Thorsten Veblen called it, is one of the deep strengths of the American character, which, if systematically weakened, undermines our society.

The principle of *democracy* is essential to improving the quality of work, but by no means a solution in itself. Studies in Yugoslavian factories have shown that democracy without individuation does not overcome the worker's alienation, and may in fact lead to a new cynicism. Democracy implies activeness, cooperation, and responsibility rather than passiveness, egocentrism, and withdrawal from responsibility on the part of the worker.

How can responsibility be instituted in industry? As Robert Dahl points out in his book *After the Revolution*,[62] there are natural constraints to maximal democracy. Full democracy is limited by the amount of time it takes, the degree of competence it requires, and the size of the group involved. Even optimal participant and representative democracy without security, equity, and the chance for craftsmanlike work is liable to become an empty form. What is the use of a say in decisions if one lacks knowledge to change dehumanizing technology? Once these other principles are estab-

62. Robert Dahl, *After the Revolution: Authority in a Good Society* (New Haven: Yale University Press, 1970).

lished, however, workers should control their own work and participate in setting work processes, hours, "hiring" and firing, etc. Only in this way can one expect activeness and responsibility on the part of the worker. In a pyramidal, authoritarian organization, it is natural for the worker to do only what he is told, and to take no responsibility for correcting errors and thinking of new ways to do things.

The concept of democracy also includes the protection of citizenship within the work place. This includes free speech and the right to be considered innocent until proven guilty on questions of discipline.

Based on democratic work groups and humanized factory technology, there are further steps toward an optimal industrial democracy. In the industrial world today, degrees of democracy in the work place range from participatory management (where the workers' views are listened to and taken into account in decision making) to systems of workers' control where the workers' authority and responsibility are institutionalized, as in Yugoslavia. In West Germany there is representative democracy, where workers' representatives serve on the board of directors. In a full workers' democracy, workers as well as consumers would have the institutionalized power to decide on all major issues of policy for the large corporations, but a workable model of such a system in the highly industrialized society still needs to be created.

Support for Restructuring Work

Who will support these principles? Given that there are more humane and healthful ways of organizing work and structuring technology,[63] how will such restructuring be achieved? The social

63. For examples of restructured technology in factories, see the work of the new socio-technical theorists such as Eric Trist and Einar Thorsrud. E. Trist, "A Socio-Technical Critique of Scientific Management" (Paper presented at the Edinburgh Conference on the Impact of Science and Technology, Edinburgh University, May 1970).

scientists and industrial engineers who pioneered in restructuring work are for the most part management consultants. Their experience of working for the progressive manager leads them naturally to believe that progress will be achieved only by gaining access to the benign prince in the guise of the corporation president. In a paternalistic organization, progress might be made in this way, but only up to the point where paternalism itself is threatened. We have seen that some of the best working conditions and participative managements exist in paternalistic companies like Oneida Ltd. or American Velvet. But fewer and fewer companies today are paternalistic.

The modern corporation which controls more and more of the economy is constructed on the machinelike principles of anonymous authority. In such organizations, changing the structure of work in any significant way requires the collaboration of both progressive managers and workers concerned with health and well-being more than the maximization of growth and profit. They are faced with the problem of changing a system, which requires political struggle, tradeoffs and compromises, as well as creative experimentation to provide concrete alternatives. Unions, which have achieved so much for workers in terms of security and equity, must enlarge their goals to include changing working conditions. These changes cannot take place unless unions work for them.

Is it realistic to believe that progressive managers will participate in restructuring work according to these principles? A number of them may join this movement for two reasons. First, many managers are dissatisfied with their own work, because it lacks security, equity, chances for personal development, and a responsible role in decision making. A recent poll of the American Management Association shows "there is overwhelming agreement among surveyed middle managers and personnel executives alike that managerial frustration and discontent with corporate life are increasing." [64]

64. The authors of the report state that "Today's manager is deeply concerned about what he regards as an increasing tendency toward greater responsibility without a corresponding increase in authority. Today's manager reports that his opportunities

As a result of this discontent, the authors report that, "Nearly half the middle managers surveyed favor a change in current labor laws which would compel employers to recognize and bargain with manager unions in business organizations where managers elected to organize." In other words, managers may unionize during the next decade, in large part because they suffer from mechanized work.

The second reason for thinking that some managers will join this movement is that so far the progressive new work projects in the United States have been developed by managers, not by unions or production workers. Moreover, based on our observation and interviewing of managers, we believe that the impulse to humanize work appeals to the most progressive side of the managerial character. Many managers are indifferent to other social issues that might concern them—such as the effects of what they produce on the environment and the public, the quality of life in their communities, military and foreign policy. But they are concerned with the quality of work, since work is vitally important to their own experience of well-being and self-realization. Since they desire secure, equitable, craftsmanslike, and responsible work for themselves, they can see the importance of such work for others.

---

for direct participation in the decision-making process seem to be rapidly decreasing in the highly bureaucratic and authoritarian structure of the techno-corporation of the 1970s." Specifically, the frustrating conditions most frequently mentioned can be grouped in terms of security, equity, individuation, and democracy, as follows:

Security: Gains secured by blue-collar unions outpacing gains of management employees (215 mentions)

Growing uncertainty about job security (160 mentions)

Equity: Low salaries or salary inequities (192 mentions)

Long hours without extra compensation (94 mentions)

Democracy: (and Equity:) Feeling of not being involved in decision-making process (128 mentions)

(and Equity:) Increased responsibility without increased authority (125 mentions)

Individuation: Little feeling of personal reward and achievement (111 mentions)

Lack of top management responsiveness to new ideas, improved methods (91 mentions)

(Alfred T. DeMaria, Dale Tarnowski, and Richard Gurman, *Manager Unions? An AMA Research Report* [New York: American Management Association, 1972]). These findings may be biased in favor of the discontented since only 1,108 of the 3,000 managers surveyed responded to the questionnaire.

A movement to reconstruct the work place will seek to influence public policy.[65] Guaranteed income, portable pensions, and improved occupational health and safety legislation will help to establish security. (For these purposes, the concept of health needs to be expanded to include emotional as well as physical well-being.) In the area of equity, legislation can establish maximum as well as minimum wages. Furthermore, government can support efforts to restructure work by giving tax credit to companies that experiment according to the four principles we have outlined. As suggested by the proposed Worker Alienation Act, funds can also be allocated for experimentation and evaluation of model projects along these lines.[66]

If such a movement to restructure the work place according to principles of security, equity, individuation, and democracy develops, what results can we expect? Ideally, as it gains momentum, it may spark the hope and liberate the energy necessary to confront other problems of postindustrial society, by demonstrating that technology can be redesigned in terms of more just and humane values.

65. See Herrick and Maccoby, "Humanizing Work."
66. U.S. Senate, *Hearings on the Worker Alienation Act*, July 1972.

Appendix

Socio-Psychological
Principles for
Reconstructing
the Work Place

Michael Maccoby
Neal Q. Herrick

Security (vs. the fear and suspiciousness of insecurity)
  health and safety
  guaranteed work
  guaranteed income
  portable pension
  reducing jobs by attrition, not firing

Equity (vs. the envy and resentment of inequity)
  fair pay differentials
  profit sharing
  more responsible work adequately rewarded
  fair promotions and job assignments

162

Individuation (vs. the boredom and hopelessness of being made a standardized part of the machine)

    craftsmanship—autonomy

    continual education

    opportunity to develop skills and abilities

    nonbureaucratic treatment of individual—respect for individual needs

Democracy (vs. the passiveness and sadomasochism of authoritarian organization)

    participative management

    self-management

    autonomous work groups

    participation in hiring coworkers and choosing supervisors

    representative democracy

    free speech in the work place

III Alternatives for Reconstruction

The contradictions identified in the first section of this book will no doubt generate a variety of proposals for reform and realignment. To the extent that people participate in developing ideas for change and act together politically, they can influence what form these changes will take. André Gorz has suggested that we look for "nonreformist" reforms which improve the situation in the short run while instilling a dynamic for further change over time. Proposals consistent with a humane reconstruction of our society must be distinguished from those that simply reaffirm the assumptions and reinforce the dynamics of the present political economy.

The essays in this section may be viewed as part of the process of struggling with such questions. All concern new modes of action by the state and new forms of economic organization. All seek to further a process of reconstruction which can slowly transform the institutions and assumptions that presently govern our work and play.

In the first article of this section, Ralph Nader and Mark Green propose another mode of regulation—federal chartering of corporations. For Nader and Green, federal chartering of what O'Connor defines as the monopoly sector offers the opportunity for stringent controls of corporate behavior. They suggest that the terms of the charters could require more disclosure of information, greater worker participation in the firm, increased legal accountability for consumer protection, and greater regulation for environmental concerns.

"Constitutionalizing" the corporation might give impetus to consumer and environmental groups, forcing greater social responsibility on corporate managers. Fuller disclosure would allow an attentive public to be far more aware of the range of corporate abuses. Furthermore, to the extent that federal chartering helps break down the notion that corporations are private free-enterprise institutions, it might create a dynamic which could lead beyond what initially can only be a very limited reform.

The shortcoming of the Nader-Green proposal is that it once again calls for government regulation to control the corporation, and thereby may be used to discourage rather than encourage citizen action. In this light, Gordon Adams' examination of the use of nationalization in advanced capitalist societies is particularly illuminating. Adams writes in response to the numerous suggestions that various industries in the United States—railroads, defense plants, transportation facilities, the energy industry—be nationalized by the federal government. He suggests that state ownership can be placed—as can federal chartering—in a broad range of state regulatory activities which in the end serve the needs of the corporate elite. Reviewing the European experience with nationalization and, more specifically, the recent takeover of Rolls Royce by the British government, Adams concludes that state ownership in Europe has never led to a redistribution of wealth or power in the society. Instead, the state firms are run hierarchically in the same manner as private corporations. Moreover, nationalization is seldom extended to profitable enterprises, and therefore even the advantages of socialized profits are lost. If a sophisticated corporate-state elite can use nationalization to maintain centralized corporate power, one must be cautious about proposals that encourage reliance on the benevolence of the state.

With Adams' admonitions in mind, the vision that Gar Alperovitz offers becomes more cogent. In searching for reforms to counter the present tendency toward a centralized corporate monopoly, Alperovitz offers a vision of a decentralized, community-controlled socialist commonwealth, combining local cooperative enterprise with regional planning. He suggests that it is possible for the economy to be run on a more human scale and to be controlled at the community level, offering greater scope for citizens to influence the shape of their lives and environment.

Alperovitz's model is rooted in present-day experiences: it takes off from the present organization of work, from a belief system of pluralism, and from our impulse for community. At the same time, one of its weaknesses is that it may underestimate the strength of certain values in our culture—manifested, for example, in the insistence of a choice of sixteen brands of soap or a wide range of consumer goods. Decentralization may assume a different value structure and a different standard of living. If this is so, such tradeoffs must be made explicit both in vision and in action.

Alperovitz is one of a group of scholars and activists which is presently attempting to define concrete alternatives to the present economic system; Geoffrey Faux is another. Faux argues that private ownership and development of land has not only resulted in irrational land use and ecological imbalance, but also contributed to the inequality of wealth which prevails in the United States. He distinguishes between small family landholdings, and the multiacre plots owned by agribusinesses or real estate developers and speculators; he suggests that the latter should be publicly owned by local communities. Community ownership goes beyond the proposal that government increase its regulation of land usage, and allows communities to benefit from the profits which accrue to those who own this scarce resource.

Faux outlines a method for the financing and maintenance of public ownership of the land, and provides examples of communities that have already begun to take over their own land. In doing so, Faux reveals the secret too often hid from public consideration. Simply, proposals to reconstruct the political economy, to make our institutions serve us instead of molding us to serve them, are not schemes devised by malcontents who seek to disrupt our lives. Rather they are serious suggestions, offered by people concerned—as everyone increasingly must be—over the inequities and absurdities of our present political economy.

The proposals offered in this section are radical, in the true sense of seeking to isolate the root of the problem, but they are neither harebrained nor sinister. They should interest all who are distressed by a centralized hierarchical economy in which power is controlled by the few and income divided inequitably. The effort to find practical ways to reconstruct our institutions and to resurrect our humaneness is a project in which virtually all can join.

7

Federal Chartering and Corporate Accountability

Ralph Nader
Mark Green

Concern over corporate activities is rising. Economic concentration and monopolistic practices, environmental pollution, product safety, occupational health, advertising and deception, corporate secrecy, corporate crime, corporate responsibility—the list of inquiry is long, as it must be. But while focusing on these behavorial effects, it is important also to consider the structural causes of corporate depredations. Where did the corporate form come from? From whom does the corporation get its legitimacy today? Who should bestow that legitimacy?

A corporation may "have no soul," as Edward Coke intoned in 1612, but legally it must have a body. In order to exist it must obtain a charter. A corporate charter is in effect an agreement whereby a government gives the corporate entity existence and that entity, in return, agrees to serve the public interest. Up until the late 1870s, states granted charters to corporations under carefully circumscribed conditions.[1] For example, corporations could not own the stock or assets of other corporations, were granted existence only for a specified period of years, and could not do business or own property outside the state in which they were chartered. These limitations, according to one commentator, reflected a prevailing fear "that a corporation was only an artificial personality and therefore did not have a soul or conscience. Lacking a conscience, it had no morals and was *prima facie* dangerous." [2] As long as corporations remained local, contained by the charter's restrictions, states still maintained the control they considered necessary for the public interest to be served.

But corporations did *not* stay local. What these restrictions aimed to avoid is precisely what occurred. In order to attract resident corporations, states made their incorporation laws increasingly permissive. The winner of the race for corporate citizens went to the state of least restriction, and the early victor was undoubtedly New Jersey. In 1866 it allowed its corporations to hold property and do business outside the state; by 1875 it had dispensed with its ceiling on the amount of authorized capital. During the 1880s, in a critical move, it allowed corporations to hold and dispose of the stock of other corporations. The result: between 1888 and 1904, 192 of the 345 American companies with capitalization in excess of $1 million took out New Jersey charters.[3] New Jersey became the home of the infamous Standard Oil Trust, and holding companies declared illegal in other states simply transferred their property to corporations organized under the law of New Jersey.

But New Jersey's dominance was only temporary; Delaware was not to be denied. As an 1899 law review article notes:

> [The citizens of Delaware] had their cupidity excited by the
> spectacle of their northern neighbor, New Jersey becoming rich

1. See, generally, James W. Hurst, *The Legitimacy of the Business Corporation in the Law of the United States, 1780–1970* (Charlottesville: University of Virginia Press, 1970).
2. R. W. Boyden, "The Breakdown of Corporations," in *The Corporation Take-over,* ed. A. Hacker (Garden City, N.Y.: Doubleday, 1964), p. 89.
3. R. C. Larcom, *The Delaware Corporation* (Baltimore, Md.: Johns Hopkins Press, 1937), pp. 13–14.

and bloated through the granting of franchises to trusts which
are to do business everywhere except in New Jersey. In other
words, little Delaware . . . is determined to get her little tiny,
sweet, round, baby hand into the grab-bag of sweet things
before it is too late.[4]

Delaware's business code of 1899, drafted by a financial reporter
and three corporate lawyers, enacted most of New Jersey's liberal
code and then some: any classification of stock could be issued, with
or without voting powers; shareholders lost rights to preemption;
there was no state transfer tax on the resale of securities; annual
meetings could be held outside the state; directors were not required
to own company stock to qualify for the directorate; state and tax
rates were set slightly below those of New Jersey; and finally,
charters permitted directors to issue new stock, change the terms of
authorized stock previous to sale, retire preferred stock, and even
change the firm's bylaws—all without obtaining shareholder con-
sent.[5] Delaware thus took over the lead in the incorporation game, an
advantage it has not to this day relinquished. As the local newspapers
christened it, Delaware became "The Little Home of Big Business."

In a sense Delaware succeeded too well, since imitative states
began to take some of its business away. Although by 1960 one-third
of the top six hundred industrial corporations were headquartered in
Delaware, the state decided to loosen its business code still more. A
revision commission, formed in 1964, attempted, in its words, "To
ascertain what other states have to attract corporations that we do not
have." The basic redrafting was done by three private corporate
lawyers working on Saturdays in their law offices. The full
commission always assumed that the state legislature, which had to
approve the new code, would be a rubber stamp. One member of the
commission called the legislature "just a bunch of farmers." No
hearings were held on the final statute, and it passed the Delaware
legislature unanimously on July 3, 1967.

4. Note, "Little Delaware Makes a Bid for the Organization of Trust,"
American Law Review 33 (1899): 418, 419.
5. Martin Lindahl and William Carter, *Corporate Concentration and Public Policy*
(3rd ed.; Englewood Cliffs, N.J.: Prentice-Hall, 1959).

The new code contained many liberalizations for corporate managers; only directors, not shareholders, could propose amendments to the charter; annual meetings need not be held; officers and directors could be indemnified for court costs and the settlement of criminal and civil cases without shareholder approval. These "reforms" achieved their purpose. Delaware had been chartering corporations at the rate of 300 a month before the new code's enactment; the figure jumped to 800 registrations a month directly afterward. By mid-1973 there were some 73,000 corporations with their corporate charters on file in Dover, Delaware, a number including one-third of all the firms listed on the New York Stock Exchange and fully 238 of *Fortune*'s top 500 industrial firms.

From a time when firms were selectively chartered and controlled by the government, private corporations have grown to huge size and power without commensurate accountability. Promoters and management—not shareholders, not employees, not the community—have vast discretion to draft and implement the governance of the corporation. How did this happen? State incorporation laws became a version of Gresham's Law, as the weaker states drove out the stronger ones. Shareholders were too powerless and disinterested, and legislative committees too ignorant and pliable, to challenge this accession of power. The task of drafting state laws remained firmly within the hands of corporate lawyers and businessmen, psychologically and financially identifying with management. A recent *Pennsylvania Law Review* article concludes:

> The sovereign state of Delaware is in the business of selling its corporation law. This is a profitable business, for corporation law is a good commodity to sell. . . . The consumers of this commodity are corporations and . . . Delaware like any other good businessman, tries to give the consumer what he wants. In fact, those who will buy the product are not only consulted about their preferences, but are also allowed to design the product and run the factory.[6]

6. Comment, "Law for Sale: A Study of the Delaware Corporation Law of 1967," *University of Pennsylvania Law Review* 117 (1969): 861.

And so long as we permit fifty-two different jurisdictions (Puerto Rico and Washington, D.C., included) to compete for corporate charters, there can be no improvement. For reform, we must look elsewhere.

The idea that the federal government should charter corporations is quite old. During the Constitutional Convention in 1787, James Madison twice proposed, unsuccessfully, that the Constitution expressly empower Congress to do so.[7] By 1791 the nation was debating whether to incorporate a U.S. Bank. Jefferson argued that such a bank would overawe the states and permit vast consolidations of economic power to dominate our economic life. Jefferson won the battle but lost the war, since great economic consolidations *did* come to dominate our economy, though via state and not federal incorporation.

In the 1880s, citizen protest built up against the economic and political power of the huge trusts. Some called for a form of federal licensing of corporations in order to control their excesses. Instead, by passing the 1890 Sherman Antitrust Act, Congress relied on competition rather than regulation. Disillusionment soon set in, as courts handed down a series of restrictive rulings that robbed the Sherman Act of its potential strength. In addition, Social Darwinists, making a virtue out of reality, approved of the trusts. Presaging today's defenders of corporate giantism, economist E. L. van Halle believed that "they [trusts] come because they must." And another prominent economist, John Bates Clark, reflecting the laissez faire philosophy of his day, said: "Combinations have their roots in the nature of social industry and are normal in their origin, development, and their practical working. . . . To accept the results of this evolution and to meet the demands of the new era is the part of wisdom." [8]

7. A. A. Berle, "Economic Power and the Free Society," in Hacker, *The Corporation Take-over,* p. 87; Federal Trade Commission, *Report on Utility Corporations* (Washington, D.C.: Government Printing Office, 15 September 1934), p. 76.

8. Quoted in G. Leinwand, "A History of the United States Federal Bureau of Corporations (1903–1914)" (Ph.D. dissertation, New York University, 1962).

But public and political opinion were turning against the protrust sentiment of the courts and the economics profession. William Jennings Bryan in 1899 went on record as favoring a federal license whenever a corporation wanted to conduct interstate business. Between 1903 and 1914, Presidents Roosevelt, Taft, and Wilson all voiced support for a federal incorporation or licensing scheme in their annual messages to Congress. The idea was endorsed by the 1904 Democratic and Republican platforms and the 1912 Democratic platform. Twenty different bills were introduced in Congress between 1903 and 1914.

Despite this array of approval, the Clayton and Federal Trade Commission Acts of 1914 became law instead of federal chartering, support for the latter never having coalesced at any one time. Taft had changed his mind about it by 1912, and the Senate Interstate Commerce Committee, after holding hearings on federal incorporation in 1913, concluded in the final committee report that it was "neither necessary nor desirable at this time." [9]

The 1930s depression brought new demands for overhauling the industrial sector. In certain respects, Franklin Roosevelt saw his National Recovery Act (NRA) as a form of federalizing corporations, since it provided "a rigorous licensing power in order to meet rare cases of non-cooperation and abuse." [10] There was brief talk during this time of going further, or replacing the NRA codes by the federal chartering of large companies and trade associations. [11] But the Securities Acts of 1933 and 1934—requiring full and accurate disclosure of material facts in a public offering and regulating the practices of the national exchanges—and New Deal regulatory schemes satisfied many who had looked to the federal government to reform corporations.

9. Ibid., p. 4.
10. Samuel Rosenman, comp., *The Public Papers and Addresses of Franklin D. Roosevelt* (New York: Random House, 1938), p. 202. ("A Recommendation to the Congress to Enact the National Industrial Recovery Act to Put People to Work, May 17, 1933.")
11. Lowe Watkins, "Federalization of Corporations," *Tennessee Law Review* 13 (1934): 89.

Nevertheless, the most sustained drive to date for federal licensing occurred in the late 1930s. Sen. Joseph O'Mahoney, a Populist from Wyoming, energetically and repeatedly promoted the idea of "National Charters for National Business." By emphasizing that "a corporation had no rights; it has only privileges," he sought to return to the days when charters policed, as well as permitted. He chaired the famous Temporary National Economic Committee hearings (TNEC) of the late 1930s, reiterating throughout his belief in federal licesing.[12] But the war checked any momentum O'Mahoney had generated.

Thus, at nearly every point in our history when federal chartering was considered, an alternate remedy was prescribed. During all these periods, federal chartering was prominent, topical and finally ignored. Clearly, it is an idea whose time has come—and come and come. Our present spectacle of corporate power abused makes it topical again.

The federal chartering of giant corporations is necessary because state incorporation has failed. Even if state business codes and authorities did not so overwhelmingly reflect management power interests, they are no match for the resources of the great corporations. (General Motors, with earnings ninety times Delaware's general revenues, could buy Delaware—if DuPont were willing to sell it.) And gross earnings can, in a variety of ways, be translated into political power.[13] "The century and a half of state failure," one observer has written, "has been the story of a battle between corporate giants and legal pygmies." [14] To control national power requires, at the least, national authority.

At a time when the federal government becomes increasingly

12. See "Final Statement of Senator Joseph C. O'Mahoney," in Temporary National Economic Committee, *The Preservation of Economic Freedom* (March 1941), p. 11.

13. See, generally, Morton Mintz and Jerry Cohen, *America, Inc.* (New York: Dial, 1971).

14. Harold G. Reuschlein, "Federalization—Design for Corporate Reform in a National Economy," *University of Pennsylvania Law Review* 71 (1942): 91.

prominent in salvaging our unstable economy, it is an anachronism for the states to create corporations which operate in national and international markets. Quite simply, state borders are not relevant boundaries for corporate commerce, and state incorporation makes as much sense as state currencies or state units of measurements. In other federal systems—German, Mexican, Brazilian—firms that do business between the states or provinces must be formed under federal law.[15]

There are procedural benefits to a system of federal chartering. At present, a charter is an IOU which the corporation signs and then files and forgets. States do not review the firms they have created for violation of their birthright, nor do they impose sanctions for charter violations. In Indiana, AT&T, Penn Central, and De Paul University all recently lost their corporate licenses to do intrastate business because they had failed to file annual reports. But no hearings were held and no fines assessed. Until the firms filed their forms, it was business as usual, although they had legally ceased to exist in Indiana. It is quixotic to expect state boards to have either the resources or the will to impose adequate sanctions. A federal chartering authority would be far more likely to do so or would be more accessible to citizens demanding that it do so.

A federal chartering agency could help to equalize the differences of burdens and benefits now experienced by corporations because of differences in state provisions. Incorporation fees, regulatory laws, charter stipulations—powerful corporations can threaten to run away to a different state if these items are not to their satisfaction. And it is easy to see why Textron in Rhode Island or DuPont in Delaware could make its host state anxious. A single federal authority could end this corporate pitting of one state against another.

15. This logic, in an increasingly multinationalized world of trade, leads to a *world* chartering authority. But until problems of national sovereignity, which involve far more than merely who is to charter whom, are resolved, world chartering is perhaps logical, but surely visionary. Short of it, existing nations are the soil in which corporations grow and trade, and they should ensure that firms are rooted as deeply as necessary to ensure corporate responsiveness and accountability.

One can anticipate some of the criticisms to this scheme. Should the government manipulate the rights of private property? Not even the venerable "freedom of contract" is absolute, as the legal qualifiers of duress, coercion, unconscionability, and minimum wage, maximum hour, and equal employment legislation have long made clear. It must be realized that private property is not a gift of the gods but a bundle of rights created by our government; it hardly seems valid to condemn the government for legally rearranging this bundle of rights when it created them in the first place. "[T]he corporation, insofar as it is a legal entity, is a creation of the state," the Supreme Court has said. "It is presumed to be incorporated for the benefit of the public. . . . Its rights to act as a corporation are only reserved to it as long as it obeys the laws of its creation." [16]

Would federal chartering merely increase the power of big government by creating yet another bureaucracy; would it be socialistic? A federal chartering agency would not be giving government power it does not now exercise. States *do* charter corporations, in a diffusion of competing jurisdictions. And since the guiding purpose of federal chartering is to encourage corporate democracy and competition, it is contrary to a centralized, planned economy. To the extent that it attempts to make private firms more accountable to their shareholders and more responsive to competitors, it is a radically conservative idea. Right now we *do* have a type of corporate socialism, in which cooperating monopolies have freed themselves from the constraints of the competitive market and much law enforcement.

The bureaucracy created would be as trim and nondiscretionary as possible. The top thousand firms or so—measured by a combination of sales, asset size, market percentage, and number of employees —would be chartered, not the hundreds of thousands of small concerns which account for a small fraction of interstate trade; *intra*state firms would not be affected. Manpower would thus be marshaled to confront the actual problem area. The kind of charter

16. *Hale v. Hendel,* 201 U.S. 43, 74–75 (1905).

provisions to be enforced would also be as objective as possible. Does the firm's percentage of the market exceed permissible limits or doesn't it; has the corporation provided profits and cost data per plant and division or has it not; did management triple its bonus without notifying the shareholders? There is no such thing as government without any discretion; if there were, we would have computers as cabinet officials. Yet excessive discretion must be avoided or else the corporate regulatees would successfully shape their supposed regulators—the situation which now obtains.

What if, because of a federal chartering law, many American firms simply left to incorporate in Bermuda or France? What if they treated us as they treat Canada: a place to do business but not to owe allegiance? Or could companies have no country at all? Carl A. Gerstacker, chairman of the Dow Chemical Company, told a White House conference in February 1972 that he looked forward to the day of the "anational corporation," one without any national ties which could, therefore, operate freely and flexibly around the world. Gerstacker revealed that Dow had for a decade been studying the possibility of locating on an island in the Caribbean. Any of these business runaways could claim that restrictions imposed on them were not required by, say, France, and would create legal conflicts with their charters there. To that, there is an effective reply: The corporation, to the extent it has assets, employees, or shareholders in this country, either complies with the conditions of the federal chartering law or it cannot trade here. Since the American market is such a large percentage of the world market, we would have the leverage, if we had the will, to make this demand of expatriate firms and foreign authorities. There are state "foreign incorporation laws" which require out-of-state firms to meet certain local standards (e.g., stringent reporting requirements) in order to do business there. The same principle must apply to firms exisiting outside our borders which wish to do business here. A final restraint could be an "equalization" tax policy making it difficult for firms to move away and then sell goods back to the United States.

Assuming that the state incorporation laws are the problem and that existing antitrust mechanisms, regulatory agencies and securities laws are inadequately checking corporate power, a federal chartering law seems the most plausible mechanism for achieving corporate accountability. What is needed is a new agency—call it the Federal Corporations Agency—to issue federal charters for firms engaged in interstate business. What is needed is not a Corporate Bill of Rights but a Corporate Bill of Obligations. A sketch of possible provisions follows:

1. *Corporate democracy* would reduce the dominance of the oligarchies commandeering most corporations. The potential areas of coverage are all those which, unchallenged, have permitted management to rule without regard to the wishes of its electorate. Such areas include: corporate loans to officers and directors and other "interested" dealings; access to corporate records and easier use of the proxy machinery; cumulative voting, indemnification and compensation schemes; shareholder rights to amend the by-laws and charter and to nominate candidates for directors; and finally, public interest directors and some form of worker participation in management decision making now seem appropriate after a century of management monopoly.

2. Strict *antitrust* standards must be a condition of the charter. No corporation (unless it clearly proved itself part of a "natural oligopoly") would be permitted to retain more than 12 percent of an oligopolistic industry (a percentage recommended by President Johnson's antitrust task force). Large conglomerates should be permitted to acquire only toehold positions in concentrated industries and should be made to spin-off assets equal in value to any they acquire.[17]

3. *Corporate disclosure* must replace corporate secrecy. What are the earnings of hidden subsidiaries and consolidated divisions; who are the real beneficial owners of the corporations; what is the racial composition of all employees and new staff; what product and safety

17. For a discussion of antitrust reforms, see M. Green, B. Moore, and B. Wasserstein, *The Closed Enterprise System* (New York: Grossman, 1972).

testing has been conducted; what plans exist to meet pollution standards? Since the public is affected so intimately, answers to all these must be made public. Shareholders, investors, and government officials need adequate information to act intelligently. If done extensively enough, a corporate information center could be developed, with data by firm, plant and product available on computer tapes to respond to significant topical questions.

4. The corporate charter should *"constitutionalize"* the corporation, in Arthur S. Miller's phrase, applying constitutional obligations to this private aggregation of power. The logic for this proposal underpins federal chartering: corporations are effectively like states or private governments with vast economic, political and social impact. A democratic society, even if it encourages such groups for private economic purposes, should not endure such public power without public accountability. Our large corporations represent just the kind of concentrated power which the Constitution and its succeeding amendments aimed to diffuse. If the Constitutional Convention were held today, it would surely encompass *America, Inc.* It makes no public sense to apply the Constitution to Wyoming and West Tisbury (Mass.), but not to General Motors and Standard Oil (N.J.).

Unions, too, are private groups which have been legislated public power, *but* on condition that they behave democratically, with safeguards of due process (that they sometimes violate such safeguards is a problem of implementation, not construction). The same principle holds true of private corporations legislated public power. When a huge corporation deals with its employees, shareholders, and outlets, "state action" principles require that it do so fairly.[18] For example, the First Amendment right to free speech means that an employee can publish material critical of the firm in a magazine or

18. *Marsh v. Alabama,* 326 U.S. 501 (1946). (A private company town, when it functions like any public municipality, must extend First Amendment freedoms of press and religion to its citizens.) Accord, *Amalgamated Food Employees Union v. Logan Valley Plaza,* 391 U.S. 308 (1968). (Peaceful picketing on private property, in a location generally open to the public, is protected by the First Amendment.) But see *Lloyd Corporation, Ltd. v. Tanner,* 407 U.S. 551 (1972).

underground corporate newspaper; Fourteenth Amendment safe-guards mean that if he refuses to perform an illegal task or if he blows the whistle on a corporate crime, he cannot be fired without a due process hearing, complete with charges and evidence; the Fourth Amendment would forbid the firm from searching his private belongings in the shop without a warrant. It is inadequate to depend merely on unions to guarantee these rights since they have enrolled less than a quarter of all employees, and hardly any white-collar employees.

Hovering over all these provisions would be graduated penalities for violation of the charter. Depending on the nature and frequency of the violations, penalties could run from small absolute fines to a percentage of sales; from management reorganization to executive suspensions; from public trusteeship to the dissolution of the charter. A scale of sanctions must be developed to guarantee compliance with the charter.

In formulating a Federal Corporations Agency (FCA), care must be taken that it does not become as unresponsive and inefficient as some of the present regulatory and enforcement agencies. Lessons should be learned from the past; at the same time, it would be defeatist and irresponsible to urge no more federal reform measures because some have failed. Many corporations go bankrupt, yet the corporation is still a viable legal structure for the production and sale of goods and services.

It is important to stress again the objective nature of the FCA's standards. It would not involve itself in the imbroglios of rate determinations which naturally invite industry lobbying and a dependence on self-serving corporate data. However, the FCA should contain liberal provisions for shareholder and citizen suits—not as now institutionalized in the Michigan antipollution law—so that interested citizens equipped with adequate tools could check agency lethargy or inefficiency. More liberal rights of intervention into government processes could similarly permit public interest lawyers to monitor any malfeasance or nonfeasance. Mechanisms will have to be provided to help insure that a "commissioner" of the FCA be vigorous, nonpartisan and independent. For example, he or she should be appointed for a fixed term, unlike the secretary of Commerce, and there should be one, visible, responsible chairperson, not a collegial body as at the Federal Maritime Commission or Civil Aeronautics Board. (Can the reader name *anyone* in either of those two collective leaderships?)

While Delaware cannot dictate terms to GM, an FCA could, but it is not inevitable that it would. Thus, a new federal agency is a necessary but not a sufficient remedy. If it is badly organized with weak powers and no citizen access and participation, it will be ineffective; if its powers are adequate and citizen access provides a prod to agency action, it can succeed. The form is crucial, and so are the powers. Its power, and ultimate success, depend on something far broader than mere federal chartering: viz., who is politically in control at the federal level. For federal chartering to succeed ultimately, the hammerlock corporations throw on political leaders must be relieved. Some form of public campaign financing as well as greater disclosure of private contributions and lobbying efforts— goals not impossible of achievement post-Watergate—are the kind of efforts needed. An interested and supportive public is a sine qua non to a vigorous and strict agency. Again, corruption such as the ITT and Watergate scandals seems to have an impact on the public conscience. While 55 percent of those responding to a 1966 Harris poll had "great" confidence in major companies, today only 27 percent do. Seventy-seven percent want the Nixon administration to be "tougher" on big business. Legal reform and popular support, then, are the cornerstones on which federal chartering must eventually rest.

8 Public Ownership and Private Benefits: The Case of Rolls-Royce

Gordon Adams

The recent nationalization of Rolls-Royce by the Conservative government in Britain illustrates the phenomenon of state ownership of production within the structure of a Western capitalist economy. This apparent conflict between "public" and "private" power raises again the question of the role of the state in modern capitalism. This article examines the function performed by the state in Europe and the United States, and the Rolls-Royce case in particular. It argues that public ownership, like other state actions in the economy, has generally been a logical response to the needs of the capitalist economy rather than a step toward the transformation of that economy toward socialism. A close examination of the state/economy relationship as currently practiced clarifies the conditions that have prevented this evolution.

The economies of Western Europe and North America are unquestionably capitalist; most of the capital resources and means of production are held in "private" hands. At the same time, in all these countries, the state plays a crucial economic role. Economists such as John Kenneth Galbraith, Robert Heilbroner, and Andrew Shonfield, whose political views fall far short of socialism, have realized that the traditional paradigm used to describe the capitalist economy—the free market—no longer accurately reflects economic relationships in modern capitalist countries.[1] Because of the activity of the state sector, these economists use such terms as "the new industrial state" or "between capitalism and socialism" to describe modern capitalism. If we accept this characterization, the techniques of state intervention in the capitalist economy can be seen as integral to the working of that economy.

Stripping away pseudo-ideological controversies over such terms as planning, regulation, and nationalization, one sees that these mechanisms exist in all capitalist countries, without changing the basic fact that a small minority of the population owns the means of production. Notwithstanding popular mythology, especially in the United States, it is clear that in all capitalist countries the fundamental decisions on social and economic issues—choices that affect incomes, prices, savings, investment, and distribution—are made by a very small group of individuals. Inevitably, this group has a major stake in preserving its power to make such decisions. Nationalization, like other mechanisms in the state sector, is implemented in a way that serves the interests of this industrial elite in capitalist countries. Nationalization fits into the twentieth-century pattern of state development as the guarantor of growth through private profits. It is simply one tool, among others, used by the state to prolong the life of the capitalist system.

Intervention by the state sector into the economy began early in the twentieth century. During the progressive era, liberal and socialist critiques of the excesses of capitalism gained support in

1. See in particular, Robert L. Heilbroner, *Between Capitalism and Socialism: Essays in Political Economics* (New York: Random House, 1970); John Kenneth Galbraith, *The New Industrial State* (Boston: Houghton Mifflin, 1967); Andrew Shonfield, *Modern Capitalism: The Changing Balance of Public and Private Power* (New York: Oxford University Press, 1965).

Europe and the United States. Economic crises, the exploitation of labor in terms of wages and working conditions, the spread of urban slums, and a series of social upheavals forced recognition of the shortcomings of the market economy. In many countries, portions of the ruling élite responded by urging the development of new functions for the state. The state was to assist capitalism by correcting its worst abuses, which capitalists were unwilling to do directly, through such policies as safety and health regulations. Additionally, the state would assume responsibilities beyond the capacity of the individual capitalist, including the prevention of severe crises and depressions, and the guarantee of controlled and relatively stable growth in industrial markets and private profits.[2]

The early influence of the industrial elite on the evolution of the modern state in capitalist countries is often overlooked. Some analysts of modern capitalism reject the argument that the development of the state's modern role in the economy was a direct response to the demands and influence of the industrial elite. Even so, they would agree that the relationship between the industrial elite and state bureaucracies is close and that it is based on shared goals: the steady, regular expansion of profits and the prevention of social or economic crises which threaten the hierarchical class structure of a capitalist society. In practice, this means the preservation of the power and position of a narrow, property-based oligarchy at the expense of the rest of the population.

In political terms, the development of the state role in the twentieth century was facilitated by the acceptance of these parameters by social democratic political movements in Western Europe. From 1914 to the cold war, the French socialists, the British Labour party, the German Social Democratic party, the Nenni socialists in Italy, and the Swedish social democrats all gradually realized that their best opportunity for gaining political power lay in accepting, rather than seeking to overthrow, the basic class structure

2. A much more thorough discussion of this early development can be found in James Weinstein, *The Corporate Ideal and the Liberal State* (Boston: Beacon Press, 1968).

of capitalism. This required participation in parliamentary and electoral politics and the development of an electoral political machine. In competing for votes with groups on the Right, these parties drew up platforms that urged no more than the amelioration of the worst evils of capitalist society. Ultimately, their representatives agreed to accept office and bureaucratic appointments in governments and state institutions dominated by the interests of the capitalist elite.

The state role which resulted from this marriage of reformists and industrial elites was intended to preserve modern capitalism. As a consequence, state mechanisms and tools were developed to serve the major goals of the dominant class. Galbraith has described the importance of order and predictability in the market for regular economic growth.[3] Andrew Shonfield has pointed out that ". . . control over the business cycle, which owes so much to Keynes's work, has been one of the decisive factors in establishing the dynamic and prosperous capitalism of the postwar era. Indeed, it is probably the single most important factor in this change. So many other developments flow from it, notably the reduction of business risks and the incentive to speed up the process of investment." [4]

A number of functions are performed by the state to help meet the goals of capitalism, utilizing a wide variety of tools, including nationalization: [5]

1. Many regulatory and legislative activities of the state mitigate the most excessive abuses of capitalism. Functionaries of the state work closely with industrial and trade union elites to develop legislation and regulations which guarantee a minimal standard of living for workers and a certain level of environmental protection.

2. A number of mechanisms are employed to counteract

3. Galbraith develops this idea in *The New Industrial State*. I disagree with his argument, however, that this search for order and regularity somehow invalidates the profit motive as the moving force of capitalism.

4. Shonfield, *Modern Capitalism*, p. 64.

5. The list of functions performed within the state sector which follows contains a certain amount of overlap. It represents the first stage of a continuing effort to classify and describe the nature of state sector activities in modern capitalism.

capitalist market disorders: commissions to supervise stock exchange operations (such as the Securities and Exchange Commission), monetary activities of national banks and reserve boards, regulatory commissions, tariff policies, indicative planning commissions, prices and incomes policies, manipulation of military and welfare spending levels, and national censuses which serve as marketing surveys for business.

3. State activities and resources are important instruments for stimulating or inhibiting investment and consumption. Fiscal and monetary policies, especially those which affect housing construction and interest rates, are particularly useful tools for influencing investment patterns.[6] Taxation and welfare policies are also central to the generation and control of industrial and consumer demand in the capitalist economy. Welfare payments, food stamps, tax benefits, rather than being a drain on capitalism, add to purchasing ability and increase the demand for industry's products.

4. The state sector in capitalist societies plays a major role in ensuring a properly trained and channeled labor supply by funding education and job training programs and through general manpower policies. Meeting future manpower needs of private capital is the acknowledged goal of these policies.

5. The state helps corporations defend their internal markets from foreign competition through tariff policies, trade negotiations, and controls over direct foreign investment.

6. The converse of this latter function is also performed in the state sector. That is, the state promotes industry's overseas expansion through military aid and action, foreign aid, subversion, the overseas sales of surplus military equipment, investment guarantees, trade negotiations, and the like.

7. The state has primary responsibility for ensuring domestic social and political order. This is a major area of state activity involving, among other things, legal measures, police activity, internal military forces, and domestic surveillance.[7]

6. Shonfield, *Modern Capitalism*, p. 21.
7. For a detailed discussion of the state's functions in the United States in this

8. The state has also assumed part of the cost of maintaining an unprofitable resource base for industry. The state often regulates, or owns outright, gas, oil, and electricity production and distribution, or provides generous tax benefits for private industry to maintain them. The state, in addition, owns or administers railroad networks, canals, and other elements of the infrastructure essential for industry. The state builds and maintains roads with public revenues, monitors the use of airspace, and supplies funds to restore productive industrial capacity after wars.

9. Closely related to this last function, the state in capitalist societies is often asked to free private capital from the burden of maintaining important but unprofitable, declining industries, such as coal and railroads. Debates over nationalization policy occur most often in this area. Recently, the state has been asked to underwrite the future growth of capitalism by subsidizing high-cost, technologically advanced industries whose capital demands exceed the capacity of the private capital market. This has meant nationalizing, funding computer industries, and supporting a large number of other research and development activities for industry. This is particularly common in industries with large overseas markets for advanced technology.

The creation of state enterprises—a concept that is sometimes linked to socialism—has only recently been accepted as a desirable function for the state. Western European countries have developed a rich experience in using nationalization, particularly since the Second World War. In France, coal, gas and electricity, railroads, the Renault automobile works, radio and television, the national bank, credit institutions for housing and agriculture, some insurance companies, and some aircraft production facilities are all owned and managed by the state. In Italy, the major state holding companies—the Instituto per la Ricostruzione Industriale (Institute for Industrial Reconstruction-IRI) and the Ente Nazionale Idrocarbure (National

domain see Alan Wolfe, *The Seamy Side of Democracy: Repression in America* (New York: McKay, 1973).

Petroleum Company-ENI)—own or have controlling power in a wide range of industries from air and sea transportation through radio and television to steel, oil, and petrochemicals. The Italian state also has a central role in the nation's banking system. Britain has had extensive experience with nationalization. Starting in 1908, the Port of London Authority was created as a state institution. By 1951, the Bank of England, coal, airlines, railroads, gas and electricity, iron and steel, and radio and television had been nationalized. West Germany has had a more limited experience of state activity, though state manipulation of tax benefits and investment capital played a critical role in the postwar restoration to power of a healthy capitalist elite.[8]

In the United States, many local authorities, such as the New York Port Authority and many urban transportation systems, are, in essence, state-dominated enterprises. On the national level, Amtrak passenger railroad services, Comsat, and the U.S. Postal Service are examples of state enterprise. Some analysts argue that the relationship between the American government and industries involved in military production approaches nationalization. Professor Galbraith has, in fact, recently suggested nationalization as the most effective solution to the problems posed by the military-industrial complex. Nationalization has also been proposed as a solution to the crisis in America's railroad industry.

The diverse experiences of state ownership in Europe and the United States should not obscure the similar functions it serves in these countries. First, many capitalist countries use nationalization to provide essential services and resources for their entire economy. Gas and electricity are resources which the industrial elite often asks the state to support and develop. This is not true of all countries, of course, since gas and electricity are sometimes profitable enterprises when owned and managed privately, as in the United States.

Second, nationalization has relieved the private sector of the

8. For a more detailed discussion of the European experience of state ownership, see Shonfield, *Modern Capitalism*, esp. chaps. 5–12, and A. H. Hanson, "Planning and the Politicians: Some Reflections on Economic Planning in Western Europe," in *Politics in Western European Democracies: Patterns and Problems*, ed. Gary C. Byrne and Kenneth S. Pedersen (New York: John Wiley, 1971), pp. 336–50.

burden of maintaining unprofitable industries whose output is still vital to the economy, or whose collapse might lead to serious unemployment and social unrest. This form of nationalization, closely related to the first, is exemplified by state ownership of railroads and coal companies in many countries.

There is a third, more recent, and little discussed purpose of nationalization which stems from the state's responsibility to ensure a steady and sufficient supply of investment capital for industry. Traditionally, in many European countries, this takes the form of the partial or total nationalization of banking and credit systems. A modern version results from the inability of the nonstate capital market to meet the extended capital requirements of advanced technological production. For example, air frame and air engine industries, as will be seen in the case of Rolls-Royce, are vital to the competitive position of a country's capitalist elite. Increasingly, however, they cannot be sustained, particularly in the research and development stage, without state aid.

Nationalization has always been used in ways that serve the interests of the ruling elite. In almost no case in Western Europe or North America has this mechanism been viewed or carried out as an alternative to capitalist relations of production. For example, nationalization has never been implemented as a part of a strategy to redistribute wealth and income. Socialists have advocated nationalization as a way for the state to control and redistribute profits. Usually, however, socialists do not control the state institutions which might take on this task. Moreover, many nationalized industries are not profitable and if they are, they are managed by the state as if they were private, competitive corporations without regard to the redistribution of profits.

Nor has nationalization been carried out in Western Europe in a manner which might permit a future assertion of power by those groups or classes which currently have little influence over the actions of capitalist firms.[9] Almost no firm has introduced a greater

9. For a discussion of the alternative possibilities of various reform measures, see André Gorz, *Strategy for Labor: A Radical Proposal* (Boston: Beacon Press, 1967).

degree of worker participation or control after nationalization. To the contrary, when a private firm is taken over, the management is either retained or other managers of private capital are brought in to run the company. Union leaders generally do not object to this, since their primary concern, understandably, is avoiding any unemployment which might result from nationalization.[10]

Parliaments provide another, though more limited, framework through which the working class could assert itself in order to transform state ownership into an alternative to—or transitional step away from—capitalism. However, most parliaments in Western Europe and North America are overwhelmingly controlled by parties whose members support the capitalist system. Moreover, nationalization is usually carried out in such a way as to avoid any increase in parliamentary or bureaucratic control over the industry in question. Parliamentary supervision of nationalized industry, in particular, is ruled out or, at best, has a pro forma character. Reformers argue that such supervision promotes inefficiency, which would weaken the industry's ability to compete and survive in the surrounding capitalist economy. Control by the state bureaucracy is also resisted and most nationalized industries stand fully outside the bureaucracies of the state sector.

To get a clearer picture of the functions performed by nationalization in the capitalist economy, let us look at the 1971 nationalization of Rolls-Royce in Britain. Rolls is a particularly interesting case of nationalization because it concerns the production and international sale of high-cost technology, vital to the survival and the future profits of modern capitalism.[11]

State ownership has been a common practice for some time in Britain and was greatly expanded by the Labour government of

10. The relations of managers and workers in nationalized industries in Great Britain are frequently described in the pamphlets published under the auspices of the Institute for Workers' Control, Bertrand Russell House, Gamble Street, Forest Road West, Nottingham, England.

11. The discussion which follows is based on a continuing research project undertaken by the author into the nationalization of Rolls-Royce, which has included a considerable amount of interviewing in Great Britain.

1945–51. The nationalizations carried out by that government represented a minimal program, much of which had already been accepted by the Conservative party.[12] The private owners of nationalized industries were handsomely compensated and prominent members of the British capitalist elite continued on the boards of the new state corporations. The resulting state firms closely resembled private corporate organizations; administrative boards ran them as commercial enterprises, though with state funds. Both worker and parliamentary participation in the planning and implementation of nationalization were kept to a minimum. Parliamentarians were permitted to make general inquiries to the appropriate ministry about corporate policies, but were prohibited from discussing day-to-day management operations. The parliamentary Select Committee on Nationalized Industries, created in 1951, was allowed to carry out only post hoc investigations. Prior to 1960, such investigations seldom took place.[13] Both Conservative and Labour leaders supported a large degree of autonomy for nationalized industry.

The Labour government of 1964–70 conformed to this pattern. It made no effort to introduce alternatives to the established pattern of productive relationships in the British economy, and Labour spokesmen prided themselves on their ability to make capitalism work better than the Conservatives could.[14] Renationalization of the steel industry was carried out in the manner described above. In addition, the government created the Industrial Reorganization Corporation (IRC) as a state holding and investment company which could encourage mergers to increase the concentration of British capital. The Wilson government also began a policy of direct state aid to high-cost advanced technology industries, such as International Computers and Rolls-Royce, where the British position

---

12. For a discussion of the willingness of the Conservative party in Great Britain to make use of the state sector, see Samuel H. Beer, *British Politics in the Collectivist Age* (New York: Knopf, 1965).

13. Shonfield, *Modern Capitalism*, p. 91.

14. For an insightful interpretation of the Wilson government's attitude toward the capitalist system in Britain, see Paul Foot, *The Politics of Harold Wilson* (London: Penguin, 1970).

on the international market was shaky or foreign investors were establishing footholds in the domestic market.[15]

Many of these instruments of state policy were used to assist Rolls-Royce long before its nationalization. Rolls, 85 percent of whose business was in air engines, had been central to the British position in this field since well before World War II, and had long received support from government contracts. Its only major competitors on the world market were, and still are, American firms: General Electric and Pratt & Whitney.

Given the highly oligopolistic character of this international market, the Rolls management and the British government were concerned that Rolls retain its competitive position. One way to ensure this was to concentrate air-engine production within Britain in a single monopoly. The Rolls management had for some time been eying their only major British competitor in this field, Bristol-Siddley, which was building the engines for the Franco-British Concorde SST. Using the argument of their greater size and the ability to break into the important American market, Rolls convinced the government that the Monopolies Commission ought to close its eyes to Rolls-Royce's absorption of Bristol-Siddley in 1966.

The next step for Rolls and the government was to ensure that Rolls had the means to compete with the American corporations. All manufacturers were convinced that the next generation of air engines would be high-thrust engines for medium-range airbuses. Two American airframe manufacturers, McDonnell-Douglas and Lockheed, were planning airbuses to suit the short- and medium-haul needs of the major airlines, most of which are also American. Discussions were also under way in Europe to build a cooperative European competitor to the Americans, the European airbus or A-300.

Given the concentration of air engine producers and the limited number of future engine contracts, the Rolls management was

15. Some indications of the state role in International Computers can be found in the *Economist*, 27 February 1971, 24 July 1971, and 2 October 1971.

convinced that the firm's only hope lay in winning contracts for the airbus engine. Research on this engine, which came to be known as the RB-211, had already begun at Rolls in 1964. The Labour government was eager to enlist in this effort, and agreed to guarantee direct launching (research and development) aid to Rolls as well as to fund the construction of a new government-owned test bed on which Rolls could test the new engine. The Wilson government was determined to prove the superiority of British capitalism and British technology. In this case, the state was an enthusiastic supporter of the British capitalist system.

Rolls' future in air engines could not be ensured solely by British participation in the European airbus. All efforts were concentrated on the American airframe manufacturers. In fact, one reason for the eventual withdrawal of the British government from the European airbus group (aside from its cost) was to avoid supporting the construction of a frame which would compete with McDonnell-Douglas and Lockheed, from whom Rolls might win a much larger order for engines.[16]

Thus, Rolls made an early decision to concentrate its sales effort on the American market and to compete directly with General Electric and Pratt & Whitney. In 1966, at a cost of $1 million, Rolls sent a large sales force to New York.[17] Teams of Rolls engineers moved from manufacturer to manufacturer and, more important, from ordering airline to ordering airline. The airframe producers were likely to order the engine which their airline customers preferred. Despite this major effort, the McDonnell-Douglas contract for the DC-10 was given to General Electric.

Lobbying activity then focused on the Lockheed L-1011 TriStar. The American engine firms and some airlines urged the American government to intervene and prevent an order for a foreign-produced engine, arguing that such an order would send

16. This suggestion was made in several of the interviews carried out in connection with the Rolls-Royce research.

17. Sir David Huddie who led the sales team was later made managing director of Rolls-Royce.

more American capital out of the United States and do further harm to the American balance-of-payments position. The British capital elite called on their own government to help counter this strategy. Several British banks and shipping firms joined forces to allow a previously small shipping firm, Air Holdings, enough backing to place an order for fifty TriStars with RB-211 engines. The income to Lockheed from this order was more than enough to offset the outflow of capital from the United States, which would result from purchase of a British engine.

The intricate financial structure of this order reveals its purpose. Air Holdings' initial deposit for the TriStar was, in fact, a secret loan from Rolls-Royce, which was thereby ensuring a contract for its engines. Even more privately, the British government guaranteed that it would make good a portion of any loss sustained by Air Holdings.[18] Largely as a result of this arrangement, Lockheed awarded the TriStar engine contract to Rolls-Royce early in 1968.

This was only the beginning of the complex involvement of the British government in Rolls-Royce and the RB-211. Direct government subsidies to the research and development costs grew after 1968. The RB-211 was based on a new design and on new materials (carbon fiber), and thus required continual testing and revision. To win the contract, the Rolls management had allowed themselves very little time before delivery of the engine was due. This meant that insufficiently tested engines went into production at the same time as the tests revealed flaws. Entire engine production runs therefore had to be scrapped at great cost, and had to be replaced with a redesigned version. Further production delays resulted from the need to abandon the use of carbon fiber for the fan blades and to revert to the more commonly used titanium, which increased the weight of the engine.

By 1969, the firm had considerably exceeded its initial estimates for launching the engine, but still had no income from sales. The firm's directors urged the government to contribute more state investment capital. The government brought in the IRC to estimate

18. From interviews.

the need for additional government funds. This led to a preliminary commitment by the IRC to Rolls of £20 million, to be paid in two annual installments of £10 million each. Before any money had been paid, however, the Wilson government was defeated in the June 1970 general elections.

The Heath government came to power at a time when part of the British industrial elite had become disillusioned with the contribution of state resources to the survival and growth of British capitalism.[19] Specifically, many were opposed to state support for declining industries, however vital to capitalism, under the rationale of "no lame ducks." If these firms could not survive the competition of the marketplace, this group argued, they deserved to die. The Heath government, reflecting this point of view, abolished the IRC.

At the same time, however, Rolls' position in the advanced technology of air engines was still important and the firm's management was demanding more state aid. Rather than treat Rolls as a "lame duck," the Heath government decided, in the fall of 1970, to bail them out once more. The one condition was that the firm's management be replaced by more efficient industrialists.[20] The government made another contribution to the launching costs of the engine and helped arrange a further loan to Rolls from the private banking system.

In January 1971, before this financial arrangement went into effect, the Rolls management told the government that the firm would have to go into receivership.[21] Rolls could not meet the RB-211 contract schedule, and was subject to severe penalties under the terms of the contract. A December-January audit showed that the contract penalties would exceed existing Rolls-Royce assets, hence the need for a receiver.

19. Since the start of the twentieth century, there have been frequent conflicts within the capitalist elite about the particular ways in which the state ought to be invoked to support the capitalist system.

20. Lord Cole, formerly of Unilever, as chairman, and Ian Morrow, already famous as a company doctor, as deputy chairman.

21. Receivership is similar to American bankruptcy, but it does not necessarily mean the liquidation of the firm.

According to the principle of "no lame ducks," the government could have allowed Rolls to go into receivership and be liquidated. A number of bureaucrats, politicians, industrialists, and bankers, however, pressured the government to preserve the firm and the RB-211 project. After some hesitation and internal debate, the government decided to follow the advice and announced that the firm would be nationalized. A short time later, the government indicated that production of the RB-211 would continue, at least on an interim basis, while a new contract was negotiated with Lockheed.

Some Americans believed that because the receivership and nationalization voided the existing contract with Lockheed, the decision was part of a plot to avoid penalty payments and obtain a new, more advantageous contract. In fact, the real motives for the decision of a Conservative government to bring under state ownership the otherwise healthy corporation were related to the critical position of Rolls-Royce in the British capitalist system. Any shrewd calculations in the decision were not directed at the contract with Lockheed, but were related to the maintenance functions of the state outlined earlier in this article.

Spokesmen for the Conservative government frequently refer to the pressures put on them by British corporate leaders who were concerned about the domestic ripple effect of liquidating Rolls-Royce and the RB-211. The air-engine division of Rolls subcontracted a great deal of work to other firms—such as Joseph Lucas (Industries) in Birmingham and Short Brothers in Belfast—which would be hurt or even forced to close some of their plants if Rolls failed and the RB-211 were canceled. The owners and managers of these firms were understandably anxious for the government to keep the doors of Rolls open.

The trade unions also brought pressure on the government. Rolls employed over 80,000 workers, 20,000 of them in some way involved with the RB-211. Workers for the subcontractors also relied on Rolls for their jobs. Liquidation would throw many of these workers into the already large pool of the unemployed in Britain.

The consequences, in terms of social unrest, could not be calculated. Trade-union leaders and Labor Members of Parliament from Derby (site of the main Rolls plant) are convinced that their lobbying efforts on this point had an important effect on the government's decision.

The importance of Rolls to the domestic British capitalist system, while clearly a relevant factor, was probably not the primary one in the government's decision. British industrial and financial elites had other motives for desiring state intervention in this case. Their counterparts in the United States were concerned about the impact of Rolls' collapse on Lockheed, the American government's largest defense contractor. Lockheed had just survived a major negotiation with the Department of Defense involving cost overruns on the C-5A military aircraft and the Rolls situation threatened disaster all over again. Cancellation of the RB-211 contract would necessitate either withdrawal from the civil aviation market altogether (by canceling the L-1011) or, more likely, redesigning the airframe to fit an American-made engine—a costly, perhaps even bankrupting, alternative.

Lockheed Chairman Donald Haughton was in London for a normal round of Rolls-Lockheed consultations when the British announced their decision. Haughton carried out an extraordinarily intensive lobbying campaign in every available corner to ensure Rolls' survival and the continuation of the RB-211. Haughton had cause for worry on the latter issue. The British government thought so little of the profitability of the RB-211 that, having decided on nationalization, the entire RB-211 section at Rolls was exempted from the bargaining over the price the government would pay the Rolls receiver for the company's assets. The RB-211 section was purchased by the new state-owned firm for only £1.

The American government backed Haughton's lobbying effort fully, including, according to rumor, an angry phone call to Prime Minister Heath from U.S. Secretary of the Treasury John Connally.[22] The strongest argument made by both industrial and

22. So many interview respondents mentioned this phone call, and its tone, that it has to be given some credibility.

governmental spokesmen from America was that dropping the RB-211 project would damage Britain's commercial reputation. This, in turn, would affect future American orders for other British products. British industrial leaders were understandably worried by this threat, as was the British government.

Concern about Britain's global commercial position also focused sharply on the country's future in the international market for high-cost technology. Rolls had received government aid for launching the RB-211 because failure to produce this particular engine might have meant complete withdrawal from air-engine competition. The Heath government feared that this would be a damaging blow to the worldwide reputation of British technology, leading to a gradual decline in the British ability to compete in the international capitalist system.

The general air-engine production of Rolls could not be allowed to collapse because it was vital to the global position of British capitalism. A large proportion of Rolls' sales were overseas; it supplied engines for over eighty airlines around the world. This made Rolls an important cog in the already vastly diminished British overseas economic position. Moreover, Rolls was an important supplier of air engines for foreign military air forces and for the British Royal Air Force. Government leaders did not wish to abandon the overseas influence this gave them, not to make their own military forces even more dependent on American production.[23]

The motives for nationalizing Rolls-Royce thus had a great deal to do with ensuring the survival, internal and external, of British capitalism, and very little to do with introducing an alternative to the capitalist system. The manner in which the nationalization was carried out is also revealing, since no effort was made to establish the nationalized firm as a model alternative. No effort was made to alter existing power relationships within the industrial system through the Rolls-Royce situation. Moreover, the nationalization was carried out

23. The British had already found themselves dependent on the United States for their submarine-based nuclear force, as Richard Neustadt describes in *Alliance Politics* (New York: Columbia University Press, 1970).

in a way that would do as little damage as possible to the previous owners of the firm.

Members of Parliament were kept in almost total ignorance of the situation at Rolls-Royce before 1971; even the extent of government involvement was concealed. The IRC investigation yielded no increase in understanding or concern in Parliament. When the crash came in February 1971, the parliamentarians reacted with ill-informed horror, as the debates and questions at the time reveal. Parliament became concretely involved in the Rolls discussions only after state officials and the corporate elite had made the key decision on nationalization. Since this required legislation, an open debate was held, statements made, questions asked, all with great cathartic effect, but with almost no impact on the choices made in the legislation.

In reading the debates, one is struck by both the members' lack of influence on the situation and the dearth of imagination revealed on both benches. In a situation which opened many opportunities for proposing alternatives, most parliamentary spokesmen rallied to the defense of the system. The left wing of the Labour party made hardly any suggestions about the future structure and productive role of the nationalized firm. The rest of the Labour ranks, whose influence on the government's decisions was likely to be minor in any case, urged the government to avert the unemployment consequences of the collapse of the firm. The greatest concern expressed on the Conservative benches was for the British commercial position and the survival of an important symbol of British capitalism and technology. Only on the fringes of the parliamentary Right was there a call for some alternative to more government involvement, i.e., to let the firm collapse and sell the assets to the highest bidder, foreign or British.

Parliamentarians had little influence on the drafting of legislation to nationalize Rolls, no role in determining the amount the government would pay the Rolls stockholders for the assets, and no voice in the structure of the new firm. The guiding consideration for the government was that Rolls be assisted as much as possible in regaining its competitive position. There were even suggestions that after the nationalized firm recovered from the RB-211 disaster, it might be resold to private enterprise.[24]

Labour and trade unions were hardly more influential in the implementation of the nationalization plan. In fact, the Rolls case is a good illustration of the difficulties faced by fairly class-conscious trade unionists in trying to design alternatives within the framework of capitalism. The Rolls workers, particularly the engineers testing the engines, probably knew of the RB-211's troubles before most of the others. Perhaps even some clerical workers had an inkling of the pending financial disaster. These workers had, of course, no way of bringing this knowledge to bear in high-level decisions. Rather, they remained ignorant of the overall picture and were the last to know about the decision to go into receivership and to discuss nationalization with the government. Once the new legal status of the firm was in effect, moreover, labor was the first "asset" to be put on the block, and the trade unions were obliged to cooperate in deciding who would be laid off in order to avoid even more serious unemployment. Understandably, the workers were anxious to continue the RB-211, since this would minimize the number of jobs lost. When it came to drawing up the order by which Rolls creditors would be repaid from the income earned from the sale of the assets to the government, the shares held by the workers, given over the years as bonuses, came last on the list.

It would have been almost impossible for the workers at Rolls to react any differently. Labor relations in the firm reflected patterns established during an earlier, more paternalistic era. The trade unions at Rolls are split into two groups: "works unions," organizing semiskilled and skilled workers; and "staff unions," representing the highly skilled engineers. The works-union members belong to a number of different national unions, but their self-described loyalty is

24. From interviews.

to the Rolls-Royce firm. The union leaders take pride in the low level of strike activity at Rolls and the regular refusal of the workers to strike against management in conjunction with the national strike actions by their unions. They recall Sir Henry Royce, whom they called by his given name, drifting through the sheds, taking a personal interest in their work.

The staff-union members of the various national trade unions have organized much more recently, since the largest expansion of the engineering staff took place in the 1960s. They have much less historical loyalty to the firm and are more responsive to their national leadership. As a result, they are much more militant and carried out a large part of the strike activity that did occur at Rolls in the late 1960s.

Fundamentally, however, both sets of workers depend on the firm and the state that supports the firm for jobs and benefits. Inevitably, when Rolls-Royce was threatened, they rallied to its defense, creating a solidarity between workers and management that amazed some managers. They grouped together to organize delegations to London to lobby cabinet ministers and Members of Parliament and demonstrate in the city.

Despite this willingness to serve the interests of the firm, the workers were still informed last, consulted last, involved last, and never included in the decisions made in Whitehall and banking and corporate boardrooms about the future of Rolls-Royce. Nor, in their dedication to the immediate issue of preserving jobs, did the unions make any effort to define an alternative to the nationalization measure being planned by the elite. Even had they done so, the legislation would probably not have reflected such alternatives. For the Rolls workers, nationalization in no way altered their role in the capitalist system; it simply brought them new bosses.

While the interests of parliamentarians and workers were poorly represented in the nationalization of Rolls-Royce, the interests of capital came in for much more careful attention. The government took over only those parts of the firm which private capital refused to maintain. The mechanisms of receivership and nationalization were defined by and serve the British corporate elite. A private accounting firm, Peat, Marwick and Mitchell, supplied the receiver to manage the affairs of the old Rolls-Royce firm, while the newly established state firm took over most of its predecessor's assets for a price to be negotiated later (an issue settled in mid-1973). Leading industrialists won immediate appointments to the new firm's board of directors. The portion of corporate assets represented by the RB-211 was removed from the negotiations over price because it was considered an unusually large loss item. The more profitable parts of the firm—automobiles, gas and marine engines, and computers—were earmarked for sale to private capital interests.[25]

Thus the nationalization of Rolls-Royce was necessary because of the vital importance of that firm to the overall position of British capitalism domestically and internationally. As the Rolls managers made clear to the government during January and February 1971, the private capital system would no longer invest at a loss the resources necessary to ensure the survival of the firm. The research and development costs of the RB-211 contract meant that Rolls would no longer earn profits, the primary interest of the industrial elite. Nationalization therefore served to preserve capitalism and was implemented in a manner that served the interests of the industrial elite.

Increasingly, nationalization is being posed as a policy alternative in the American setting, most recently in the case of the railroad industry in the eastern United States, and in Galbraith's proposal for the future ownership of defense industries. One should not be misled, however, into thinking that the increasing involvement of the state in the capitalist economy constitutes a step toward the fundamental alteration of the structure of the ownership of production. As the Rolls-Royce case illustrates, state and industrial elites work closely to ensure that no significant changes take place when the state assumes

25. A public offering of shares in a new firm, Rolls-Royce Motors Holdings, Ltd., was made May 7, 1973.

responsibility for a part for the productive apparatus. To serve as a mechanism of transformation, nationalization must be accompanied by redistribution of profits and power in the firm. The key issue, surpassing by far the question of the role of parliaments in nationalized firms, is that of the role to be played by workers. If nationalization is to have any redistributive impact, it needs to be planned as part of a general movement for workers' control of industry. These issues of redistribution and workers' control must be raised every time the state is urged by the ruling elite to take over a particular industry. If it is not raised, nationalization will be handled as a technical matter; and it will continue to be designed to suit the interests of the powerful.

9

Notes
Toward
A Pluralist
Commonwealth*

Gar Alperovitz

It is perhaps time—as Galbraith's loose assertion that the "Democratic Party must henceforth use the word socialism" should warn—that Americans interested in fundamental change begin to define much more precisely what they want.[1]

Where to begin a dialogue on long-term program? Historically, a major radical starting point has been socialism—conceived as social ownership of the means of production primarily through nationalization. Although the ideal of socialism involves the more encompassing values of justice, equality, cooperation, democracy, and freedom, in practice .it has often resulted in a dreary, authoritarian political economy. Could the basic structural concept of common ownership

---

* This essay is excerpted from the forthcoming *A Long Revolution* by Gar Alperovitz. For a more extended discussion see the author's *Strategy and Program* (Boston: Beacon Press, 1972).

1. John Kenneth Galbraith, *Who Needs the Democrats? and What It Takes to Be Needed* (New York: Signet, 1970), p. 67.

of society's resources for the benefit of all ever be achieved, institutionally, in ways which fostered and sustained—rather than eroded and destroyed—a cooperative, democratic society?

My primary concern in these "Notes" on alternative program is with economic and social issues. There must obviously also be discussion of political institutions capable of preserving (and extending) positive elements which, though badly corroded, still inhere in aspects of the Western democratic traditions of freedom. The central question at this point, however, is the structural organization of the economy. Achieve a valid solution, and various political alternatives may be possible (though by no means inevitable); without it, the power thrust of the economic institutions is likely to bypass whatever more narrowly political forms are created. . . .

State Socialism

Some of the main issues may be posed by reviewing the now familiar critique of state socialism:

One major problem is that the concentration of both economic and political power in a centralized state produces what might be called an "economic-political complex," an institutional configuration not very appealing at a time when there is increasing awareness of, and concern over, the dangers of bureaucratic government. The Soviet and East European experience attest to as much, and the dreary history of British nationalization (to say nothing of America's own recent federal takeover of rail-passenger transportation) is fair warning that the structural principle of nationalization is not in itself sufficient.

A second problem is that classical state-socialism's dynamic tendency toward hierarchy and centralization reduces individual and social responsibility, and thereby destroys the basis both for freedom and for a practice and ethic of voluntary cooperation: to the extent decision making is centralized to achieve the planned allocation of resources, alienation appears to increase. Individuals become ciphers in the calculus of the technocrats; hope of humanism based on the equality of individuals working together fades. Arbitrary party directives or (in some cases) the worst forms of market competition then naturally become dominant modes of administration—for there must be some means of regulating the often inefficient, irrational, and irresponsible practices of bureaucracies set up to achieve "efficient," "rational," and "responsible" control of the economy.

State socialism, thirdly, largely precludes maintenance of an underlying network of local power groupings rooted in control of independent resources—a political-economic substructure which might sustain a measure of restraint over central authorities. . . . In instances of error or blatant injustice (as in Poland in late 1970) the citizen's recourse is to violent rebellion—now against precisely those agencies which were supposed to administer resources on the basis of new principles of equity! . . .

For such reasons—and also because of restrictions on political freedom, the absence of a sense of equitable community, and the drabness and sheer monotony of most existing socialist societies—it has become extremely difficult to imagine the Old Left objective of nationalization ever alone achieving many ideals. This image is especially difficult for young radicals who affirm a new vision of personal fulfillment and who urge "let the people decide" in their own local environments. Centralized state socialism as the center-piece of radical program would make a mockery of such principles, especially in continent-spanning America which, by the end of the century, will encompass 300 million individuals.

In sum, although the concept of socialism involves a broad humanist vision, it has yet to be demonstrated how in advanced industrial settings the abstract ideals might be achieved and sustained in practice. While some form of social ownership of capital and the planned use of society's wealth may be necessary to deal adequately with many economic issues, the question remains, precisely what form? We return to the basic issue: Could society ever be organized equitably, cooperatively, humanely, so that wealth benefited every-one—without generating a highly centralized, authoritarian system?

Alternatives to Centralization

A number of traditions have attempted to confront difficulties inherent in the centralizing tendencies of state socialism; consideration of some of their alternatives suggests an initial approach to defining elements of a positive program:

It is helpful to acknowledge frankly at the outset that some traditional conservatives (as opposed to rightist demagogues) have long argued correctly that centralization of both economic and political power leaves the citizen virtually defenseless, without any institutional way to control major issues which affect his life. They have objected to state socialism on the grounds that it destroys individual initiative, responsibility, and freedom—and have urged that privately held property (particularly that of the farmer or small capitalist entrepreneur) at least offers a man some independent ground to stand on in the fight against what they term "statism." Finally, most have held that the competitive market can work to make capitalists responsible to the needs of the community.

Some conservatives have also stressed the concept of "limits," especially limits to state power, and (like some new radicals) have emphasized the importance of voluntary participation and individual, personal responsibility.[2] . . .

Few traditional conservatives or members of the Libertarian Right, however, have recognized the socialist argument that private property and the competitive market as sources of independence, power, and responsibility have led historically to other horrendous problems, including exploitation, inequality, ruthless competition, individual alienation, the destruction of community, expansionism, imperialism, war.

A second alternative—also an attempt to organize economic power away from the centralized state—is represented by the Yugoslav argument for workers' self-management. Whereas private property (in principle if not in practice) implies decentralization of

2. See especially Nisbet's *Community and Power* (original title, *Quest for Community*, 1953) (New York: Oxford University Press, 1962).

economic power to individuals, workers' self-management involves decentralization to the social and organizational unit of those who work in a firm. This alternative may even be thought of as a way to achieve the conservative antistatist purpose—but to establish different, socially defined priorities over economic resources.

The Yugoslav model of decentralization raises a series of difficult problems: Though the Yugoslavs proclaim themselves socialists and urge that the overall industrial system must benefit the entire society, the various workers' groups which actually have direct control of industrial resources are each inevitably only one part of society. And as many now see, there is no obvious reason why such (partial) groups will not develop special interests ("workers' capitalism") which run counter to the interests of the broader community.

Indeed, problems very much akin to those of a system based on private property have begun to develop in Yugoslavia. Overreliance on the market has not prevented inequality between communities, and has led to commercialism and exploitation. Both unemployment and inflation also plague Yugoslavia. An ethic of individual gain and profit has often taken precedence over the ideal of cooperation. Worker participation, in many instances, is more theory than practice. Meanwhile, as competitive tendencies emerge between various worker-controlled industries, the need for some central coordination has produced other anomalies. The banks now control many nationwide investment decisions, severely reducing local economic power and the Yugoslav Communist party takes a direct and often arbitrary hand in both national and local decisions. In general, it has been extremely difficult for social units to develop a sense of reciprocal individual responsibility as the basis for an equitable community of mutual obligation. . . .

The Yugoslav model recalls the historic themes of both guild socialism and syndicalism. It is also closely related to the "participatory economy" alternative recently offered by Jaroslav Vanek, and the model of workers' participation proposed by Robert A. Dahl.[3] All

3. See, for instance: Jaroslav Vanek, *The Participatory Economy* (Ithaca: Cornell University Press, 1971); *The General Theory of Labor-Managed Economics* (Ithaca:

alternatives of this kind, unfortunately, suffer from a major contradiction: it is difficult to see how a political—economy based primarily on the organization of groups by function could ever achieve a just society, since the various structural alternatives seem inherently to tend toward the self-aggrandizement of each functional group—as against the rest of the community.

The point may perhaps be most easily understood by imagining workers' control or ownership of the General Motors Corporation in America—an idea close to Dahl's alternative. It should be obvious that: (1) there is no reason to expect white male auto workers easily to admit more blacks, Puerto Ricans, or women into "their" industry when unemployment prevails; (2) no internal dynamic is likely to lead workers automatically or willingly to pay out "their" wages or surpluses to reduce pollution "their" factory chimney might pour onto the community as a whole; (3) above all, the logic of the system militates against going out of "their" business when it becomes clear that the automobile-highway mode of transportation (rather than mass transit, or simply less transit—and more planned collocation of functions) is destructive of the community as a whole though perhaps profitable for "their" industry. . . .

Some basic distinctions must be confronted. First, while management by the people who work in a firm should be affirmed, the matter of emphasis is of cardinal importance: "Workers' control" should be conceived in the broader context of, and subordinate to, the entire community. In order to break down divisions which pose one group against another and to achieve equity, accordingly, the social unit at the heart of any proposed new system should, so far as possible, include all the people—minorities, the elderly, women, youth—not just the "workers" who have paid "jobs," and who at any one time normally number only some 40 percent of the population and 60 percent of the adult citizenry.

Cornell University Press, 1970); Robert A. Dahl, *After the Revolution?* (New Haven and London: Yale University Press, 1970); Kenneth Coates and Anthony Topham, *Industrial Democracy in Great Britain* (London: MacGibbon & Kee, 1968).

A second, perhaps more difficult, point: The only social unit inclusive of all the people is one based on geographic contiguity. This in the context of national geography, is the general socialist argument; the requirement of decentralization simply reduces its scale. In a territorially defined local community, a variety of functional groups must coexist, side by side. Day-to-day communication is possible (indeed, individuals are often members of more than one group); and long-term relationships can be developed. Conflicts must inevitably be mediated directly by people who have to live with the decisions they make. There are, of course, many issues which cannot be dealt with locally, but at least a social unit based on common location proceeds from the assumption of comprehensiveness, and this implies a decision-making context in which the question "How will a given policy affect all the community?" is more easily posed.

When small, territorially defined communities control capital or land socially (as, for instance, in the Israeli kibbutz or the Chinese commune), unlike either capitalism or socialism, there is no built-in contradiction between the interests of owners or beneficiaries of industry (capitalist or local workers) as against the community as a whole. The problem of "externalities," moreover, is in part "internalized" by the structure itself: since the community as a whole controls productive wealth, it, for instance, is in a position to decide rationally whether to pay the costs of eliminating the pollution its own industry causes for its own people. The entire community also may decide how to divide work equitably among all its citizens.

Although small-scale ownership of capital might resolve some problems it raises others: the likelihood that if workers owned General Motors they might attempt to exploit their position—or oppose changes in the nation's overall transportation system—illuminates a problem that a society based on cooperative communities would also face. As long as the social and economic security of any economic unit is not guaranteed, it is likely to function to protect (and, out of insecurity, extend) its own special, status quo interests—

even when they run counter to the broader interests of the society. The only long-run answer to the basic expansionist tendency of all market systems is to establish some stable larger structural framework to sustain the smaller constituent elements of the political economy. This poses the issue, of course, of the relative distribution of power between small units and large frameworks, and of precisely which functions can be decentralized and which cannot.

Some of the above questions may perhaps be explored most easily in the context of the alternative to centralization represented by the localized practice of cooperative community socialism in the Israeli kibbutz—a historically agricultural institution that is now rapidly becoming industrialized.[4] The many existing variations of the model suggest numerous alternative ways to make decisions involving not only workers' self-management but community (social) uses of both capital and surpluses. Some approaches have been successful, some obviously mistaken and wasteful. . . .

Within the best communities one major point deserves emphasis: Individual responsibility—to act, to take initiative, to build cooperation voluntarily—is a necessary precondition of a community of mutual, reciprocal obligation, and, ultimately, the only real protection against bureaucracy. When the ethic of an equitable, inclusive community is achieved, the efficacy of true "moral incentives" is dramatically revealed; individuals are neither paid nor valued according to their "product," but simply because of their membership in the community. But there are huge problems even in the best settings, not the least of which is that small communities tend easily to become overbearing and ethnocentric. If they are to break out of conformity they must allow a range of free individual initiative—without waiting for majority approval. And they must find ways to achieve flexibility and openness to prevent provincialism and antagonism against outsiders or (all) "others."

4. The kibbutzim demonstrate, incidentally, that small industrial units can be highly efficient—contrary to theorists who claim large scale is a technical necessity. The kibbutz movement has continued to grow in Israel, although the proportionate role of this sector has diminished as huge migrations have swelled the capitalist economy since 1948.

The kibbutzim as a group have experimented with confederation, an idea which begins with democratic decentralization as a first premise, and attempts to build a cooperative structure between small units yet remain responsible to them. The confederate framework in part—but only in part—also helps deal with the issue of economic insecurity and the self-aggrandizing expansionist logic of market systems. The kibbutz experience is of course not transferable directly to advanced industrial society. However, it is highly suggestive. . . .

One may raise objections to practical failings of the existing models or to theoretical aspects of the various traditions, but it is hard to disagree with the judgment that centralization through corporate capitalism, fascism, or state socialism has destructive implications for local communities—for all people, that is, except the managing elites (and for them, too, in more subtle, insidious ways). Accordingly, whether one accepts the conservative view that individuals must control capital, or the Yugoslav that workers must, or the radical Israeli or anarcho-communist view that "communities" smaller than the nation-state must, we are compelled to come to terms with the general proposition that political power has in some way to be related to decentralized economic power, at least until the postindustrial era.

A Pluralist Commonwealth?

To review and affirm both the socialist vision and the decentralist ideal is to suggest that a basic problem of positive alternative program is how to define community economic institutions which are egalitarian and equitable in the traditional socialist sense of owning and controlling productive resources for the benefit of all, but which can prevent centralization of power, and, finally, which over time can permit new social relations capable of sustaining an ethic of individual responsibility and group cooperation upon which a larger vision must ultimately be based.

A major challenge of positive program, therefore, is to create "common-wealth" institutions which, through decentralization and cooperation, achieve new ways of organizing economic and political power so that the people (in the local sense of that word) really do have a chance to "decide"—and so that face-to-face relations establish values of central importance to the larger units of society as a whole.

Small units are obviously only part of the answer. My own view is that it is necessary to (1) affirm the principle of collective ownership or control of capital (and democratically planned disposition of surplus), and (2) extend it, at least initially, to local communities, the subunits of which are sufficiently small so that individuals can, in fact, learn cooperative relationships in practice. These, however, should be conceived only as elements of a larger solution—as the natural building blocks of a reconstructed nation of regional commonwealths.

The sketch of a long-term vision might begin with the neighborhood in the city and the county in the countryside (and pose as a research problem which industries—from shoe repair to steel refining—can usefully be decentralized and which cannot, and what scale—say, between 30,000 and 100,000—is appropriate for "communities" (with still smaller subunits at the level of neighborhood). Its longer thrust, however, is more complicated: In place of the streamlined socialist planned state which depends upon the assumption of power at the top, I would substitute an organic, diversified vision—a vision of thousands of small communities, each organized cooperatively, each working out its own priorities and methods, each generating broader economic criteria and placing political demands on the larger system out of this experience. The locality should be conceived as a basis for (not an alternative to) a larger framework of regional and national coordinating institutions.

In its local form, such a vision is obviously greatly supportive of the ideal of community proposed by Percival and Paul Goodman in their book *Communitas.*[5] More specifically, a community that owned substantial industry cooperatively and used part of its surplus for its own social services would have important advantages: It could

5. See especially Scheme 2. Percival and Paul Goodman, *Communitas* (Chicago: University of Chicago Press, 1947).

experiment, without waiting for bureaucratic decrees, with new schools, new training approaches, new self-initiated investments (including, perhaps, some small private firms). It could test various worker-management schemes. It would be free for a range of independent social decisions based upon independent control of some community economic resources. It could grapple directly with efforts to humanize technology. It could, through coordination and planning, reorganize the use of time, and also locate jobs, homes, schools so as to maximize community interaction and end the isolated prison aspects of all these presently segregated units of life experience.

Communities could work out in a thousand diverse localities a variety of new ways to reintegrate a community—to define productive roles for the elderly, for example, or to redefine the role of women in community. They could face squarely the problem of the "tyranny of the majority" (and the concomitant issues of minority rights, and individual privacy), and experiment with new ways to guarantee individual and minority initiative. The anarchist demand for freedom could be faced in the context of a cooperative structure. The issue of legitimate leadership functions might be confronted rather than wished away; and various alternatives, including rotation, recall, apprenticing, etc., might be tested. . . .

In their larger functions communities would obviously have to work together, for both technological and economic reasons. Modern technology, in fact, permits great decentralization—and new modifications can produce even greater decentralization if that is a conscious objective. In cases where this is not possible or intolerably uneconomical (perhaps, for example, some forms of heavy industry, energy production, transportation) larger confederations of communities in a region or in the integrated unit of the nation state would be appropriate—as they would be for other forms of coordination as well.

The themes of the proposed alternative thus are indicated by the concepts of cooperative community and the Commonwealth of Regions. The program might best be termed "A Pluralist Commonwealth"—"Pluralist," to emphasize decentralization and diversity;

"Commonwealth," to focus on the principle that wealth should cooperatively benefit all. . . .

Levels of Community

"The crux of the problem," Kenneth Boulding observed in 1968, "is that we cannot have community unless we have an aggregate of people with some decision-making power. . . . It is easier for a relatively small unit to have some sense of community. . . ." [6] Although Boulding offered his argument in connection with management of traditional municipal services, in my opinion his point applies in many instances to economic matters as well:

Could conflicts of interest within communities, for instance, be more rationally resolved by new cooperative principles of ownership without engendering local bureaucracies?

If each community were restructured so that it might engage its own development more directly, how, more specifically, might it establish a basis for cooperative trade between communities, and for control of larger industry?

How might large scale planning, investment, trade, economic balance, and ownership/control issues be wisely addressed?

There is no doubt that cooperative development proceeds best in communities sufficiently small so that social needs are self-evident. Voluntarism and self-help can achieve what centralized propaganda cannot—namely, engender group involvement, cooperative enthusiasm, spontaneity. This is a primary reason to emphasize small-scale local structures at the outset—even if it may entail short-term disadvantages. The hope is that thereafter, with the benefit of a real basis in some cooperative experience, it may be possible to transcend

6. Kenneth E. Boulding, "The City as an Element in the International System," *Daedalus* 97 (Fall 1968): 1111–23, 1118.

historical starting points in the longer development of a larger framework.

A key question is how to prevent local centralization of power: Individuals as well as small groups must obviously retain some power as opposed to the local collectivity as a whole. (And the organization of individuals and small groups *is* power—power to prevent bureaucratic domination, even in small settings.) One answer is self-conscious individual responsibility—and therefore another requirement is the achievement of local practices and relationships that build the experience of responsibility at the same time they constrain bureaucracy. This will require a further breakdown into smaller subgroupings organized both by function and neighborhood geography within communities. (A "city" might be understood as a confederation of smaller communities.[7]) Another answer might be to distribute "vouchers" to individuals so they could freely choose different forms of public services like education and medicine.[8] Such a financial mechanism might—if properly designed—permit substantial freedom of operation for a variety of semicompetitive, nonprofit service institutions. . . .

The need for a larger-scale framework becomes obvious when problems of market behavior are considered more closely. What if every community actually owned and controlled substantial industry? . . . Community industry would vie with community industry, neighborhood vs. neighborhood, county vs. county, city vs. city. If communities were simply to float in the rough sea of an unrestricted

7. The Israeli kibbutz confederation, with units dispersed throughout the geographically compact nation, hints at how small neighborhood communities might conceivably agglomerate into a larger decentralized city when telescoped, conceptually, to more compact local sites.

8. This approach is already in use, obviously, in Medicare payments and in some transferable higher education scholarships. It will surely be extended for health care. "Tuition vouchers" for elementary education have been proposed by a diverse group ranging from Paul Goodman to Milton Friedman and Christopher Jencks; and an OEO experiment may test a version in the near future. Housing "vouchers" are also now being tested. The "voucher" approach may perhaps be best understood as a "transition mechanism" (to facilitate the establishment of a variety of voluntary and community controlled institutions), rather than as a final solution to the problems of public bureaucracy.

market, the model would likely end in "community capitalism," trade wars, expansionism, and the self-aggrandizing exploitation of one community by another. As in modern capitalism, there also would likely be both unemployment and inflation, ruthless competition and oligopoly, and so forth. (And, within communities, one result would be a tendency to exploit wage employees, as some kibbutzim exploit Arabs.)

Such problems can never be fully resolved unless a context of assured stability is established. Above all, the conditions of insecurity in which local expansionism and exploitation arise as defensive strategies, even when the best intentions prevail, must be eliminated. A larger structure capable of stabilizing the economic setting is necessary, and, if it is to rationalize the economic environment facing each community, it will have to control substantially much wholesale marketing, longer-term capital financing, and taxation.

Other issues that cannot be resolved alone by one community point up further functions of a larger framework and a larger decision-making body. These include managing the ecology of a river system, deciding the location of new cities, establishing transportation between population centers, committing capital in large societal investments, and balancing foreign trade. (And, of course, unless such a larger framework is established, it is hard to see how the insecure conditions out of which international expansionism and imperialism grow can be eliminated.)

Since the socialist argument for a large unit appears to be correct in all these instances, the issues become: How large? And how might it be established without generating a new dynamic toward centralized power? A governing, continental scale "state" would be far too large for any hope of democratic management by localities—and totally unnecessary for technical efficiency save, perhaps, in continental transportation and some forms of power exploitation. (But cooperation between areas is feasible, as present international air transport or American tie-ins with Canadian energy sources illustrate.)

. . . Some intermediate unit larger than a "community" but smaller than a nation of 300 million people appears to be required. For many economic matters the present states are too small, and more, they lack a tradition of direct economic responsibility. The unit must be capable of taking over directly (and decentralizing!) capital and productive functions now controlled by, say, the five hundred largest economic corporations—without escalating to the scale of the entire social system. In America today, though extremely limited in function, the most obvious suggestive example of a regional unit is the Tennessee Valley Authority, but we should begin to conceive of a system in which this nation, by the end of the century, might be broken into eight or ten confederated regions of 20 to 30 million people, each region made up of confederated communities. . . . (The TVA, of course, is not offered as a "model"—as its failure to resolve many issues [from participation to ecology] warns.)

Part of the answer might also involve regional units of different sizes for different purposes. The metropolitan area as a unit, for example, might control certain heavy industries or specialized public services such as intraurban transportation. Some state units might control power development and, building on the state park tradition, could also appropriately manage expanding recreational industries like skiing. A grouping of regions like New England and Appalachia might control electric-power production and distribution; the Pacific Coast and the Mountain States might unite for a variety of functions, particularly for rational ecological planning and watershed control. In such instances, organization *across* regions is more rational. Black Americans and other minorities may for political reasons also wish to establish racially organized associations across the nation. The point of regional organization as a guideline is not to exclude collaboration but rather to attempt to solve some problems of cooperation and power by building up units of rational scale which are still manageable by the localities implicit in a decentralist vision.

Planning, Power, and Process

Within the larger unit, decisions should reflect the needs of real (that is to say, local) communities. But to avoid wastes and inequalities, higher-order planning is obviously also necessary. The issues then are: Who controls the planners? And how are fundamental planning criteria determined? The thrust of the argument is that controlling criteria should in part be generated out of expressed community needs and experiences, out of specific demands for goods and services—over time, through stages—and that these must be bolstered by the development of independent local bases of power. . . .

In general, the difficult broader principle in a three-level vision of cooperative community, economic region, and confederated nation is to anchor units in new social structures which preserve sufficient independence of decision and power (without which neither freedom nor responsibility is possible), but which are not so powerful as to produce unrestrained competition and deny the possibility of a substantial measure of rational planning. The rule should be to leave as many functions as possible to localities, elevating only what is essential to the higher unit.

A critical problem is to define specific ways in which people living in localities might constrain larger-order systems without making it impossible for them to function. Here, some clues are available from modern American experience. In the Tennessee Valley Authority, for instance, local corporation farms (and other private business interests), rather than "communities," to a great extent keep the bureaucrats in line, serving their purposes—but TVA authorities still retain sufficient power rationally to control much river development.[9]

What if communities were the power base or building blocks of a new political economy? They might reduce regional units to more

9. The way military contractors and the various services often partially "coopt" the federal civilian defense bureaucracy, paralleling the corporation forms of the TVA, is also instructive. Only in imagination do Defense Department bureaucrats simply "order" the corporations, the services, and their congressional allies to do their bidding.

limited roles, largely responsible to (in part "coopted" by) the interests of the people—organized in new cooperative community forms. Given the proper social basis, a large unit such as a region might be kept in check. Its ultimate role would then be partly simply coordination; its broad policy-making and administrative functions would depend upon the development (and acceptance) of a rationally articulated political program. A two-chamber legislature might perhaps represent the organized communities, on the one hand, and the interests of the people at large, on the other.

In this setting, several other basic questions could be addressed: What, for example, might be the best process for making decisions over such fundamental issues as how population should be dispersed; whether to make major new society-shaping investments, as in one or another transportation system; how much should be allocated to prevent the destruction of the environment (directly, or indirectly through the greater allocation of time entailed by some—but not all—voluntaristic methods); how much of society's resources to allocate between consumption and investment (which also entails many ecological considerations, including the question of a zero growth rate).

"Planning" is obviously required here, too, but again it is important to recognize that in this sketch of an alternative program, the process of central "planning" would be quite different from that of the rationalized state or the Soviet "command economy." It would be developed through local processes in each community, and then "integrated" subsequently through regional and national politics generated out of local experience. Ultimately, the central regional and national bodies would have to resolve conflicting claims about resource allocation through the more broadly representative political processes.

To identify socialism with streamlined, computerized planning, as some do, is a fatal error. "Planning" would more likely be an "iterative" phenomenon involving: first, information, priorities and criteria generated at local levels; next, an integration at a higher order

"planning stage"; then, the implications calculated; a return to
smaller units for reconsideration; and finally back up again. (The
Chinese call a similar process "two ups and two downs"; and some
large U.S. corporations have developed sophisticated linear program-
ming models for their decentralized internal management which are
relevant.)

One must recognize that decentralized, democratic planning
inevitably involves inefficiencies and considerably more time. If
successful, however, the gains in released energies, to say nothing of
the quality of life, are likely to more than compensate for what is lost.

But this returns us to the question of whether the basic social
units in which day-to-day life occur are, in fact, likely to sustain new,
more humane experiences of community. . . .

There are no easy answers to this question, and very little
guidance available from foreign experience or past history. Chinese
and Israeli developments suggest that communities may be able to
sustain and deepen the quality of internal social relations at the same
time external relations involve both the limited use of market
competition and a larger framework. Marxist theoreticians as
different as Charles Bettelheim and Paul Sweezy agree, too, that the
use both of a limited competitive market and planning seem
inevitable at certain stages of development under all forms of
socialism.[10] Competition can then be viewed not as a method of
exploitation but as a tool of rational administration. One challenge, it
accordingly appears, is to be able to recognize the latter and eliminate
the former, and (if the social system is to overcome its origins in
capitalism), to attempt shrewd tradeoffs between competition and
cooperation at different stages of development, as a new experiential
basis emerges, as mutual needs develop, as larger national political
possibilities open up, and as a new vision is created.

In such a long process of development, as Martin Buber urged,

10. See, for instance, their exchange in *Monthly Review* 22, no. 7 (December
1970): 1–21. For an introduction to Chinese practices, see John G. Gurley, "Capitalist
and Maoist Economic Development," *Monthly Review* 22, no. 9 (February 1971).

the permissive environment which may be attainable if localities are not totally subservient to central agencies is more important, initially, than the apparent top-down rationality of centralized planning systems. The conservative, the Yugoslav, the Israeli, the Chinese, and the anarchist all seem right also to argue that a degree of local autonomy and a degree of competition must be assured if freedom and spontaneous innovation are to continue over time. . . .

Precursors and Prefigurations?

A variety of existing youth communes and collectives point in the direction of small-scale cooperative community. Affluent white youths' need to transcend isolated individualism seems to be generated systematically out of the sterility of high-income suburban (and nuclear family) life, out of the collectivizing experience of migration to the (university) ghetto, and out of the general contradiction between liberal expectations for fulfillment and American realities. Hesitant and beleaguered though they are, collectives and communes all over the country are experimental arenas in which some cooperative "common-wealth" values are being learned in practice—and in which the outlines of a new social vision are beginning, however falteringly, to emerge. . . .

Far more significant developments related to the concept of a Pluralist Commonwealth are to be found in parts of the black community, particularly in a few areas which are politically far ahead of the nation. Increasing numbers of black Americans today are attempting to articulate the idea of "the community" and are beginning to experiment with ways to institutionalize the notion that its interests should take priority. Here, the collective ideal and higher expectations seem rooted partly in earlier agrarian traditions, partly in collectivizing migrations to the (urban) ghetto, the experience of rising income levels (as compared with the rural South), and the contradiction between raised hopes and brutal denial and repression.

All have been important (and are continuing) conditions out of which a new vision is slowly being forged. . . .

In most ghettos the notion of "community" has for the most part been expressed as a demand for control of institutions in existing neighborhoods, like Harlem or Hough. The emerging concept of the "community corporation" is taking on increasing importance in this context—and may become a critical element in an "alternative program" if it transcends the limitations of the inevitable initial compromises.

The mechanisms of a democratically controlled neighborhood corporation involve little more than drawing a legal line around a neighborhood or rural area to establish a geographically defined corporate entity which may undertake a variety of social, economic, and political functions. The crucial feature is democracy—either through the principle of one person, one vote; or through confederations of local block clubs, churches, and action organizations.

Though sometimes conceived only as OEO vehicles or instruments of "neighborhood government," such institutions become of much greater long-run interest when they assume ownership of industries and stores collectively in the name of the entire community, as they are now doing in many areas. The terms "community union," "community cooperative," or "community development corporation" (CDC) are then more accurate descriptions. Instead of letting individual capitalists buy businesses and absorb the profits themselves, a CDC either distributes small dividends to all members or, more significantly, it uses proceeds collectively for such community-building services as day-care centers, recreational programs, or training activities.

Some CDCs (e.g., FIGHT, in Rochester, New York) are already operating community-owned electrical manufacturing plants of substantial scale. In Los Angeles, Operation Bootstrap has established a cooperatively owned toy factory; in the Chicano community of New Mexico there are a variety of cooperatively owned industries ranging from farming and cattle feeding to furniture and wood products manufacturing; in Cleveland, a rubber molding factory is collectively owned; in Philadelphia there is already a large community-owned shopping center (and one which is to be more broadly based in the community is in the planning stages in Cleveland).[11]

In one or two instances, particularly in the New Communities, Inc., experiment in southwest Georgia, the vision of community has been developed much further, and has led to the purchase of land for a black, collectively owned city based on communitarian ideals—similar in hope, if not yet in practice, to the Israeli *moshav*. Obviously, none of the experiments represents the achievement of a fully developed alternative vision; their significance is only as possible "precursors" and "prefigurations" in a long process which might conceivably transcend what must begin as "community capitalism."

Two distinct ways of organizing power to bolster these community efforts have emerged: In many cities demonstrations, sit-ins, and other militant protests have successfully wrenched control of housing and even urban renewal from public bureaucracy—and placed ownership and control in the hands of community groups. Elsewhere, a more traditional form of power which attaches to the voting strength of well-organized groups has forced many concessions. In New Mexico, for instance, at one point state authorities were brought to direct state schools and hospitals to give preferential treatment to the purchase of vegetables from local community cooperatives.

The linkage between a local, community-owned vegetable cooperative and a higher-order political authority is of special interest in that it illustrates in skeletal outline what might be thought of as a two-tier Pluralist Commonwealth model. In this instance, the local community-based economic effort is fortified by political-economic decisions made by the higher unit—however, given the power relationships, it is forced to be responsive to a coalition of smaller-

11. For information on these and other efforts, write to the Center for Community Economic Development, 1878 Massachusetts Avenue, Cambridge, Massachusetts 02140.

scale units. The relationship of the mayor to community groups in Cleveland, Ohio, suggests similar possibilities may emerge elsewhere. Community corporations are only one illustration; throughout the nation, from Berkeley, California to Madison, Wisconsin to Rockville, Maryland; municipalities are also experimenting with public ownership of land, utilities, real estate. . . .

Hannah Arendt has urged that we give renewed attention to the history of the "council" movement—the spontaneous eruption in history of local, people's governing bodies. The contemporary trend toward community control is, in fact, best understood as part of a tradition which includes Jefferson's idea of "ward republics," and extends through the Paris Commune, the *soviets,* the Mexican *ejida,* the Algerian *autogestion* system, and the like.[12] Though not the result of national upheaval, some of the new American institutions, moreover, emphasize explicity (as did not all the previous institutions) the socialist concept of direct (local) common ownership of property. That community-owned efforts are at this stage only fragmentary and partial is obvious; their importance may be more as educative vehicles which teach basic concepts related to the vision of a Pluralist Commonwealth than as ultimate structures. . . .

Long-Term Program—And Strategies of Change

Space does not permit a full discussion of the crisis facing the American system, nor of the potential opportunities for change we may confront. Long term programs obviously, however, make sense only if related to serious strategy. The following is offered merely as a potential *framework* for the discussion of the relationship between program and strategy in the emerging context of the 1970s.

Immediate reforming demands which can achieve small victories

12. See her *On Revolution* (New York: Viking Press, 1963). That the historic movements largely failed is reason to consider carefully not only their great importance, but what must be added to the tradition to make it relevant and viable in the specific conditions of our own technological development and historical period.

(and real improvements), illuminate tensions inherent in the political economy, and—if linked with an explicit strategy—help suggest the limits of the present system and the need for a fundamental transformation:

1. Specific organizing efforts including neighborhood confrontation, municipal electoral campaigns, referenda, etc., to secure popular local control over—and redirection of—a variety of such public programs as: education, medical care, urban renewal, rent control, public housing, transportation, etc.
2. Specific efforts, including both direct action and political organizing, to obtain positive local, state, and national legislation to expand resources in such programs (and in adequate income maintenance programs) as a matter of right.
3. Broader national efforts to end military, political, and economic interventions, reduce military spending, and shift resources to programs structured along the above lines so far as possible.
4. *Simultaneously:* organizing efforts by public employees (teachers, sanitation workers, administrators, etc.) to secure equitable higher wages and more public-service jobs under worker/community control—demands that may both bring immediate gains, and, again, increase pressure for a redirection of state resources to legitimate purposes.

All of the above combined with efforts to tap that huge share of society's income and wealth now controlled by elites and corporations—in order to benefit the vast majority, illuminate inequities, and explicate contradictions of the present system, and help pose the fundamental issue of what could be achieved if society's income and wealth benefited the entire community directly.

5. *Simultaneously:* specific programs to reduce or end taxation not only for the "poor" but progressively for a majority of citizens, up to incomes in the $12,000–$15,000 range—again, demands

designed to obtain specific gains, and, strategically, to increase awareness that a major restructuring of state finance is necessary. Especially, an end to sales taxes, property taxes on housing, and social security levies.

6. *Simultaneously:* efforts (activist, political, legislative) to shift the tax burden onto the elite (minority) top 15–20 percent of the income pyramid, with steeply progressive taxation above $20,000—and, onto the major corporations.

Especially heavy taxation of dividends, rents, profits, inheritances, and other unearned receipts derived solely from title to property; a sharpening of the distinction between "earned" and "unearned" income.

The uniting of both taxpayers' organizations and public employees (e.g., teachers) in common efforts: lower taxes for the majority and better pay—made possible through taxation of the elites and corporations, and, ultimately, through community ownership of revenue-producing enterprise (housing and development corporations, land trusts, municipal power, etc.).

7. The latter efforts accompanied by a strategy *to constrain private corporate control of economic surpluses*—including programs (and coordinated national organizing) to prevent corporations from shifting wage increases and taxes to the consumer through higher prices: price controls, not wage controls, except above $15,000–$20,000.

Especially efforts to exploit local opportunities for community control of prices (rents) in tenant-occupied housing—again, both to secure specific improvements in geographically defined organizing areas and to apply pressure against exploitative private landlords; simultaneously, development of parallel cooperative and community owned housing to illustrate a structural alternative to private property. Similarly: efforts to strengthen control of gas and electric prices combined with parallel development of cooperative or municipally owned utilities. The same strategy applied ultimately to all significant productive enterprise—locally, regionally, nationally.

8. Strikes and other actions by working Americans (blue and white collar) to secure higher minimum-wage laws, higher wages for those below $12,000–$15,000, and control over working conditions—all (together with demands for price controls and increased taxation) to help set limits on corporate control of economic surpluses.

Actions also to constrain corporate investment abroad—both to halt interventionism and to underscore how such (and other) private investment decisions contribute to domestic unemployment and other irrationalities.

The above efforts—which in part coincide with a "New Populism"—combined with long-range educational programs to suggest the inherent limitations of movements which (despite positive intent) do not confront the basic power realities; hence, the need ultimately for a fundamentally different economic system—one which, as a matter of structural principle, does not (as now) permit the elite top 20 percent regularly to garner 40–46 percent of society's income (leaving the 80 percent majority to make do on what is left); which does not permit less than 2 percent to own 80 percent of the corporate stock held personally, 90 percent of the corporate bonds, virtually 100 percent of state and local bonds; which does not permit concentrated private corporate control of society's main productive wealth by 200–500 giant firms, etc.

9. *Simultaneously*, therefore: all of the above coupled with activities which seek public control over a variety of irresponsible corporate practices—from Ralph Nader's limited (but at this stage attention-focusing) demands for responsible production and tougher regulation, to specific ecology, urban, and other anticorporate direct-action campaigns.

But, also, education to suggest the demonstrable limitations of such approaches (despite their intent); hence, again, the need to establish a dialogue that moves progressively beyond them (even as their immediate educative value is acknowledged) to more fundamental alternatives.

10. Broader national efforts demanding jobs (and meaningful work) and an end to inflation—coupled with long-term educative efforts to increase understanding that a corporately organized, profit-motivated economic system is substantially incapable of fulfilling such demands; that, accordingly, a new publicly responsible system is needed.

Efforts to establish preliminary positive experiments that illustrate a basic structural alternative, slowly prefigure the elements of a new society, and, over the long haul, tie in with attempts to mobilize an effective new social movement and political alliance rooted in the vast majority.

11. All of the above accompanied by the buildup over time of alternative institutions capable of meeting immediate needs (free schools, clinics, day care, etc.), especially institutions which, through cooperative community control of productive capital, new community technologies, and public services, begin to suggest economic principles and structures related to a society-wide commonwealth vision.

Cooperatives, community development corporations, various municipal ownership efforts, and cooperative housing major priorities—above all those which use some surpluses directly and illustratively (in contrast to taxes on the majority) to provide some community services.

But also, communes, small-group encounters, and self-transformation efforts which teach voluntary cooperation, a sense of community, and, generally, awareness of one's personal responsibility for the existential, social, political, and economic consequences of one's actions (or inactions).

Special efforts—as in attempts to establish radically new communities—to offer paradigmatic demonstrations of how an integrated vision of a new community (implicit in the ideal of a new society) might actually function in practice (southwest Georgia, New Communities, Inc., an important beginning

effort; Cambridge Institute New City Prospectus, a suggestive
initial sketch). . . .

12. Specific attempts to bring together subgroupings of such alli-
    ances within the geographically defined area of the region—in
    political organizing around parallel demands in education,
    housing, medical care, welfare, and other matters (The North-
    east Model Cities Citizens' Union in New England, an
    illustration); in common regional cooperative marketing ar-
    rangements; in demands for public regional control of ecological
    issues (especially river systems), land use, transportation, energy
    (electric power and gas and oil pricing), and (ultimately)
    large-scale productive industry (Appalachia, a strategic area for
    developing new regional models). . . .

This framework rests on the belief that in the specific conditions
of late-twentieth-century American capitalism, despite the obvious
barriers to change, a new approach is both necessary and possible.
Notwithstanding the many failures of modern social movements—
and the resulting pessimism—the 1960s should at the very least have
taught us to question fashionable predictions that nothing can ever
change. It is important at the very outset to reaffirm the legitimacy of
self-evident human needs, and the legitimacy, too, of demanding a
society that can meet them. In each instance, therefore, rhetoric must
give way to clearly defined program. The relationship between some
radical-militant activities and some liberal approaches and even (as in
tax and decentralization issues) some traditionally conservative efforts
must be clearly articulated. The broader near-term objectives are to
bring people together around common interests, to achieve specific
improvements, to raise public consciousness of the limits of the
present system, to narrow the power range of corporate institutions,
to illuminate the need for fundamental change, and to begin to
suggest the specific content of a basic alternative.

The points here outlined also involve the judgment that as the
brief remaining decades of the century are traversed new alliances
with various groups, now not often regarded as possible, may well be

practical—if issues are formulated with a view both to immediate problems and to the logic of the long-term dilemmas facing the American system. . . .

10 Reclaiming America: Land Reform as a Means of Reconstruction

Geoffrey Faux

Land reform has not made much headway in America. For most of our history, there has seemed to be enough land for everyone. Can't get land in Pennsylvania? Move to Ohio. Can't find enough in Ohio? Move to Missouri. The availability of land was the single most important economic fact that distinguished the New World from the Old. The myth that we would never run out of land was so strong that it relegated the most original economic thinker the nation has produced—Henry George—to the crackpot bin of history. Today, long since the frontier has disappeared into the Pacific, the myth prevails.

It was lust for land that destroyed the native Americans, united the revolutionary colonies, and financed the westward expansion. What did it matter that our history became one episode of land fraud and swindle after another? Land was the one thing that the nation could afford to give away, and it did. During the nineteenth century two-thirds of the land in what is now the forty-eight continental states was transferred from public to private ownership.

No region of the country has escaped the sad pattern of speculation, corruption, and monopoly that accompanied and followed this transfer. In the West, railroad companies have built huge empires on land held in clear violation of the original grants made by the U.S. Congress to finance the laying of track. In the South, small farmers, black and white, have been driven off the land through credit manipulations of the banking system. In Appalachia, coal and timber companies have engaged in an orgy of strip mining and clearcutting on land that they have filched from mountain people through legal swindles. Even New England, which began with a tradition of encouraging small landholdings, has seen its initial pattern of small townships run by free, economically independent yeomen destroyed by the same familiar tale.

The rationale for abuses of the land was often rooted in Jeffersonian visions of a nation of small freeholders. Thus the Homestead Act of 1862 and the Reclamation Act of 1902 were ostensibly designed to assist the homesteading of small resident farmers. For a while they did. But in the end much of the land that was set aside for the support of small farmers ended up in the hands of corporate giants that are the very antithesis of the Jeffersonian ideal.

As a result of all this, America's land is more and more owned and controlled by a concentration of private corporate powers. The top twelve pulp and paper companies directly own 35 million acres of land and probably control at least twice that amount. (In Maine a dozen timber and pulp companies own more than half the state.) The top eight oil companies own 65 million acres of land. And the potential profits from recreation and second-home development have lured companies such as Chrysler, Gulf and Western, ITT, CBS, Eastman Kodak, and others to buy up huge chunks of real estate all across the country.[1]

1. For an excellent survey of the concentration of land ownership, see Peter Barnes and Larry Casalino, *Who Owns the Land?* (San Francisco: Center for Rural Studies, 1972).

Nor has the dreary tale been limited to the countryside. Land speculation and the resultant corruption of the political process have been a driving force behind the urbanization of America. In their book *The Ultimate Highrise*, the staff of the San Francisco *Bay Guardian* give a fascinating account of how this interaction works in one of the country's most sophisticated cities.[2] Each highrise that goes up simultaneously raises the value of the surrounding land and decreases the value of the surrounding buildings (which then become less attractive space because of competition with the highrise). This means an increase in tax assessment, which can be countered only by higher densities, which in turn means tearing down the older, shorter buildings and putting up new highrises. The "ripple effect" spills over into residential areas, where it drives out the low- and moderate-income people who cannot afford the high tax and rent levels. Moreover, since the developers have the political clout to get tax abatements, the taxes on residential property move up even faster than they otherwise would. Thus while the assessed valuation in the downtown area of San Francisco rose 67 percent between 1950 and 1970, it rose 191 percent in the inner "arc" of neighborhoods surrounding the downtown, 190 percent in the middle "arc," and 137 percent in the outer "arc."

A New Constituency

If the case for alternative systems of land ownership and control in the United States had to rest solely on the facts of corporate ownership and abuse, the outlook would be dim. Over the past century the magic of private property has been so well sold to Americans that any abrogation of the rights of the International Paper Company to abuse the land and the people on it seems to threaten the right of every homeowner to plant his tulips where he wants. When the magic of private property is combined with the

2. Bruce B. Brugmann, Greggar Sletteland, and *Bay Guardian* staff, *The Ultimate Highrise* (San Francisco: Bay Guardian Books, 1971).

myth of equal opportunity, you have a powerful combination: "I don't care what J. Paul Getty gets," said a working man to me the other day, "as long as I get mine." In the face of such powerful sentiments, even the worst abuses rarely call into question the basic rights of property. Those interested in protecting the land and its tenants tend to concentrate their energies on preventing the most outrageous abuses rather than on changing the basic structure of private ownership.

The political economy of the United States, however, is not static. In recent years the concentration of land ownership has resulted in a great many Americans getting less and less of "theirs." Some of these people have never had a large share of America's bounty—farmworkers, small farmers, inner-city minorities who can't get decent housing, rural people in Appalachia or northern New England, and so forth. But they are being joined by others as well. Young families cannot obtain housing even though they make a decent salary (in New England a family must make about $12,000 to swing the cheapest conventionally financed house). Environmentalists watch the failure of attempts to regulate land development. Working- and middle-class urban people see their neighborhoods overrun by speculators catering to racial fears of homeowners. Middle-income suburban residents are trapped in the inefficient and irrational patterns of suburban sprawl. Not enough to make a national effort—yet. But enough of a potential to start thinking seriously, for the first time in our history, of the possibility of land reform.

At present the political manifestations of these groups' concerns are usually limited to demands for greater public regulation of private development. How this works out can be seen in a typical recent example—the controversy in Boston surrounding Park Plaza, a proposed luxury highrise and commercial center. On one side of the controversy are the developers, the Chamber of Commerce, the building trades unions, the professional architects, the Boston newspapers, the mayor, the governor, and a number of politicians who get their sustenance from the building boom. (Jesse Unruh, the

California politician, once said that "money is the mother's milk of politics.") Opposing the project are neighborhood people, environmentalists, and some local politicians. The project was rejected twice by the state commissioner of community affairs on the grounds that it was financially weak and would therefore require future subsidies, would cast dark shadows on the Boston Common, had an inadequate plan for relocating the neighborhood residents, and would probably cost the public treasury much more than it would contribute. One analysis suggested that it would be at least seventeen years before the project could possibly begin to make contributions to the city's tax base.

Although the logic was on the side of the commissioner, the clout was on the side of the developers. After the second rejection, the commissioner was forced to resign, paving the way for final approval of the project.

Similar fights are going on in rural areas. In Maine, for example, the Maine Land Use Regulation Commission (LURC) was established in 1969 after a long political struggle. Its proponents were mostly environmentalists, though in the end they were joined by some conservative sportsmen who didn't want to see any more public land despoiled. The law that established LURC is generally regarded as one of the more progressive in the nation.

The Maine Land Use Regulation Commission is the kind of agency that many environmentalists would be overjoyed to see operating in their state. But LURC is doomed to fail, as was the Massachusetts Department of Community Affairs in the Park Plaza case. A result of a compromise, LURC is politically fragile. A small nudge in the direction of the large landholding interests will nullify the agency's ability to retard land abuse, and all it takes is a few decisions to destroy the barriers that the agency is trying to build against the developers. The election of a more conservative governor and the appointment of a pro-timber-company director could result in the despoiling of acreage over a few years that would take a century to rectify.

Also, the agency's public image is necessarily mostly negative. It has the power only to say no, to deny "progress," to oppose job-creating development. Like all government in a capitalist society, it can at best deny, while the private sector is always seen as bringing benefits. In this context the comments of the governor of Massachusetts and an aide in response to the Park Plaza controversy are revealing:

> *The Aide:* We've had a policy that said "no" in so many different places—transportation, parking, the Port Authority—but there are limits to this.
> *The Governor:* We cannot allow the state to become an obstacle to progress.

The Limits of Public Control

The public does of course have the right to plan, but no right to implement. Thus the fate of a plan is almost always in the hands of the developer, as the history of America's suburbs over the past two decades suggests. A tour of the files of towns and counties on the outskirts of any metropolitan area in the nation will find scores of large, pretty, neatly designed plans for the orderly development of the area. And a drive through the countryside will show how little good all the planning has done.

The failure of planning and regulation is not primarily a matter of personal corruption. In many cases good, honest people sitting on the zoning board give away development rights because they are eventually outlasted and outmaneuvered by the developers. Developers apply year after year for zoning variances or changes in land-use classifications, each time to be confronted by resisting planners and neighborhood opposition. And then one night it happens. The neighbors don't show up. Or the surrounding area has been spot-zoned, making this new request for rezoning more logical. Or the developers promise some new amenity. Or a new board more sympathetic to the real estate interests is elected. Or, like the governor of Massachusetts, the board simply cannot continue to say no to everything. And in one night the political efforts of a decade are lost forever.

Beyond the immediate problem of the failure of regulatory measures to control land use, there is the fundamental antisocial character of private land ownership. Because the supply of land essentially is fixed, its ownership involves monopoly control. Not only are there natural monopoly profits, but the competition among would-be monopolists to capture these profits (speculation) further raises land prices putting access to it out of the reach of more and more of the population. Speculative changes in land prices are a major contributor to the internal migrations that generate social upheaval and more social costs. As the San Francisco illustration shows, the quest for monopoly profits, *which is built into the system of private land ownership,* fuels irrational building booms which destroy poor and working-class neighborhoods. Small business is eliminated and the residents are shoved into older more dilapidated housing whose owners can take advantage of their own strengthened monopoly situation to raise rents and increase densities. Since taxes and costs are also rising as a result of land speculation, many landlords would be forced into raising rents even if they personally would prefer not to do so. In many cases, the result of the process is that landlords abandon buildings while a large proportion of the population is without adequate housing.

Another irrational result of private landownership is illustrated in the massive migrations of black rural working people from the South as a result of the mechanization of the cotton fields during the late 1950s and early 1960s. The system of private ownership of the plantations ensured that the landowner would automatically receive *all* the benefits of the increase in productivity caused by the public subsidization (through the federal subsidies for agricultural research and development) of the cotton-field mechanization. The suddenly unneeded sharecroppers and farm workers automatically absorbed all the costs—social and political as well as economic—of the change. And when the resultant migration wave broke upon the cities of the North and West, the public sector had to bear the additional costs of the damage. Moreover, the gain went primarily to landowners who by virtue of their large holdings were more able to finance the introduction of machinery into their field. Thus private concentrated landownership resulted in the siphoning off of practically all of the direct gains from productivity growth to the landowners and shifted the costs to the public and the working classes.

For the most part, zoning and land-use regulation have not been aimed at distribution of wealth objectives. They are concerned with more rational land use, with primary emphasis on environmental and "quality of life" considerations. As our society becomes more urban and more complex, environmental concerns require more planning in the public interest. But when the power over land is private, the land will be used to further private interests.

The limitations of zoning and regulation are becoming apparent. Gradually some cities and municipalities are beginning to understand that there is little alternative to public ownership if the public wants to assure control. Public land banks to buy, hold, and resell land are now being proposed in a number of large cities, such as Kansas City, Saint Louis, and New York. Smaller towns, like Arlington, Massachusetts, are considering a similar agency empowered (in this case) to buy "land, buildings, or interest in any real estate within the Town of Arlington at its fair market value." After the purchase, town-meeting members would have a chance to approve or disapprove specific actions which, if disapproved, would be resold. Rising land values help ensure that the town will not lose money in the real estate transaction. In Rockville, Maryland, the city purchased a 152-acre farm, 40 acres of which the city decided to develop itself in an explicit effort to capture the increase in land value for the city treasury. (Over the last two decades, average assessed land values in Rockville have increased more than 500 percent.)

Another clear case of a rejection of the conventional liberal alternative in favor of a more radical but sensible approach occurred recently in the coastal town of Georgetown, Maine. The people of this conservative village overwhelmingly voted against zoning in their 1972 town meeting. They then agreed to permit the town to buy up 50 acres of the town's waterfront, including its only wharf, and hold it for future development.

Corporation Socialism

A number of established urbanologists and assorted corporate entrepreneurs have understood the need for more public ownership and more effective public control of land. Their goal is rational economic planning (not to be confused with economic justice). Examine, for example, the following quotes:

Robert Wood, former secretary of HUD and now president of the University of Massachusetts:

> Fundamentally, we are at the point where public ownership and public planning are probably the essential components for a genuine land reform program. Certain levels of density no longer make tolerable private ownership and development even though zoning and planning requirements are available to affect them directly. Only a general plan with land ownership and control being the decisive forces in critical areas can do the job. . . . If we fall victim to the belief that the only thing that government does well is raise taxes and redistribute them, we are indeed at the mercy of the marketplace.[3]

David Rockefeller, chairman of the board of the Chase Manhattan Bank:

> I have been giving considerable thought as to how the process of promoting new towns can be expedited. I have come to the conclusion that additional legislation will be required as well as added financial support.
>   Specifically, it seems to me that two steps are needed. . . .

3. Robert Wood, *The Necessary Majority* (New York: Columbia University Press, 1971).

To deal with the problem of land acquisition—and perhaps provide guidance in terms of national land use planning—we need either a new federal agency or an existing agency supplied with special additional powers for planning and obtaining sites for new towns. . . .

The plan would call for a federal agency with the ability to determine sites and projects in a manner consistent with the economic needs and goals of the communities involved as well as those of the nation. Thus, a single agency would handle land acquisition and site location.

The second agency, either private or quasi-public, would be organized on a non-profit basis to provide the pre-development financing. Possibly a new kind of bank could be devised which would seek its capital from commercial banks, insurance companies, industry and other sources.[4]

Few people should have any illusions about what kind of role the Rockefellers envision for the public sector. Like urban renewal, like the Housing Act of 1968, like the port authorities of any number of our seacoast cities, like hundreds of similar public institutions, programs designed by the bankers, businessmen, and their professional allies will above all facilitate the making of profits for private pockets. It would be difficult to draw any other conclusion from a proposal by the head of the Chase Manhattan Bank that the government expand its role as financier.

The problem that Rockefeller and the others have come up against is that private property is threatening to undo the planned orderly environment that the large banks and firms need to maximize their profits and power. Listen to Rockefeller on the dangers that stubborn property owners pose to the big-time capitalist venture:

In the case of Columbia, a few parcels could not be acquired and, in the end, the planners just had to design the city around them. If more parcels had been held out, or if they had been in more critical locations, this could have undercut the whole project. *The chanciness related to land acquisition is much too great as things now stand.* [Emphasis added.]

4. David Rockefeller, "New Towns and Satellite Cities" (Address before the Regional Plan Association, New York, February 16, 1971). Mimeographed.

It is a manifestation of the point that economic thinkers such as Schumpeter, Galbraith, Heilbroner, and others have been making for a long time: that as the economy becomes more complicated, and as power becomes more concentrated, the private sector will demand the use of government powers to support and finance private economic development.

Public ownership of land *is* an indispensable element of land reform. Regulation has failed, and history tells us that simple redistribution would eventually lead to the same kind of monopoly control now prevalent. The corporate sector's new interest in public ownership—whatever its intent—may be an opportunity to get over the largest single obstacle to socially responsible land policies: the scare of socialism.

We all have been subject to incessant propaganda on the evils of socialism. More important, the public sector itself in the United States is largely a passive tool of the private sector, or a repository for the failures of our society. It is an "employer of last resort," a pork barrel for corrupt politicians, the giver of welfare, the place where failures of society are provided with cheap, depressing services by people who have no pride in their own jobs. With an image like that, no wonder people cringe when the word socialism is mentioned. Do we really want the country run by the people who run the Boston school system? Or the state of Mississippi's Department of Welfare?

The answer, of course, is that public ownership does not *necessarily* mean incompetent bureaucracy or Stalinism. It can be designed to be sensitive, efficient, and effective. If the brains and talents of those bright people who spend their lives designing missile systems and helping rich men thread their way through the eye of a tax loophole were put to work on new forms of public ownership, there is little doubt that they could do better. In fact, when the rich and powerful need an efficient public vehicle to further their own ends, they are able to attract smart, hardworking people to the public sector, as with the port authorities, NASA, and so on. The key is to create a system where there is an incentive for working in the public interest. This can be accomplished by raising the rewards for public service, diminishing the rewards for working in the private interest, or a combination of both. The task then is to break down, to demystify, the power that the word socialism has to destroy every rational effort at restructuring society. One way to do it is to put the monkey on David Rockefeller's back. The demands of corporations for more public-sector involvement offer a way to break down the myth that the Chase Manhattan or any other large accumulation of capital operates in a free market. Perhaps then a more serious discussion of various forms of social ownership and control might begin.[5]

The consequences of *not* socializing the land are profound. The rape of the countryside and its people will continue. And without public ownership of land, the contradiction between demands for a higher standard of living and the need to conserve the environment can never be reconciled.

For example, business firms have been given huge federal, state, and local subsidies—as well as granted the right to pollute in violation of environmental standards—for the purpose of luring them into depressed areas. When they do move in, they typically fail to deliver the benefits they promised. For example, of 4,000 new jobs created by one Chrysler plant in West Virginia, only 600 went to local workers. Of some 8,000 jobs created in Indian reservations by federal subsidies in past years, Indians got less than half. Studies of subsidized economic development in the Ozarks have concluded that the bulk of the new jobs went to outsiders. More outsiders means shortages in housing and education, and a higher cost of living. When the cycle ends, local people are often worse off than before it began.

But since there is no visible alternative to private development, there is nothing for the unemployed and underemployed to do but to support more development (and more pollution) in the hope that one of these days a job for them will come along. It is not enough to tell them that they are caught in a self-defeating cycle. The developers at least offer them a promise, the antidevelopers offer them nothing.

5. The situation in which the private market has become so inefficient that it no longer serves the needs of corporate capital is not limited to land. Transportation is another one. Communication may be another. Energy is a fourth.

Public ownership of the land by itself will not solve this issue. But it is a necessary condition to give the public control to exercise effective planning that will break this cycle.

Land-reform Programs

Demonstrating the socialist character of modern corporate activities is easy stuff compared with the difficulties of coming up with some credible alternatives. But without an alternative there is little hope for organizing a constituency against the corporate powers. As André Gorz has observed: "That socialism is a necessity has never struck the masses with the compelling force of a flash of lightning."

What land should be reformed? Any land-reform effort should make clear that it does not intend to put the property of the small homesteader and homeowner under public control. There is probably no greater incentive for care of the land than pride of ownership in small doses. It is observable in city and country, among whites and nonwhites, rich and poor. Moreover, Jefferson's insights into the benefits to political democracy of small-scale land ownership are as valid today as they were two hundred years ago. People who own their own small plots of land are more likely to care about their community and to participate in its governance than are those without such ties. One study of voting patterns among black people in Mississippi in the 1960s showed that home ownership was more closely associated with participation in elections than all of the common socioeconomic factors such as income, education, and occupation.[6] Finally, the sense of independence and other psychological values attached to owning a small piece of property are more American than apple pie, and threats to it will undo any political effort.

Beyond the principle of hands-off the small homesteader, the

6. Lester Salamon, "Family Assistance: The Stakes in the Rural South," *New Republic*, 20 February 1971.

determination of what land should be included in a land reform strategy might follow the following taxonomy, listed in no particular order of priority.

1. Land where speculative pressures are causing economic hardship, e.g., urban slums, rural land being converted to recreation and other activities that force out the nonfarm rural poor (the Maine coast, eastern slopes of Appalachia, Indian reservations in the Southwest and the rural South). Politically, these crisis areas should be the places that draw the most support for a land reform movement. There is a natural constituency for redistribution as well as public ownership on the part of those who suffer in both urban and rural areas. In addition, there is hope for support from liberals whose experience with less radical approaches to solving these problems has been frustrating.

2. Land held in violation of statute (e.g., all irrigation lands reclaimed by the authority of the Reclamation Act of 1902 and which are owned in excess of 160 acres or are owned or operated by an absentee landlord; unsold land held by railroads in violation of original grant conditions). There is less of a natural political constituency in these cases. However, the stark fact that corporate wealth is based on a continuing violation of the law makes it a possible target for political action.

3. Land in the clear path of development that will automatically increase the value of undeveloped land (e.g., land outside the major metropolitan areas). The long-run purpose of a strategy aimed at such areas would be to deny the rich and powerful the speculative profits that are generated by natural growth in demand for land. Public ownership of these lands together with an aware political constituency would give the public control over the future directions of economic growth in local communities which up until now have been dictated by the speculators.

4. Land held in concentrated amounts by so few large corporations

that economic freedom of other groups is restricted (e.g., timberlands, large corporate farms, land held by large mining and oil companies). This involves a direct confrontation with the centers of monopoly corporate power. Thus the political risks and possible gains are both relatively large. In all probability it will require a sophisticated alliance between environmentalists and those for whom the land issue is a way to raise the question of wealth distribution in general.

How might land reform be financed? It is unlikely that public ownership of U.S. land now in private hands can be accomplished through confiscation without payment. Somehow the land must be paid for. The history of condemnation sales of land suggests that the specific prices paid are as much a function of the political strength of the seller as they are a function of the value of the land.[7]

Thus we can expect that the price the public pays for land will depend upon the political power of the land reform movement to staff the land purchase courts with people sympathetic to the cause. Land reform will have to be generally accepted as a public goal if existing property holders are not simply to be bailed out at high prices.

The capital necessary to finance a successful land reform effort can be raised in two ways—through tax revenues or through self-financing.

Purchase of land through taxation requires an institution to receive the proceeds and purchase the land in a sort of land trust. The amount of land a land trust can buy would be limited to the amount of tax revenues that are either earmarked or pledged by the legislature. Since its revenue is free to the land trust there is no economic pressure on the trust to dispose of the land in any specific way. The authorizing legislation could require a certain pattern of

7. Determining the value of condemned land is clearly a political art. In Maine, assessing of timberland is done by a private firm owned by the family of a Republican state senator which also does work for timber companies. They assess the same timberland at $3 to $5 per acre for tax purposes and $25 per acre if the land is to be sold to the state.

disposal, but it is certain that the bureaucracy administering the trust would have great discretion.[8]

A system whereby the purchase of the land is financed from future revenues from the land is more of a land bank. A land bank would borrow money by pledging the future rents (or sales to another public body, e.g., sales of parks to municipalities) as repayment for the bondholders. Thus there is always pressure on the land bank to generate a sufficient amount of revenue to cover the mortgage payments on the land. If the bank should default to the bondholders, either the legislature would have to make up the difference, the bondholders would lose income, or the bondholders would have the right to take over the assets—the land—of the land bank.

The clear advantage of the self-financing land-bank system is that the huge amounts of capital required for taking over the land are more easily raised. Given the massive social needs of the country, a political movement advocating radical change runs the danger of not being able to raise the money necessary to pay for its social reforms. Poverty programs, housing for low- and moderate-income families, public-service employment, a national medical care system, antipollution programs, and so forth, must for the most part be financed out of taxes. And given the acute demands for the above, it is unlikely that a radical constituency would permit its immediate needs to take a back seat to a land reform effort. In addition the alternative of a tax-supported land trust carries with it no internal requirement for resource allocation. Being free of the requirements to cover the cost of the money gives the land trust a great deal of arbitrary bureaucratic power.

On the other hand, the economics of land banking require that the land be put into productive use right away, thus lessening its ability to achieve conservationist goals. Moreover, self-financing encourages the bank to release the land to the highest bidder. The land trust, not pressured to return interest and principle to its

8. See, for example, Peter Barnes, "Buying Back the Land," *Working Papers* 1 (Summer 1973): 43–50.

financiers, would have more freedom to pick and choose those to whom it wanted to rent according to social rather than purely economic criteria.

Given the heavy demands on tax revenues for the remainder of this century, it is likely that successful land reform will have to be self-financing. But some taxation will inevitably be needed to cover start-up costs and early down payments to landholders. And the tax/trust model could still be the most applicable route for environmental preservation trusts, subsidized recreation, and similar purposes that reasonable policy would not expect to be self-financing.

Those taxes that are used to finance land purchase should be aimed at reducing the price of land so it will be cheaper for the public sector to purchase it. For example, a tax on the unearned increment to land value would have the effect of reducing the expectations of speculative profits and therefore the land price itself.[9]

A progressive property tax would have the effect of making large landholdings less valuable vis-à-vis small ones. To avoid getting very complicated such taxes would have to be applied on a locality-by-locality basis since the economic significance of a given amount of landholdings varies from place to place. On the other hand, localizing the tax would permit people with many modest-size plots spread over a number of localities to escape the tax. Whatever the level on which it is applied, any progressive property tax would require strong disclosure laws to avoid concealment of property holdings.

Who Gets the Land?

As the history of mining and timbering in the national forest suggests, public ownership of the land is not sufficient to assure that it will be treated with respect and that its benefits will be equitably distributed. It is not enough for the public to own land; the public

9. Ibid.

must be responsible for its exploitation as well. Since there is little in the way of a public enterprise tradition in the United States, new institutions will have to be developed.

To encourage responsiveness, it is wise that these institutions be as decentralized and as democratically controlled as possible. It is not necessary, nor perhaps even desirable, that they be public in the sense of being controlled by the state. A complete system of state enterprises would concentrate bureaucratic power to a much greater degree than is healthy for a free society. What we need are institutions controlled by a local community of citizens or small producers, but which act as independent (although hopefully cooperating) economic units.

Thus, while local municipal ownership may be appropriate for a number of enterprises such as utilities and recreation, it is in general best to maintain some separation between the technocrats and the politicians. The destructive influence of political patronage is reason enough to find alternatives to a simplistic system which would put all organized activities under the same socialized roof.

Models of alternative institutions already exist. Over the long run they might evolve into community-controlled enterprises strong enough to utilize leased land from a federal or regional land bank.

One model is the cooperative. Cooperatives have always been an important part of our agricultural tradition and would therefore be a natural form of organizing for a number of rural activities. Although there are some exceptions, cooperatives have generally implied common marketing and purchasing by farmers who own their land privately and who work it on an individual basis. There are few successful examples of cooperatives whereby the farmers actually produce cooperatively, since farmers who work the same crop in the same area normally need the manpower and the equipment at the same time.

In conventional terms, marketing and buying cooperatives have been reasonably successful in U.S. agriculture. There are seven such organizations listed in *Fortune* magazine's list of the top 500 corporations in the nation. Unfortunately the fact that they are cooperatives has not meant that they respond much differently to market forces than do traditionally organized firms. It does suggest, however, that there are economic advantages to cooperation that conventional economic and business analysis ignores. In fact, the large cooperatives have been so successful that the U.S. Congress is now considering removing some of the tax advantages that cooperatives have traditionally enjoyed.

Inasmuch as returns to scale in agriculture level out at relatively modest acreages, it is clear that the advantage of large farmers over small ones lies primarily in their ability to obtain credit and technical help, to a large extent from the U.S. and state departments of agriculture. As one California small farmer put it, the big farms "farm the Department of Agriculture better than I can." A system of cooperatives that could effectively furnish this assistance to smaller farmers would give them a much greater chance of survival, and in concert with a tax structure designed to support land reform on a large scale, reverse the seemingly inevitable trend to the destruction of the family farm.[10]

The cooperative form is not limited to agriculture. It can be used in any situation where there is a large number of small private producers, such as the timber industry. Typically, the labor force used in the woods to cut pulp consists of a large number of independent cutters—men who have their own truck and saw, and who hire out on a piecework basis to the large pulp and paper companies. By treating these men as independent contractors, the large firms escape responsibility for fringe benefits, industrial accidents (in a highly accident-prone industry), and the seasonality

10. Those interested in exploring the "government-business" partnership in agriculture might examine the Nixon administration's decision to abandon farm subsidies and the recent failure of large corporations to produce field crops successfully. Most agribusiness firms have now concluded that there are more profits to be made by processing and distributing than by growing. (See Dan Cordtz, "Corporate Farming: or A Tough Row to Hoe," *Fortune*, August 1972.) The Nixon decision, which should cheapen the cost of farm products to processors and distributors, fits neatly into that strategy.

of employment. It also makes it difficult for the pulpcutters to unionize.

Since the pulp and paper companies control the market, they are able to maintain economic pressure on the pulpcutter. The cutters, who have to finance their trucks and equipment, average poverty wages in many areas of the country. Over the past few years many have organized into pulpwood associations, and there have been strikes in at least three states (Maine, Wisconsin, and Mississippi). The strike in Mississippi against the Masonite Company was the most successful, but even there a combination of political and economic pressures has damaged the internal unity of the pulpcutters association.

Given this labor force of worker-entrepreneurs, cooperatives' associations might provide a way in which the workers can gain some control. There is at least one example—in Minnesota—of a cooperative lumber mill operated by independent woodcutters.[11] With a positive national policy of encouraging such cooperation—plus some technical aid and financing—the woods could be turned over to the woodsmen themselves.[12]

A model of broader local community-controlled enterprise is the community development corporation (CDC). CDCs might be particularly appropriate for the development of urban land. They are local institutions created and controlled by the people of a designated neighborhood. They can operate with the flexibility of any business corporation to buy, produce, and sell, but the benefits and the ownership are limited to the people in the neighborhood. In various forms and in a variety of sponsorships CDCs are functioning in close

11. "EDA Teams with Minnesota Town to Build New Mill and Restore Economy," *Economic Development*, September 1972; publication of U.S. Department of Commerce.

12. The existence of twenty-one worker-owned plywood mills in the Pacific Northwest suggests that the lumber industry may be among those that are relatively more conducive to cooperative institutions. See Carl J. Bellas, *Industrial Democracy and the Worker-Owned Firm: A Case Study of Twenty-one Plywood Companies in the Pacific Northwest* (New York: Praeger, 1972). [This would also be consistent with efforts proposed by Maccoby and Terzi for "independent" work. See chapter 6 of this volume. Editors' note.]

to a hundred neighborhoods and cities in the United States. They operate shopping centers in Philadelphia and Cleveland, supermarkets in Watts and Durham, light manufacturing plants in Roanoke and Rochester. And in Brooklyn, Chicago, and a number of other cities, they are using their political influence to gain control over land.

Up to now the CDC has been seen as a poverty program aberration, a marginal institution outside the mainstream of the American economy. And to a large extent this is correct. Even those most sympathetic are hard pressed to imagine the CDC being able to survive without federal or foundation grants as long as it insists that ownership and control be limited to the neighborhood. Owners of capital are typically not anxious to invest in community-owned enterprises, and the community itself does not have the funds. The availability of inner-city land might solve that problem. The land bank or trust could grant to the people of the urban neighborhoods the right to develop their own land. Given the continued urbanization of the nation, the economic value of the land—and therefore opportunities to develop it—are sure to increase over the long run. The CDC would be the mechanism for capturing those benefits for the people.

Community development corporations are also applicable to rural areas. Some of the most promising are operating in eastern Kentucky, northeastern Oklahoma, in Hancock County, Georgia, and in the Mississippi Delta. They are also being developed in a number of Indian reservations, and in several are operating a successful tourism and recreation complex where the jobs and income go to members of the tribe. Where appropriate, CDCs could be established on a regional basis to take advantage of the large scale of operations that might be required in sparsely settled rural areas.

Finally, in some land-based industries with organized labor forces (coal, oil, electric power) worker ownership might be an appropriate form of business organization. The United Mine Workers, for example, which is not only a strong, well-organized union but which also owns a bank to provide the financing, might be a good place for worker ownership to begin.

Any set of community-controlled economic institutions will need to be supported by a system of financial and technical aid. Ultimately this system too will probably have to be publicly owned, or at least publicly controlled to a large extent. Although there are a few exceptions, the history of private bankers in assisting even the mildly reformist efforts of the past two administrations to set up blacks and other minority people in business is not auspicious.[13] This experience suggests that private control over financing makes it difficult to develop cooperative or socialist islands in a capitalist sea. Without a sympathetic banking system to furnish long-term capital for development, the likelihood of a successful land strategy based on community-controlled landowning institutions is considerably diminished.

Here, too, however, we may have the beginnings of an alternative system. The Farmers Home Administration and the Small Business Administration are bureaucracies established to serve those whom the private banking community cannot or will not serve. Neither is a radical institution, and the record of both in serving the small farmer and businessman, let alone the community-controlled enterprise, is woeful. But their existence at least means that the *principle* of a separate, government-sponsored banking system has been established.[14]

The most useful existing model for a system of land-based community-controlled enterprises might be the Farm Credit System, which is made up of the locally operated Farm Land Bank Associations and the Production Credit Associations. In 1969 the system provided 24 percent of the long-term and 17 percent of the short-term credit needs of American farmers. It also includes the Bank for Cooperatives, which has provided the capital for the ex-

13. Arthur Blaustein and Geoffrey Faux, *The Star-Spangled Hustle* (Garden City, N.Y.: Doubleday, 1972), chaps. 10 and 11.

14. For a discussion of how many of these existing government institutions can be used by community-controlled enterprises, see "Note on Community Development Corporations: Operations and Financing," *Harvard Law Review* 83 (May 1970): 1558–1671. The present cutbacks by the Nixon administration make much of the material obsolete as a practical guide.

pansion of many marketing and purchasing cooperatives into conglomerates. The system has many attractive features, not the least of
which is that it is for the most part owned by its membership: since
the establishment of the system in 1917 by the Federal Farm Act,[15]
borrowers have been required to buy shares in local land-bank
associations which in turn buy shares in the national system. The
national system in turn lends money to local associations who lend
out to the borrowers. The entire system became controlled by its
constituent local land-bank associations by 1968.

First Steps

The picture that emerges of a systematic land-reform program
is technically reasonable. A vast amount of acreage is now in private
hands which, by any standard of rationality and the public interest,
should be owned by the public. The financing of the transition from
private to public ownership through the creation of a land-bank or
trust system (and a supporting system of taxes and self-financed
bonds) is not beyond our technical and managerial capacity. Even the
most difficult part of the system—the development of local community-controlled institutions and attendant support mechanisms—is a
practical possibility, though it would clearly take time. Unfortunately, of course, this grand vision of a cooperative, publicly
responsible system of land tenure is for the moment completely
unrealistic for the obvious political reasons. A National Land Reform
Act will not be passed this year. But working for that goal in the near
future is our only alternative. The history of land use and abuse in
America clearly indicates that the conventional liberal solutions of

15. The Federal Farm Act is itself a useful document to study. Its preamble
declares that it is the policy of the Congress to encourage "the organization of
producers into effective associations or corporations under their control for greater
unity of effort in marketing and by promoting the establishment and financing of a
farm marketing system of producer owned and producer controlled, *cooperative*
associations and other agencies." (Emphasis added.)

zoning, planning, regulation, and taxation cannot by themselves save the land or the people on it.

The purpose of creating a model of land reform (of which this article is only a rough start) is not to lay out a blueprint, but to suggest some general principles (e.g., public ownership, decentralization, democratic control) upon which a large number of people seriously interested in social change can agree. This then can be used as a guide by which to judge the various turns and detours along the way. Short of violent revolution, significant social change is a political process. And since the political process—no matter how radical—requires compromises and small interim steps, such a guide is critical. Without it, it is too easy to lose the way, too easy to be satisfied with partial reforms, and too easy to overlook the kind of contradictions that characterized (for example) the Great Society programs.

Assuming that the above outline of a land-reform program is a general goal, what might be the interim steps on the way toward achieving it?

The first and most critical step is the continuous process of creating a larger and larger network of people willing to work for land reform over a long period of time. In addition to the constituencies already mentioned, it would be well to include people within the present bureaucracies who can in their day-to-day activities support existing efforts to create alternative institutions. These people make grants, make loans, write regulations, and otherwise wield small amounts of useful power. And at certain times this sort of network within the bureaucracy could be crucial. This is not to say that one can expect the bureaucracy to lead us into the new world, simply that a serious long-term effort at restructuring society cannot afford to ignore this source of allies, particularly when established economic powers will have to rely more and more on public sector bureaucracies to achieve their profit objectives.

Over the long term, we also need to build support for the many efforts at community-controlled development going on throughout the country. And we need to encourage more, even though they do not at this stage represent the perfect model. (Or, as is usually the case, the people operating the models do not see themselves in a radical context.) New alternative institutions cannot be developed overnight. Nor can the people who will run them. Nor will the general public accept the notion that community-controlled institutions can in fact operate business enterprises, unless they see some examples.

There are two critical steps on the evolutionary road to a socially responsible system of land ownership. The first is the acceptance of public ownership. But the purpose of public ownership should not be to make land assembly easier for the private sector or simply to protect some land from development. It should be to control the development process itself, to capture the gains in unearned value for the public, and to assure rational land use. Thus land banks, such as those now being proposed, *might* be a reasonable first step *if* there is sufficient public accountability. Without these elements, land banks inevitably will be the handmaiden of corporate interests.

The second step is the acceptance of the need for public enterprise to assure that the land is in fact used in a rational and humane way. This will take longer, and is partly a function of the degree to which alternative community enterprise can be made credible. But it is essential. In the end, land reform will succeed when people are convinced that just reforming land is not enough.

Bibliography

Part 2 Contradictions in the Political Economy

A. General works on the political economy of advanced capitalist societies

Blair, John M. *Economic Concentration*. New York: Harcourt Brace Jovanovich, 1972.

A good work that surveys the extent to which monopoly pervades the U.S. economy. Blair is a former chief economist of the Senate Subcommittee on Antitrust and Monopoly.

Edwards, Richard C.; Reich, Michael; and Weisskopf, Thomas E., eds. *The Capitalist System*. Englewood Cliffs, N.J.: Prentice-Hall, 1972.

A large collection of basic articles on the theory, structure, and operation of capitalism. It includes lucid introductory comments by the editors, and a section on alternatives.

Ellul, Jacques. *The Technological Society*. New York: Random House, 1964.

An assessment of the increasing technological dependence of both capitalist and socialist societies. It warns that technology requires ever-closer coordination between the state and industry, which can lead to total planning where technologists become the rulers.

Galbraith, John Kenneth. *Economics and the Public Purpose*. Boston: Houghton Mifflin, 1973.

The latest entry in the author's perennially revised interpretation of American capitalism, this volume more fully than his others tries to reconcile the irrationalities posed by the lag of the competitive sector. His "solution" is to encourage the growth of monopoly in this sector, and then to control monopoly with increased government planning—which is what he calls socialism.

Gorz, André. *Strategy for Labor*. Boston: Beacon Press, 1967.

A leading French socialist's analysis of contemporary capitalism with special regard for the role of labor. In examining the repressive functions of consumerism, state regulation, technology, and planning, he elaborates on the problematic of reforms which are consistent ("reformist") and those which are inconsistent ("non-reformist") with modern capitalism.

Heilbroner, Robert L. *Between Capitalism and Socialism: Essays in Political Economics*. New York: Random House, 1970.

An argument for a new perspective on both politics and economics which sees the two areas as inextricably linked. Further questions the use of the notion of "private" in light of the growth and impact of large corporations. However, the author considers socialism only in terms of state ownership.

Kolko, Gabriel. *Wealth and Power in the United States*. New York: Praeger, 1962.

An analysis of the unchanging distribution of wealth and income in the United States since the 1920s. It illustrates how taxes contribute to inequality with a lucid discussion on the distinction between wealth and income.

Miller, Herman P. *Rich Man, Poor Man*. New York: Thomas Y. Crowell, 1971.

A graphic description of the extent of poverty and the distribution of poverty in the United States by use of data from the U.S. Census Bureau. Of little utility beyond its data as the author assumes the causes of poverty lie with the faults of the poor.

Miliband, Ralph. *The State in Capitalist Society: An Analysis of the Western System of Power*. New York: Basic Books, 1969.

A major contribution to the study of the political economy of capitalist societies, the author applies a Marxist framework to the examination of how state power is used to maintain the viability of corporate capitalism. It considers the role of institutions such as schools, parties and legislatures in this light, and critically assesses the activities of "socialist" administrations in western capitalist societies.

Olsen, Mancur. *The Logic of Collective Action*. Cambridge, Mass.: Harvard University Press, 1965.

Although rooted in a capitalist framework, this tightly argued treatise undermines the validity of pluralist assumptions about group formation. It helpfully distinguishes between exclusive and inclusive goods and related costs of membership to the nature of benefits of groups.

Parkin, Frank. *Class Inequality and Political Power*. New York: Praeger, 1971.

An analysis of social stratification theory with a critical assessment of its uses in both capitalist and socialist countries. In relating stratification to political power, it provides a strong argument for a "class" analysis rather than a stratification framework.

Shonfield, Andrew. *Modern Capitalism: The Changing Balance of Public and Private Power*. New York: Oxford University Press, 1965.

Probably the most thorough introduction to the liberal view of the evolution of private capital and state planning since the end of World War II. Assesses the impact of technology and full-employment policies, though is a bit dated in this regard.

Warren, Bill. "Capitalist Planning and the State." *New Left Review*, no. 72 (March/April 1972): 3–31.

Examines the spread of goal-oriented planning by governments

in capitalist countries, with particular reference to Britain and
France. It assesses the limits of the efficacy of such planning.

Weinstein, James. *The Corporate Ideal and the Liberal State*. Boston:
Beacon Press, 1968.

A critical analysis of the role of the state in a capitalist society,
this study argues that federal regulation of the economy during
the "Progressive Era" served the needs of the owners of large
corporations as it worked to overcome problems created by
expanding industrial employment and cutthroat pricing.

Wolfe, Alan. *The Seamy Side of Democracy*. New York: David
McKay, 1973.

An important introduction to the nature of repression in a
capitalist society. The author explores the bias of the "democratic" state, the mechanisms of state repression, and the
political consequences of private repression. It provides a useful
framework for further analysis.

B. *Further reading on fiscal policy, global corporations and work*

   1. Fiscal policy

Mattick, Paul. *Marx and Keynes: The Limits of the Mixed Economy*
Boston: Porter Sargent, 1969.

Contrasts Marx and Keynes with particular reference to value
theory. Highlights his argument by evaluating contemporary
Marxists in light of the problematic he sets forth.

O'Connor, James. *The Fiscal Crisis of the State*. New York: St.
Martin's Press, 1973.

A major study of the dynamics of state and private power,
which argues that the state is being forced to use its resources
beyond its capacity—i.e., to spend more than it has, hence, a
fiscal crisis—in order to maintain the profits and control of one
sector of the economy. Technically sophisticated, the book is
written from an economist's perspective that considers state
operations principally in terms of budget questions.

Pechman, Joseph, and Okner, Benjamin. *Individual Income Tax and*

Erosion by Income Classes. Washington, D.C.: Brookings Institution, 1972.

An empirical study that attempts to measure the degree to which the basis for government resources in the individual income tax is being eroded. Analyzes the ethical question of tax burden by suggesting formulas based on what people pay.

Schumpeter, Joseph. "The Crisis of the Tax State." *International Economic Papers* (1954).

Views taxation in political terms, both as a political instrument and as a reflection of the dialectics of the society.

2. Global corporations

Babson, Steve. "The Multinational Corporation and Labor." *Review of Radical Political Economics* 5 (1973): 19–36.

A general review of the relations between unions and multinational corporations vis-à-vis the global activities of the latter. It outlines the debate and offers a critique of the positions of both sides.

Galloway, Jonathan F. "Multinational Corporations and the Military-Industrial Complex." Lake Forest College, 1972. Mimeographed.

One of the few studies that considers seriously the role of multinational corporations in the military-industrial complex. Relates this role to the tension between nation-states and the corporations.

Hymer, Stephen. "International Trade and Uneven Development." In *Kindleberger Festschrift*, edited by Jagdish Bhagwati et al. Cambridge, Mass.: MIT Press, 1970.

———. "Internationalization of Capital." *Journal of Economic Issues* (March 1972).

In these two articles the author argues that global corporations markedly differ from previous forms of international corporations and are more than merely large firms. The firms reproduce national capitalist systems on a global scale with the consequence of increasing inequalities between world areas, in-

creasing specialization, and the dominance of capital as a criteria
for economic decisions.

Levinson, Charles. *Capital, Inflation and the Multinationals.* New
York: Macmillan, 1972.

A labor economist examines the impact of multinational
corporations on labor and argues that wages and prices are
controlled on a global scale by the corporations, and not by
supply and demand and market pressures.

Müller, Ronald. "Poverty Is the Product." *Foreign Policy*, no. 13
(Winter 1973–74): 71–102.

A readable econometric analysis which demonstrates that
corporate investment in Third World countries relies on the
native capital of the country and so does not introduce new
capital. The investment does serve to contribute to uneven
development, though, and unemployment.

Stephenson, Hugh. *The Coming Clash.* New York: Hill & Wang,
1973.

A general overview of the nature and implications of multinational corporations. Though it stops short of in probing deeply
many of the issues raised, this essentially journalistic account
does lay them out.

3. Work

Blumberg, Paul. *Industrial Democracy: The Sociology of Participation.*
New York: Schocken, 1969.

A detailed overview of workers' control experiments in several
countries, though with special emphasis on Yugoslavia. Examines the theoretical literature on participation, and provides
ample empirical material.

Fromm, Erich. *The Sane Society.* New York: Fawcett, 1955.

A major assessment of the impact of social structure on
character development. The noted psychologist here examines
the effect of capitalism on personal development and identifies
the marketing orientation as a significant element in the
alienation prevalent in capitalist societies.

Herrick, Neal, and Sheppard, Harold. *Where Have All the Robots Gone?* New York: Free Press, 1972.

An analysis of the relationships between the nature of work, political attitudes, and emotional attitudes. Based on data collected in several studies of industrial workers, the book attempts to catalogue the shifting nature of the workforce in the United States.

Sennett, Richard, and Cobb, Jonathan. *The Hidden Injuries of Class.* New York: Vintage, 1973.

A rich exploration into the pain and degradation which work inflicts on industrial workers. Based on in-depth interviews, the authors skillfully adumbrate the way in which ideology serves to alienate workers. Despite a weak definition of class, the work proves provocative.

U.S. Department of Health, Education, and Welfare. *Work in America.* Cambridge, Mass.: MIT Press, 1972.

A broadly detailed presentation of the effects of work on workers, this report provides data on job discrimination, the situation of older workers, and the consequences of stress. Brings together recent research from a University of Michigan survey and older reports.

U.S. Senate, Subcommittee on Employment, Manpower, and Poverty. *Hearings on the Worker Alienation Act.* Washington, D.C.: Government Printing Office, 1972.

Includes a wide range of reports, analyses, proposals and data relevant to worker alienation. See, especially, Maccoby, Michael and Neal Herrick, "Humanizing Work: A Priority Goal of the 1970s."

Wachtel, Howard M. *Workers' Management and Workers' Wages in Yugoslavia.* Ithaca: Cornell University Press, 1973.

A solid analysis of the nature and effect of workers' councils in Yugoslavia, within a well-defined theoretical framework. The study explores the uneven development in Yugoslavia that results apparently from reliance on market mechanisms for distribution, and the unequal participation in work-place decisions.

Part 3   Alternatives for Reconstruction

Barnes, Peter, and Casalino, Larry. *Who Owns the Land?* San Francisco: Center for Rural Studies, 1972.
An examination of the patterns of land ownership in the United States, with a detailed proposal for transforming the system of ownership into community control through land trusts and land banks.

Bowles, Samuel. "Cuban Education and the Revolutionary Ideology." *Harvard Education Review* 41 (1971): 472–500.
An examination of the changes in the educational system in Cuba during the first decade of the Castro regime. The author provides good conceptual framework for understanding the often contradictory needs which the educational system had to serve—to create a "new Cuban man" with a communistic outlook while providing for highly skilled workers to develop the self-sustaining capacity of the country.

Brecher, Jeremy. *Strike!* San Francisco: Straight Arrow Press, 1972.
A healthy corrective to the notion that American workers have been docile and lack an activist tradition, this book reviews the history of spontaneous worker uprising and organization. Provides examples of non-American uprisings as well.

Buber, Martin. *Paths in Utopia*. Boston: Beacon Press, 1958.
A brilliant review of anarchist literature and anarcho-communist thought which finds the need for a socialism rooted in decentralized communities based on common work and common life. A critique of Leninism, this work argues that common experiences in socialism, developed over time in reconstruction, must precede a "revolution."

Coates, Kenneth, ed. *Can the Workers Run Industry?* London: Sphere Books, 1968.

A collection of analytical articles and case studies of workers' control in British industries. It includes some studies of workers' management in public enterprise firms, and national health units.

Feder, Ernest. *The Rape of the Peasantry.* Garden City, N.Y.: Doubleday, 1971.

An examination of land reform in Latin America, this work points up the necessity for seeing land reform within the context of other economic factors. The results of land reform reflect the relative bargaining positions of various groups, not simply features of the land itself.

Goodman, Paul, and Goodman, Percival. *Communitas: Means of Livelihood and Ways of Life.* New York: Random House, 1947.

Two of the leading humanist theorists review the history of urban planning here, and formulate a plan for communities based upon people living, working and playing in the same area. They relate this to the development of production on a humane scale.

Gorz, André. *Socialism and Revolution.* Garden City, N.Y.: Doubleday, 1973.

A series of essays by a leading French socialist which explore the meaning of socialism in Western "democracies." He provides a brief assessment of the "May Revolution," but most interesting is analysis of limiting situations relevant to a politics of transformation.

Harrington, Michael. *Socialism.* New York: Bantam Books, 1973.

The former head of the American Socialist party provides a scholarly and thorough history of socialism in America in order to assess the possibility and meaning of socialism today.

Hubbard, Benjamin. *A History of the Public Land Policies.* Madison: University of Wisconsin Press, 1965.

The standard reference on public land policies, this work traces the way in which the state and federal governments disposed of land in their possession or used it for a variety of ends.

Kotler, Milton. *Neighborhood Government*. Indianapolis: Bobbs-Merrill, 1969.

An argument for the reconstitution of cities into the autonomous, historically and territorially defined neighborhoods from which they derived in order to secure personal liberty that was abrogated by downtown "imperialism."

Mansbridge, Jane. "Town Meeting Democracy." *Working Papers* 1 (Summer 1973): 5–15.

Based on an empirical study in a New England town, the author argues that within a capitalist society town-meeting democracy has limitations, that there is differential participation and this is related to wealth and status. It provides a serious caveat in considering the possibility of decentralized socialism.

Kirschner, Ed, and Bass, Peter L. *New Town Development: Costs, Revenues, and Alternative Sponsorship Arrangements*. Berkeley: University of California, Department of City Planning, 1971.

A technical study which takes new towns as an illustrative example of what might be done if a community were to own and control property and productive assets in its bounds.

Mumford, Lewis. *The City in History*. New York: Harcourt Brace Jovanovich, 1961.

A comprehensive study of the evolution of cities in terms of their economies, legal forms, architecture, and quality of life. Readable and basic.

Nader, Ralph, and Green, Mark, eds. *Corporate Power in America*. New York: Grossman, 1973.

A collection of essays based on papers presented at a conference on corporate responsibility, the book ranges from the nature of corporations and corporate democracy to the limits and possibilities of controlling corporations with antitrust efforts.

Raskin, Marcus. *Being and Doing*. Boston: Beacon Press, 1973.

A philosophical analysis of the structure and constraints of American society that develops a notion of colony in all elements of our lives. Further provides a framework for thinking about reconstructing our colonized lives, by attempting a synthesis between pragmatic and existential philosophy.

Shepherd, William G. "Re-examining Public Enterprise." *Working Papers* 1 (Summer 1973): 62–71.

Reviews the various forms of public enterprise, from nationalization to subsidization, and relates them to the ability of a people to control the enterprise and its activities in order to assess the limits of public enterprise. Proposals for change are sophomoric, though.

Vanek, Jaroslav. *The Participatory Economy: An Evolutionary Hypothesis and a Strategy for Development.* Ithaca: Cornell University Press, 1971.

A theoretical analysis, based on economic efficiency models, of how a worker-managed economy might be made operable and under what conditions.

Waskow, Arthur. "The 1990 Draft Constitution." In *Futures Conditional,* edited by Robert Theobold. Indianapolis: Bobbs-Merrill, 1972.

In this essay from a larger work in progress, the author describes what a decentralized society might look like. Through the correspondence of two old friends he takes an historian's trip along the path of social change from the 1950s to 1999.